Small Nation Survival

*Political Defense
in Unequal Conflicts*

V. V. ŠVEICS

Centuries ago the conqueror Tamerlane realized a truth applicable to today's Space Age nations, but one not fully understood by their leaders: "Good politics can accomplish more than heroism, a shrewd idea is more valuable than an army. An arrow shot with the weapons of politics at the opportune moment finds without fail its place in the heart of the enemy."

This political insight was completely lost on Stalin when he said, "I shall shake my little finger—and there will be no Tito!" And on Hitler who, declared, "The day of small states is past!" After World War II a German general admitted, "The German mistake was to think that military success would solve political problems." The United States is painfully discovering that truth in Vietnam today.

In this timely book V. V. Šveics sets forth his theory that small states can successfully defend themselves against the overwhelming military might of the superpowers. The weapons are political rather than military. To illustrate his point, the author cites the conflict between Russia and Finland, Russia's failure to control Yugoslavia and Romania, French loss of Indochina and Algeria, the British defeats in Ireland and Cyprus and the present grave difficulties of the United States in Vietnam. In each instance political power has proved more potent than military force.

The *political* failure of the Russians at the time of their 1968 invasion of Czechoslovakia illustrates this point. "International conflicts," the author writes, "are political

Small Nation Survival
Political Defense in Unequal Conflicts

V. V. Šveics

An Exposition-University Book

Exposition Press   *New York*

EXPOSITION PRESS INC.

50 Jericho Turnpike   Jericho, New York 11753

FIRST EDITION

LIBRARY OF CONGRESS CATALOG CARD NUMBER: 76-136980

0-682-47163-1

To my FATHER and MOTHER

Contents

Introduction

When a great power, or a militarily far stronger enemy, uses his forces against a small nation, the struggle can be called an unequal conflict. Such unequal conflicts often have their own rules. One of the accepted rules is that the giant always wins.

Unequal struggles—open as well as concealed—are raging in Europe, in the Middle East, in Southeast Asia, and in other places. Yet the outcome of these struggles is often in doubt, although the strength of a big power is directed against a militarily far inferior opponent. Will the Russians break the resistance spirit of the Czechs and the Slovaks? Will they be able to annul the independence of Romania? And will the Americans escape a major defeat in Vietnam and the adjoining areas? Only the future will tell.

The big powers unquestionably exert a decisive influence on the pattern of international relations. Smaller members of international society appear to be at the mercy of the leading states. Consequently, big-power strategy is widely discussed and accepted as generally valid by political and military writers, while the strategic problems of small states do not receive adequate attention.

Yet a considerable portion of the globe belongs to small states and nations, whose role is far from insignificant. They have been able to survive even in a postwar Europe divided into two spheres of influence by the superpowers. Does their influence not seem to be increasing, while empires are breaking apart? Does the theory of the omnipotence of the great powers really fit the facts?

Is the unexpected vitality of small nations in the present

world a passing trend? Can small nations continue to exist merely at the sufferance of the great powers, or as members of international organizations and military alliances dominated by the great powers? Or would they be able to defend their independence even against the giants? These questions are of importance in the unfolding of world politics.

The problem can be approached in many ways. One way is to focus on international organizations—on their past record and expected future reliability as protectors of small nations. Another approach is to ascertain whether military alliances adequately protect the interests and guarantee the inviolability of their minor partners. The third approach is to examine whether small nations can survive even if, as may well happen, they must rely on their own strength. Since international organizations and alliances, just like the gods, help mainly those who can help themselves, even the first and the second approaches ultimately point to the third. In the last century, as well as the last few years, often the only protection available to small states was their own fortitude.

This study examines the rather neglected problems concerning the defensive capabilities of individual small states, both in deterring and in actively resisting aggression. The key question is: How can they defend themselves in a world dominated by the great powers?

I begin with the tantalizing Czechoslovak resistance. The background includes a look at the present defensive posture of small nations like Switzerland and Sweden, their strategic dilemma and need for a new kind of defense; the role of the small states in military history and theory; the European resistance movements during World War II. A discussion focused on Europe can use widely known and well-documented examples, while remaining within manageable limits. The Czechoslovak struggle reveals hitherto unrealized possibilities of intelligent political resistance against the military forces of an invading superpower.

Despite the wide variety of reviewed cases, a search for

conditions favorable to the survival of small nations reveals many similarities, common patterns and principles. The primary factors appear to be political: the nature and strength of the political community and its leaders. Military power is merely a secondary factor. This study examines some of the political elements in the defense of small nations as a counterweight against the threat or use of military force.

In order to avoid treating every related strategic and tactical problem of both political and military nature, the study is limited on four counts:

(1) It stresses *political* elements, while giving the military aspects secondary place; *nations* rather than small states in general, or other entities; a strategy of *defense;* and examples from the experience of *small* nations.

(2) The approach used is that of a small defending nation fighting on its own, not as a member of an alliance. Thus, defense means essentially self-defense; the struggle goes on inside the contested area; the crucial political relationships involved are those between the citizens, the political leaders, the community on one side and the intruders on the other. The strategy applied is a true small-nation strategy.

(3) The problem of nuclear attack is omitted. It does not affect the primacy of socio-political factors in planning a defensive strategy for small nations. Furthermore, resistance within a political community does not offer any targets for nuclear attack.

(4) I write as a protagonist of small nations, searching for means that give them a reasonable chance of resisting attacks on their internal and external freedom. Many of their problems, as well as their strengths and weaknesses, differ so significantly from those of other states that they are best studied separately.

The narrow limits are necessary to reduce the volume of the study. But they have a negative effect: they prevent the examination of many practical problems connected with the total defense of small nations.

To compensate for this disadvantage, I attempt to apply

the study, at least by implication, to a greater number of actual cases:

(1) Wherever possible, I examine the more difficult situations; the less difficult ones can then be included by an argument *a fortiori*. For instance, a small nation may suffer various degrees of outside pressure, subversive activities, a regime imposed by an alien power and/or a military invasion; since invasion is the most difficult to deal with, it is discussed in more detail than other forms of intervention. Similarly, I do not consider outside help.

(2) I give more attention to political strategy than to tactics, because the former is wider in scope. Where the defending nation takes the correct strategic position, the tactical possibilities—as the ingenious Czechs and Slovaks proved—are practically unlimited.

(3) Some methods of defense (organized and spiritual resistance, for example) can be varied to apply in all situations—from the least to the most favorable.

The basic argument is as follows:

Modern international conflicts have become increasingly more political. Formerly centered around military threats and hostilities, they now include political struggles that begin before, continue simultaneously with, and go on long after a military interlude that includes anything from implied threats of force to outright conquest. Even the ultimate aim of modern invasion is to gain effective and uncontested political control.

Political control can be attacked or defended directly by political means, but only indirectly by military force and terror.

The strategy of the great powers seems to rely on military superiority to gain and hold political control.

A correct strategy for small nations—like the one used by the Czechoslovaks in 1968—is to use political strength to neutralize the aggressor's military preponderance. An extended political resistance must aim to deny political control to the intruder.

This type of defense is *political* (in the original sense of the term, signifying matters connected with the *polis*—the political community) because (1) it is a struggle within the national community, (2) for the control of that community, and (3) it brings to bear the typical assets of a politically organized nation. National loyalty and cohesion; the groups and organizations of a pluralistic community; the shared traditions and goals—all are political elements contributing to the strength of national defense.

National resistance must be based on defensive strategy, operational flexibility, tactical dispersion and diversification, and an extensive spiritual preparation.

The best defense is a ubiquitous struggle that extends far beyond the limits of classical wars and even guerrilla operations.

The plan of the study can be summarized as follows: Chapter I describes briefly the surprising success-defeat-success pattern of the Czechoslovak resistance against Russian military invasion and political attacks. Chapter II stresses the dilemma of small-nation defense, their inability to resolve it within the present-day strategic framework. Chapter III explores the urgent need for a new general strategy of small nations; how to gain a political goal with political means. National resistance, in its broadest sense, is such a strategy—a political opposition, rooted in spiritual strength and propelled by a strong will to resist. Chapter IV sketches the politicizing of warfare, particularly the defense of small nations, from the great revolutions; the resistance of Spain, Rome, and Prussia in the Napoleonic Era; the Arab revolt in the First World War; to relevant strategic theories of A.H.D. von Bülow, Carl von Clausewitz, and T. E. Lawrence. Chapter V touches on the relation of force and violence to political control and concludes that force, if correctly resisted, does not secure control. Chapter VI discusses nationalism and other sources of political strength, as well as the political leaders and active fighters. Chapter VII concerns spiritual and technical preparation for resistance (predisposition), both in the deterrence stage and after enemy attack. Chapter VIII discusses the advantages of an extended defensive opposition and the use of free resistance components. Chapter IX reviews the organizational and administrative, as well as some military, aspects of specialized conflicts. The Conclusion evaluates the material in the light of new insights for unequal conflicts in the future between small-nation Davids and big-power Goliaths. The Goliaths, it appears, do not always win. . . .

In short: International conflicts are political by nature and have political objectives. This favors small nations in deterring and resisting an attack. Within their own borders, mobilizing the political strength of the citizens, they can apply their political superiority to prevent an aggressor from securing control of the country.

Small nations can hardly hope to resist a stronger power if they neglect to use every available element of their political strength. A new defensive strategy, using primarily political means to achieve political ends, is best suited to exploit their strength fully.

Even states relying on military power should not neglect the political factors. Military power can be decisive, at most, only in the second phase of the conflict. In the first phase—before military threats or hostilities start—and in the final phase—after military operations recede—political elements are the decisive ones. They determine the outcome of defense far more effectively than military fighting.

My bias in this study is in favor of small nations: (*a*) I believe that their existence and interests are just as important as those of the great powers, that it is politically myopic to disregard the rights of the small nations. (*b*) And I believe that nationalism among nations is a phenomenon as positive as individualism and the will to live are among individuals.

The four military-political writers discussed most in this study are, in chronological order, A. H. D. von Bülow, C. von Clausewitz, T. E. Lawrence and B. H. Liddell Hart. European resistance movements during World War II, events in Finland, Poland, Hungary after the war, French experiences in their less than successful revolutionary wars and the disastrous American troubles centered on Vietnam provide the examples. The history-making successful resistance of the Czechs and the Slovaks, in

1968, and their setbacks, in 1969, shed new light on the political elements of small-nation defense.

Obviously, there is no plausible answer to the perplexing questions about Czechoslovakia and Vietnam in military terms. Modern wars cannot be adequately discussed as military phenomena—either as big wars or as small wars. Without due regard for the vital political elements, the unequal conflicts remain largely unintelligible.

This study aims at providing a partial framework for a political analysis of unequal conflicts.

by nature and have political objectives. This favors small nations in deterring and resisting an attack. Within their own borders, mobilizing the political strength of the citizens, they can apply their political superiority to prevent an aggressor from securing control of the country. . . . In Czechoslovakia, the successful defense strategy turned out to be exactly of this type. The armed formations remained passive but hostile—an ambiguous strategic threat. Russian military forces were deprived of all targets. The resistance was fought with exclusively political weapons, against which the invaders could pit only a few hundred collaborators and imported agents. The Russians had planned it as an unequal military struggle with all the advantages in their favor; it turned into an unequal political struggle with all the advantages against them. Small nations, facing the mass armies of an invader, can resist effectively—they can transfer the struggle to the higher level of politics. Their strategic success is to stay above the effective range of military force and violence."

Students of international affairs will find this work interesting reading. For political and military leaders, indeed for all citizens concerned with national defense, it will be an enlightening experience.

CHAPTER I

Three Surprises in Czechoslovakia

An era in the life of Czechoslovakia ended with the year 1967. Political and religious oppression, economic stagnation, personal and national rivalries finally united a sufficient number of top Communists against the arbitrary rule of Party boss and President Novotny. After a prolonged struggle, the Stalinoid leadership was forced to step down.

Between January and April, 1968, more and more liberals replaced hard-liners in the apparatus of Party, State, and Government.

The population greeted the changes with united enthusiasm.

The new leadership, carried forward by this powerful national sentiment, adopted an increasingly liberal program. It promised free elections—at least within the ruling Communist Party of the Czechoslovak Socialist Republic (C.S.S.R.); a government based on popular support; restoration of citizens' rights; and envisaged "a socialism with a human face"—all of these features absolutely irreconcilable with a Communist regime patterned on the Soviet model.

The Stalinoid reaction was immediate. A few weeks after it had come to power the new leadership was almost deposed by a military coup that collapsed at the last moment.

Disappointed, the Russians now started a massive campaign to intimidate the new leaders into discontinuing all reforms and clamping down rigid controls. The threats began as suggestions. They continued as flagrant pressure through political channels and concerted press attacks from Moscow, Warsaw, and East Berlin. They escalated into a series of military demonstrations along the borders of Czechoslovakia. In June, Russian troops

entered the C.S.S.R. and refused to withdraw at the end of the
"maneuvers," calling repeatedly on the "healthy" reactionary
elements in the country to use their presence to stage a coup
and openly assuring them of "all the brotherly help required" to
oust the liberals.

In July in a speech in Moscow, Brezhnev pointedly praised
the 1956 suppression of the Hungarians with tanks. The Soviet
press by implication threatened economic sanctions that might
bring about the collapse of Prague's economy. Soviet agents
planted—and "discovered"—weapons in Czechoslovakia; the an-
nouncement of the find was intended as a signal for a formal
invasion."[1]

Surprisingly, the Czechs and Slovaks could not be intimidated.
Supported by a united public opinion, and by the sympathies
of Yugoslavia, Romania, and the Communist Parties of Western
Europe, the national leaders refused to yield to Soviet pressures.

Massive forces of the Russians and their allies, posed for
attack since the end of May and held back in mid-July at the
last moment only by disagreement within the Kremlin, rolled
across the borders of Czechoslovakia on the night from August
20 to 21.

The invasion of Czechoslovakia, patterned on the successful
suppression of Hungary, proceeded with impressive speed and
efficiency. Its Army did not fight. There was no armed resistance,
no attempts at sabotage. The entire country was occupied within
hours. Russian troops reached all objectives; they arrested and
deported liberal leaders of Government, Party, and Parliament.
It was a complete *military* success.

The first, and by far the most startling, surprise in Czechoslovakia was the complete *political* failure for the Russians:
Political resistance erupted hours after the attack. The invaders
now found themselves unable to suppress the countrywide protests, to install a collaborator regime, or to control the country
effectively on their own. Moscow had to release the arrested
national leaders and to negotiate a settlement with them. After

---

[1] *The New York Times*, August 8, 1968.

five days of occupation, the resistance newspaper *Reporter* described the situation as follows:

> It is clear that the moral victory is ours. The aggressors have encountered such a single-minded resistance by the two nations of our country that there is no precedent for it in history. They are desperately seeking some authoritative collaborationists to provide a semblance of "legality" to the aggression after the fact. There simply are none. The occupation army is totally isolated, helpless, completely rejected. The country is anonymous and mute. Arrest warrants and lists of victims have become worthless. The occupiers have seized our printing houses, but newspapers keep appearing several times a day with full freedom of expression. They have seized the radio, but the broadcasts go on in freedom. They have seized the television but failed to silence it, too. Already in these first days, the occupation has been politically defeated, defeated morally and psychologically, defeated and rendered ridiculous before the eyes of the whole world.[2]

Hitler, in 1939, and Stalin, in 1948, had taken over everything without any complications. Why did not the same type of assault by Stalin's heirs succeed in 1968? In the past, both Czechs and Slovaks had lacked fighting spirit in similar situations. And the two nations were, in addition, divided among themselves. The invasion was well planned and prepared. There was an impressive show of "invincible" Russian military might; days before Russian secret police had been brought to Prague, the collaborators had been informed; the leaders and the people were caught by surprise; by the time the citizens arose the occupiers had arrived.

Surprisingly, the Czechs and Slovaks showed great political maturity and an instinctive ability to choose the best form of resistance. The attacks, rather than dividing them, had united them against the alien intruder as never before. When they discarded any ideas of armed opposition but concentrated all their energies on political resistance, the situation for the invaders had not only gotten out of hand—it had gotten out of the range

---

[2] Reprinted in R. Littell (ed.), *The Czech Black Book* (New York: Praeger, 1969), p. 211.

of military force. Thus, the Russians simply lost control of the situation.

Despite continuous Russian political pressure, merciless threats, and feverish subversive activities, the united population and the leaders resisted successfully all through 1968. By the beginning of 1969, Czechoslovakia was succeeding in the political combat: although occupied, it was in fact a free country; the Russians had been able to extort nothing but a few insignificant concessions. Full seven months after the invasion the political battle raged undiminished, but the Czechs were still undefeated.

The second surprise came early in April, 1969, when—as a result of another round of the now familiar Russian threats and subversion—the unity of the country's Communist leadership cracked and the invaders could force a collaborator regime on the disunited Party and Government bureaucrats.[3] Rapidly, a Stalinoid rule was re-established. Patriots were expelled from Party and Government positions. The invader's agents began attempts to destroy popular groups and organizations, imposed totalitarian censorship of the information media, closed the country's borders, arrested or dismissed from their jobs thousands of citizens for political reasons.

The third surprise was that, despite the oppression of the invader's servants, the Czechs and the Slovaks maintained their spirit of resistance. The unity of the people did not suffer; they did not acquiesce. The workers, the youth of the country, practically all strata of the population rejected the invasion and the regime. Their support of liberal leaders and their demands for freedom became, if possible, even stronger albeit not always openly expressed. Their opposition to the present regime is determined and not likely to change in the foreseeable future.

A political victory remains safely out of the reach of the occupiers and their retainers. Their only support is the invading army.

What does the case of the C.S.S.R. mean for the defense of other small nations? What does it teach about other unequal

---

[3] *Der Spiegel*, April 28, 1969.

conflicts? The fact that the Czechoslovaks won a political victory, and held on to it for more than seven months, means that small nations *can* resist a military invasion—even the invasion of a superpower—by political means. This insight is an important breakthrough in small-nation strategy.

It has been traditional to consider as exceptions the cases in which small nations succeeded, and as the rule those cases in which they failed. In the following chapters I shall explain why I disagree with this pessimistic fatalism. The Czechs, just as the Hungarians, the Algerians, the Cypriotes, and the Vietcong, lost the military contest. But the Czechs and Slovaks refused to fight on the battlefield, relying on their political superiority.

Can a small nation turn the political superiority into a decisive strategic element of an unequal struggle against a military invader? We saw that the nations of Czechoslovakia were successful as long as their leaders did not turn against each other. And that the people are still undefeated. This is a significant insight for other small nations who may have to fight in similar conditions: if they can muster a stronger leadership, their national resistance can succeed.

In the past, small nations have often failed to find the strategy most likely to let them prevail against a powerful aggressor. The Czechoslovak experience suggests the correct political strategy for defending small nations in unequal struggles.

The greatest surprise may still be the discovery of the political strength of small nations and the political weaknesses of aggressors.

CHAPTER II

The Dilemma of Small Nations

Two superpowers have dominated the world since 1945. Other states merely clustered around them for protection or hoped to save themselves by withdrawing passively to the sidelines of world politics. If some countries expected to achieve independent strength, they attempted that by joining regional unions aspiring to become great powers sometime in the future.

Small nations seemed to be but appendages of the spheres of great-power influence, helpless fragments likely to be swallowed by the giants at will. This view remained unchanged even after Russia failed to take over Finland in 1948, or to prevent the assertion of Yugoslav independence in 1948 and of Romanian independence in 1964; after France could not hold Algeria; and after the United States accepted the collapse of her probe against Cuba in the Bay of Pigs. The strategic impotence of small states was still held to be both unprecedented and permanent.

Curiously, the general tendency still is to define *a priori* as exceptions all cases in which small nations prevailed and as the rule the cases in which they perished. It may be well to test this dogmatic assumption. Is it not possible that the small nations of our time could defend their existence and independence, despite the great disparity between their strength and that of the military giants? What are the dangers for small nations? How can they counteract the dangers?

The danger is that a great power, or any other state having disproportionate military strength, may act to deprive in whole or in part a small nation of its physical existence, national identity, or independence. The threat extends all the way from (1) outright incorporation into another state, (2) turning a small nation into a colony or satellite, (3) imposition of an unpopular regime, (4) subversion, (5) undue influence over a small nation's internal or (6) its external policy. The chief means of the aggressors are threats and the use of military force against weaker members of international society.

The great misfortune for the small states is that they have adopted great-power strategy as their own.

A. THE STRATEGY OF GREAT POWERS

In the twentieth century, the generally accepted strategy evaluates international conflicts according to the relative strength of the opposing military formations. Superior numbers and technical capacity of weapons, a greater mass of divisions with tanks and planes, must decide the issue on land and in the air; a navy with more and better-equipped vessels controls the seas. To conquer, one must concentrate greater numbers against a weaker point of the enemy. The problems are more or less mathematical: more means victory, less means defeat.

According to this great-power doctrine, military power decides international conflicts: their outcome depends exclusively on the results of battles between mass armies. The theoretical basis of the doctrine is the stress on total war, derived from a misinterpretation of the teachings of Clausewitz.

World War I was the outstanding example of mass strategy in the twentieth century. Foch, Haig, Brusilov, Ludendorf, and other generals of the opposing great powers handled armies of millions of men. They staged gigantic battles, with casualty figures often reaching half a million. By such standards, small nations did not rate at all. Bigness was the criterion of greatness.

In the period between the World Wars, political and military experts considered the dominance of great powers to be self-evident. As soon as postwar life began to normalize, everyone was thinking mainly in terms of large states and their "legimate interests." Small nations did not seem to have such interests. At times they seemed nothing but an irritant in a world that, without them, could be ruled so smoothly by the empires of Britain, France, Japan, the U.S.A., Hitler's Germany, and Stalin's Russia.

Even Mussolini's Italy, a musical-comedy empire, was counted among the masters of the world!

Aggressive pressures and the initial successes of expansionism impressed the world. "The independence of small states, and indeed of all states save the largest and richest, is impracticable now that a mechanized army and air force belonging to a great state can simply sweep aside all resistance," wrote a leading political scientist, accurately expressing the consensus of people in politics, the military profession, and the news media. "In a world in which appeal to force still lies at the back of international relationships, the sovereign state which is utterly unable to defend its borders is an anomaly."[1] The strategy of the big powers was firmly based on similar assumptions.

What about the small nations? The Irish, the Greeks, the Swiss, and the Romanians may have found it a trifle sad to accept the idea of theirs being an "anomaly," but cold numbers of men and weapons seemed an uncontrovertible argument. The people in Helsinki, Warsaw, Riga, and Budapest concluded that their sentiments were wrong, that they could not reasonably expect to preserve their freedom.

Famous strategists, among them two very able ones, agreed that military hardware was decisive. "The most virile nation might not be able to withstand another, inferior to it in all natural qualities," wrote one analyst, "if the latter had decisively superior technical appliances."[2] Another stated it even more strongly: "Tools, or weapons form 99 per cent of victory. Strategy, command, leadership, courage, discipline, supply, organization and all moral and physical paraphernalia of war are nothing to a high superiority in weapons—at most they go to form one per cent which makes the whole possible."[3] These theories sounded impressive and were accepted.

---

[1] G. D. H. Cole, *Europe, Russia and the Future* (London: The Macmillan Co., 1942), pp. 13, 69.

[2] B. H. Liddell Hart, *The Revolution in Warfare* (New Haven: Yale University Press, 1947), p. 37.

[3] J. F. C. Fuller, *Armament and History* (London: C. Scribner's Sons, 1945), p. 31.

In this regard, World War II and the subsequent developments changed very little. As before, the strategy of great powers envisions military giants grinding forward, destroying every resistance in their path. A division equals a division, a battery of missiles and warheads equals another with the same technical capacity, etc. As before, the practice is to abide by the result of a military contest. Once the troops have won on the battlefield, all contests are decided. As in the old-fashioned history books, the emphasis is on battles, killing, and violence.

Militarily inferior opponents receive little attention in the strategy of great powers. Hitler did not value the Poles sufficiently to have a single expert on their culture and language at his headquarters in September, 1939.[4] "How many divisions does the Pope have?" Stalin inquired sarcastically. Later he declared: "I shall shake my little finger—and there will be no Tito!"[5] The giants are expected to win—always.

According to orthodox strategy, conflicts are analyzed in purely military terms, without regard for the people concerned. The Berlin Crisis of 1961–69—in a metropolis with 3,500,000 inhabitants, surrounded by a nation of more than seventy million whose interests were directly affected by every move—was evaluated exactly in this fashion. One calculated what the Soviet Army was doing or planning, what the Western Allies were trying to do, how the Red Volksarmee and the West Berlin police would behave. People and nations, obviously, belonged to the items that could be safely disregarded in this strategic calculation.

The conclusions for small nations are simple: They cannot survive. An aggressive great power can always concentrate more power and force a military decision in its favor. To insist on opposing the formidable masses is unreasonable obstinacy.

From the point of view of the great powers this is, of course, quite in order. To stress orthodox theory and military force, the

---

[4] Peter Kleist, *Zwischen Hitler und Stalin* (Bonn: Athenaeum Verlag, 1950), p. 155.

[5] Nikita S. Khruschev, *The Anatomy of Terror: Revelations About Stalin's Regime* (Washington, D.C.: Public Affairs Press, 1956), p. 55.

bases of their strength, wisely furthers their interests. They are following the safest road to preponderance by making bigness count for most, by exploiting a military superiority over smaller and weaker opponents. If bigness is greatness, they are the winners.

But what happens to the small nations?

B. THE INADEQUACY OF SMALL-NATION DEFENSE

How can small nations counter the various threats from interference in their affairs to outright absorption into an empire?

Orthodox military strategy, unfortunately, does not tell how a small nation could hold off a great power: a strong and fast attack cannot be prevented from reaching the defender's nerve centers and occupying the country. Hitler only restated with his typical bluntness what logically follows from the principles of great power stategy: "The day of small states is past!"

But the danger that small states may be threatened and attacked is always present. A momentary stability in certain regions does not guarantee future safety, especially if the equilibrium is not based on their own strength but on a stalemate between the ambitions of great powers. Any change in a constellation of power—be it a shifting of the respective spheres of influence, a reshuffling of alliances, the direction of interests to another area, a deal or agreements between the nuclear powers, a breakthrough in military technology, etc.—increases the fluidity of the situation, and leaves small nations at the mercy of the locally dominant giant. If they cannot defend themselves, their freedom is in danger. This is the dilemma of small nations today.

Reference to the Swedish situation may illustrate the point. Sweden is a rich and highly developed country with a good strategic position and other defensive advantages. Her people are eager to preserve her independence. Her armed forces are stronger than those of her neighbors. She has a homogenous population, a solid national tradition, a considerable economic strength, a high level of education, a good living standard, and an internal political and social stability that can be the envy of many other states. The picture is completed by a marked absence of significant minority groups or dissatisfied elements. Her territory includes large mountainous regions; almost 70 per cent of it is covered by forests, lakes, and rivers; 15 per cent lies north of the Arctic Circle. Road and rail communications, especially in central and northern Sweden, are few and most of them could be easily interrupted by sabotage. Strategically important mines and industries can be rendered useless to an invader by systematic destruction.

Yet despite all the advantages, Sweden would be helpless against a great power, even against a conventional attack. What are the basic tasks of Swedish defense? Can the Swedish Army accomplish the tasks? In case of attack, the first basic task is (1) "to prevent the enemy from putting his foot on Swedish soil." However, (2) "if the enemy forces succeeded in obtaining a footing, they must be dealt with promptly"; and (3) "if they cannot be defeated at the start, offensive operations must be delayed until the appropriate moment."[6]

Sweden could, in optimum conditions, mobilize 600,000 men; but her peacetime army consists of conscripts trained seven and a half months. (The service lasts ten months, "whereof 75 days are lost because of weekends, holidays, leave, illness, etc.")[7] Liddell Hart wrote that even men who spent twice that time in the army "can hardly be reckoned as really trained—and the risks of relying on semi-trained men in modern warfare have been shown."[8] In addition, Sweden has a Home Guard, made up of boys and older men who get twenty hours of Sunday training each year, and some local defense units. A semi-official Swedish publication admits that even if mobilization were accomplished before an attack, combat units could not simultaneously be ready for action in all the possible points of invasion.

---

[6] Anders Grafström, *The Swedish Army* (Stockholm: Hörsta Förlag, 1954), pp. 6, 11.

[7] *Ibid.*, p. 95.

[8] B. H. Liddell Hart, *Defence of the West* (London: Cassell, 1950), p. 225.

"It would be a flight of fancy to suppose that an aggressive power would give us time to mobilize. At worst we must be prepared for an enemy attack to be launched before we had time to mobilize."[9] Hardly a very impressive outlook, it is all a small state can do.

Since the Swedish Army may not be ready for a considerable time, who will resist the enemy? The local Home Guard with twenty hours of training, and at some places also some local defense units (but most of the latter will be ready only after a few days). They will have to face the enemy's elite troops. The country's defense may depend, in many sectors, on the Home Guard (assisted, if possible, by hopelessly outnumbered Air Force and Navy units), for as long as the whole first week of the war, or longer. The first task, obviously, cannot be accomplished, failing ample advanced warning or the landing of inferior enemy forces in the middle of a concentration of Swedish training units (there are no other standing units). The second task is equally impossible for the Home Guard and local units, the only ones ready for action during the first days. Remains the third: to concentrate adequate forces for a full-scale counterattack. But that could not start earlier than a week, in most cases even longer, after invasion. By that time the advantages would no longer be on the side of the Swedes. By that time Sweden would have lost.

An aggressor could select the conditions most favorable for himself and force the defenders into a strategically hopeless position from the beginning. He could choose the time, place, and type of attack; use numerous elite troops, and exploit the element of surprise. A former German general, working for the Russians, revealed how Sweden could have been occupied, in World War II. "A sudden attack with a strong concentration of fire from all arms if undertaken by assault forces with war experience and modern equipment," he wrote, "should be able to direct a heavy blow against Sweden's Army and Air Force, and take the sap out of her, already during the first days of

---

[9] Grafström, *op. cit.*, pp. 84, 147.

attack."[10] Hitler's Wehrmacht did tip the scales against Poland, Denmark, Norway, Holland, Belgium, Yugoslavia, and Greece in a matter of days. Even France was lost after Guderian's breakthrough, on the fifth day of the attack. What Germany could do then, another aggressor can do now. The Russians did take Czechoslovakia in a few hours.

In fact, no expert has seriously claimed that Sweden could repulse an invasion. Her Defense Minister called only for "such strategy and tactics as to force an attacker's minimum cost of occupying Swedish territory up as high as possible." He implied that occupation was unavoidable. The Commander-in-Chief of the Swedish armed forces wrote in a memorandum to the Government that Sweden could be attacked both over land and from the sea. But with the military means at her disposal, he stated, she could repel an attack only from one of the two directions, not from both.[11] The calculated costs may dissuade an enemy from attacking, but once he does attack the outcome is not in doubt.

One must conclude that a successful defense is impossible. Yet Sweden is, it should be emphasized, one of the strongest small nations in Europe. Most of the others are weaker. Switzerland is probably stronger.[12] But with their present defense posture, none of them is safe; they are likely to succumb within a few days, if not hours.

What is more: a fast collapse of their military defense may be preferable to a longer struggle. In the unlikely case in which a small nation can concentrate sizable units for a counterattack, it would lose them against the aggressor's superior force. The

---

[10] Ernst Jungstedt, " 'Polarräven' en Tysk anfallsplan mot Sverige under andra Världskriget," *Krigshistoriska Studier* (Stockholm, 1950), p. 100. All translations from works whose titles are quoted in French, German, Swedish, and Danish are mine (V.V.S.).

[11] *Dagens Nyheter* (Stockholm), March 17, 1961; "Ur OB-svaret 62," *Tidskrift för Värnpliktiga Officerare*, 5 (1962), 7 ff.

[12] An excellent study of practically every aspect of Swiss defense is Hans Rudolf Kurz, ed., *Die Schweizer Armee Heute* (Thun: Verlags-AG, 1964).

invader may even permit, or *induce*, the concentration to destroy the defender's last reserves faster and more thoroughly. The result? A short while after mobilization the mass of the nation's best men would be in prison camps, helpless captives abandoned to physical and psychological assaults of the enemy. A defense built according to the criteria of great-power strategy can achieve little more than this unfortunte result. The conqueror himself could not have planned a more complete paralysis of opposition.

Small nations would do well to ponder the best use of their forces. The Norwegian Army, to take but one example, has existed since 1905. It was needed for the eighteen months between the autumn of 1938 and the spring of 1940, when it speedily collapsed after a military *beau geste* without significance. As a matter of cruel fact, Danish, Belgian, and Dutch armies could impede the occupation of their countries just as little as the grand-ducal forces could protect Luxemburg! Danish Defense Minister Andersen recognized this and advised surrender when Germany attacked in 1940: "If one sees that the result is already clear, I consider that further sacrifices must be prevented, and I am ready to assume a share of responsibility for it in the present situation."[13] There was absolutely no sense in "slugging it out" with the Wehrmacht.

The only practical value of small-nation armies lay in the experience their cadres brought to resistance movements. Norway, for one, may have made a stronger showing, in 1940, if she had omitted a mobilization against Germany but prepared for a purposeful resistance. Elite units, extremely mobile and placed at crucial points of the rugged country, could have specialized in quasi-military action, held out indefinitely, and encouraged the nation. Liddell Hart reviewed the experiences of 1939–45 and advised small states to use subtler, non-violent means. The resistance that counted "only began after their armies had been overthrown. The gesture of keeping forces to offer battle was superfluous extravagance."[14]

---

[13] Walter Hubatsch, *Weserübung* (2d ed.; Göttingen: Musterschmidt Verlag, 1960), pp. 128-29.

[14] Liddell Hart, *Revolution in Warfare*, pp. 98-99.

Extensive partisan warfare is seldom a better solution. If the enemy is strong enough to destroy the defending military forces, guerrilla actions are not likely to defeat him. To expect victory from a mere irritant is illusory. (In exceptional circumstances a guerrilla war can, of course, be decisive; and violent attacks, or urban guerrilla campaigns, may well reinforce political resistance.)

At the present time, the defense policies of small nations are caught in a vicious circle between well-intentioned preparations that do not assure their survival and a feeling of futility, a resignation that "nothing can be done." Orthodox strategy (the strategy that now guides defense planning and preparations) holds out no hope for them; it only rationalizes their unavoidable collapse. As with most cancer treatments now and the polio antidotes of twenty years ago, at the end there is only death or paralysis. The predestined doom is inescapable.

This strategy has too many defects; it does not make any sense for the small nations to rely on it for their salvation: (1) It does not even attempt to explain why some small nations have survived and defended themselves, while others were subdued and exterminated. (2) It does not show how they can counter the wide variety of political and military pressures—beginning with diplomatic threats, subversion, and limited incidents—available to aggressive great powers. The alternatives either to fight a defensive war and guerrilla actions against each threat, or to surrender without opposition—the only choice great-power strategy gives them—are entirely insufficient. (3) It does not teach small nations how to use defensively their greatest strengths: in the case of Sweden, they are a homogenous population, solid national tradition, political and social stability, high level of education, etc. Obviously, a strategy must be useless if it ignores a nation's greatest assets.

To cling to such obsolete dogma is a potentially fatal strategic blunder. One hundred years ago, in an equally dangerous situation, the Swedish scholar and poet Victor Rydberg said: "It is our own fault if we prepare our defense setup in a way, or develop it further in a direction, that makes the greatest part of our forces useless in the hour of need."[15] The Prussian military expert A. H. D. von Bülow censured the leaders who brought his country to defeat by "repeating without thinking what others, who also did not think themselves, have said before." And Karl Marx wrote that "a nation fighting for its liberty ought not to adhere rigidly to the accustomed rules of warfare, to the etiquette of war."[16] A drastic change is as imperative now, as it was in their times. "Since the founding of the Republic," wrote a Czech resistance newspaper, "we have had a strong army, but have never been allowed to use it. Every time we want to mobilize the army for our defense, the act of mobilization itself would threaten our very national existence."[17]

The leaders of small nations should reject the outmoded strategic *Weltanschauung* of the great powers.

But what can be put in its place? How can the small nations escape the dilemma their defense is facing?

---

[15] Victor Rydberg, *Huru kan Sverige bevara sin sjelfständighet?* (Göteborg, 1859), p. 10.

[16] F. O. Miksche, *Secret Forces* (London: Faber and Faber, 1950), p. 25; quoting *Neue Rheinische Zeitung*, April 1, 1849.

[17] *The Czech Black Book*, R. Littell, ed., (N. Y.: Praeger, 1969), p. 108.

CHAPTER III

The Defense of Small Nations

A. A NEW STRATEGY

Small nations can escape the dilemma concerning their defense if they find a new strategy that lets them exploit their strengths and the weaknesses of their adversaries, and to counter the wide variety of political and military pressure available to the aggressors. It must be a defensive strategy of their own, measured to the needs of the small nations.

They must, first of all, break out of the vicious circle of futility and despair. They must recover their self-confidence and determination. They must realize that not absolute strength determines victory, but the best use of their resources,. "Experience taught me that a clever plan does more than an army of 100,000 warriors," said the conqueror Tamerlane. And Mao Tse-tung succeeded by following the principle that the enemy's advantages can be reduced, and his shortcomings aggravated, by one's efforts. Mathematical superiority does not decide conflicts; correct strategy does. Clausewitz wrote that "the privilege to dictate the rules of the contest to the enemy makes a difference in gaining time and strength, and in various secondary advantages that become very substantial in the long run."[1]

Many a spectacular victory was won by a militarily weaker side able to impose its rules on the struggle. The nationalists of Ireland, the saintlike Gandhi, the Communists Mao and Giap defeated powerful enemies. Colonel Geneste guessed the secret

---

[1] Carl von Clausewitz, *Vom Kriege* (17th ed.; Bonn: F. Dümmler's Verlag, 1952), Bk. VI, Ch. 25.

of Vietminh victory—they had "changed the rules of the game."[2]
They imposed their own strategy on the French. Grivas dictated
the conditions to the British on Cyprus. The Algerians placed
France (a great power, compared to the F.L.N.) in an impossible
strategic situation. In Europe, Hungarian revolutionaries forced
Russian divisions to retreat and destroyed alien political control
of the country in 1956. The subsequent reconquest of Hungary
was possible only because the Freedom Fighters had a faulty
strategy: they accepted the rules of great-power warfare and
abided by the military decision. In Czechoslovakia, the successful
resistance against invasion in 1968 was an undeniable political
victory for the patriots—the result of unexpectedly intelligent
strategy exploiting their own strengths and Russian weaknesses.

The last four instances, by far not the only ones of this kind,
saw nuclear powers defeated. (Another contest is still going on
in Vietnam, where the world's strongest superpower—the U.S.A.
—is having considerable difficulties.) These lessons are highly
instructive. The fact that they were *political* victories does not
depreciate them; it makes them truly modern and significant.
It shows that correct strategy prevails over mass, destructive
power, and military hardware.

The Russian General Tatarchenko remarked cleverly that
"the battleship did not replace the cruiser, nor the minelayer,
nor the cutter, not even the rowboat."[3] Even more can be said:
If the competition is a rowing contest, a battleship cannot win.
And by 1970, battleships are obsolete, while rowboats are still
quite useful. Similarly, nuclear bombs do not replace other forms
of military and political struggle; they do not even render raiding parties obsolete. Empires do not replace nations, nor does
great-power strategy preclude a success of small-nation strategy
—no matter what the worshipers of bigness may claim. The
strategic principles of Sun Tzu are still valid (Mao and Giap

---

[2] "Guerrilla Warfare," in Franklin Mark Osanka (ed.), *Modern Guerrilla
Warfare* (New York: Free Press of Glencoe, 1962), p. 265.

[3] Quoted in Raymond L. Garthoff, *Soviet Strategy in the Nuclear Age*
(New York: Praeger, 1962), p. 225.

gained much by applying his teachings); so are those of T. E. Lawrence, more than ever.

Many small nations are closely knit national communities. Their best policy is to rely on this socio-political strength, to defend themselves within their own borders, among their own people. Within the patriotic nation, the cause of its freedom is superior to any other; every alien invader is strongly detested and resisted.

History has repeatedly demonstrated how exposed an invader's weaknesses are in a resisting country. Napoleon's brother Joseph vividly expressed the political hopelessness of the French in Spain in a letter to the Emperor:

> One hundred thousand scaffolds are needed here to keep in power a Prince condemned to rule under you. I do not have a single supporter here. I have as an enemy a nation of twelve million brave, utterly enraged people. No, Sire, one does not know this nation; every house will be a fortress, every man will adopt the common cause. Not a single Spaniard will serve me if the country is conquered; we will not find a single guide, not a single spy. . . . Sire, you are making a mistake; your glory will be wrecked in Spain.[4]

Exactly one hundred and fifty years later, George Kennan stressed the same political factors when he suggested a new defense policy for European nations: armed forces, he wrote, should be paramilitary and not regular military units. The training should aim "to prepare them not only to offer overt resistance to a foreign invader but also to constitute the core of a civilian resistance movement in a territory that might be overrun by the enemy." He considered the main defense tasks to be the elimination of possible collaborators; strengthening of "the united and organized hostility of an entire nation"; making the stay of occupation forces unpleasant, costly, and "without favorable long-term prospects."

A small country should be able to tell the possible aggressor that he will be facing exactly this type of defense, said Kennan,

---

[4] Octave Aubry, *Napoléon* (Paris: Flammarion, 1936), p. 209.

if he were unwise enough to invade. The respected scholar offered "personal assurance," certainly not without having weighed his words well, "that any country which is in a position to say this to Moscow, not in so many words but in a language of military posture and political behavior, will have little need for outside help to assure its immunity."[5]

The Czechoslovak case by no means disproves Professor Kennan's theory: the Czechs never spoke clearly about defending themselves either by military or by any other means. Nor did the Russians have any reason to expect the united and determined resistance they actually had to face. A clear Yugoslav determination to fight obviously deterred Stalin from attacking in 1948–52. A Romanian threat to resist by all means may have deterred his heirs from invading Romania in September, 1968.

Small nations should not waste their human and material wealth fighting battles where the enemy can easily defeat them. A far better policy is to prepare for political defense, their own kind of strategy. They should fight with maximum advantages on their side, maximum disadvantages on the enemy's! The resistance of a nation in its own country against an alien comes close to that ideal. There a small and united nation is strongest, and the aggressor's political disadvantages are greatest.

Small nations must create their own strategy and impose it on the struggle. They should disregard the rules of the enemy, adopting the attitude described by Lin Piao: "You fight in your way and we fight in ours; we fight when we can win and move away when we cannot. You give full play to your superiority and we give full play to ours; you have your way of fighting and we have ours."[6] To prepare a political defense of their own should be the major goal of the small nations. Such a strategy will even permit them to retaliate against the invaders: no matter how strong, each of the great powers has an Achilles' heel or

---

[5] George Kennan, *Russia, the Atom and the West* (New York: Harper, 1958), pp. 63-65, *passim.*

[6] Lin Piao, *Long Live the Victory of People's War!* (Peking: Foreign Languages Press, 1965), p. 36.

two. The United States has its Negro problem, and the Soviet Union has difficulties with its subject nationalities; but neither Lichtenstein nor Andorra has such weak points. The small nations should concentrate on politics, where both their fundamental strength and the fundamental weakness of the enemy can be found.

In short: The contest must be transferred to the political arena, and a strategic success against aggression must be sought there. It can be achieved if (1) the defending nation finds elements of political strength that correspond to the intruder's weakness; if (2) it successfully exploits this strength against that weakness to gain a political superiority; and if (3) it can give this superiority sufficient weight to annul the impact of the enemy's military preponderance. Strategy is, after all, the art of making one's own superiority decisive.

A defending small nation can be vastly inferior militarily—it can refuse to oppose the invader—and still defeat him if it sticks to a national strategy and makes its political advantages prevail. My thesis is that many a small state can achieve a decisive political victory even in the "nuclear age." The Czechoslovak success, in 1968, was not a special case but a generally valid example: it was not unique, it was merely the first clear instance of political victory despite military inferiority in postwar Europe.

B. CONFLICT, RESISTANCE AND VICTORY

Why can political elements become strategically decisive? Because modern warfare is marked by the ascendancy of politics over war; because both the nature of modern conflicts and their objectives are basically political. Even wars, properly understood, are political conflicts between states and nations. Our age could quite accurately be described as the political era.

In modern conflicts one can distinguish a preliminary political stage, an interlude marked by the threat or the use of force, and a final political struggle. The contest—the adding of ingredients to the compound, the product of which will ultimately be victory or defeat—continues through all three phases. It may begin long before military or other forceful measures start and go on long after they have ended. But the decision falls in a political stage: only then do the final results of the entire conflict become apparent; only then is it revealed who won the struggle, including the stage when force was used.

The study (logos) of modern conflicts (polemos)—the *polemology*—is a political, not a military subject. Historiography may still present wars as a series of battles. The big powers contribute to the misconception that military force decides victory and defeat when they stress the destructive effect of their weapons. But other elements—economic, demographic, etc.—already receive more attention than before. Sooner or later politics must be recognized as the decisive factor.

All conflicts are a part of politics. In A. H. D. von Bülow's view the revolutionary wars in America and France established politics as the most important and political strategy as "the highest strategy." War was but one function of politics: "A war not governed by a political aim must be considered the silliest of all absurdities!"[7] The Napoleonic wars confirmed Clausewitz's view that war and politics are interdependent, that politics penetrate every campaign and battle, that no strategic plan or situation is purely military: "War belongs in the sphere of social life. It is a conflict between great interests. It could be compared with commerce, which is also a conflict of human interests and activities; and much closer to it stands politics."[8]

T. E. Lawrence demonstrated the primacy of politics. In the beginning, he recalled, "my vision of the course of Arab war was still purblind. I had not seen that the preaching was victory and the fighting a delusion." Later, he disparaged battles as a "mistake" and relied on diathetics, calling the enemy's presence a mere "secondary matter."[9] And Mao Tse-tung paraphrased

---

[7] A. H. D. von Bülow, *Der Feldzug von 1805, militärisch-politisch betrachtet* (Berlin, 1806), pp. xiv-xv.

[8] Clausewitz, *op. cit.* Bk. II, Ch. 3.

[9] T. E. Lawrence, *Seven Pillars of Wisdom* (New York: Dell Publishing Co., 1962), pp. 167, 200.

Clausewitz: "Politics are bloodless war, while war is a politics of bloodshed."[10]

Modern conflicts are multiform: their basic elements and ends remain political, but they may include an unlimited variety of secondary elements or means, not excluding military ones. Bourgès-Maunory, a former French Defense Minister, described modern war in one word—*polyvalent*.[11] James Burnham referred to the tools of war as "sticks, stones, and atoms": "In the nuclear age stones function as weapons a good deal oftener than nuclear bombs—and have won many more battles."[12] It is important to keep in mind this distinction between means and ends and to realize that, whatever the means, they are all part of a strategy to achieve political goals: "The object of war among civilized states is not to bring home heaps of scalps, it is to achieve new and more favorable *political* arrangements."[13] President Kennedy spoke of the U.S. armed forces as "a complement of our diplomacy," as a "deterrent" and a "symbol."[14]

The polyvalent nature of conflicts leads to the conclusions that any means, of whatever nature, may be useful in reaching political goals; and that one kind of technique or tool may be substituted for another. In Prague a Russian military weapon, a tank, turned into a Czech political weapon when painted with slogans and swastikas. . . . A military success is one possible means, but it is neither a necessary nor a sufficient condition for political victory. And it can be entirely dispensed with. The distinction leaves one free to select the best weapons, techniques, tactics, and strategy for each operation. It also leads to the conclusion that a political goal can be reached directly—and more effectively—by political means. Centuries ago, Tamerlane

---

[10] Mao Tse-tung, *On Protracted War* (Peking: Foreign Languages Press, 1954), p. 83.

[11] Quoted in *Modern Guerrilla Warfare*, p. 428.

[12] James Burnham, "Sticks, Stones, and Atoms," in *Modern Guerrilla Warfare*, p. 418.

[13] R. W. van de Velde, "The Neglected Deterrent," *Military Review* (Fort Leavenworth, Kansas), XXXVIII (1958), 3.

[14] *The New York Times*, June 7, 1962.

knew this from experience: "Good politics can accomplish more than heroism, a shrewd idea is more valuable than an army. An arrow shot with the weapons of politics at the opportune moment, finds without fail its place in the heart of the enemy."[15]

The goal of a conflict is to achieve political victory or to avoid political defeat. Clearly, not fighting but victory is the proper aim of all contests, including war. Just as clearly, the end is not a preliminary success, but a final victory which secures a decision. "There is only one success," according to Clausewitz, "namely, final success. Until then nothing is decided, nothing won, nothing lost."[16]

A military triumph does not, of itself, bring political victory, although occasionally it may facilitate a political decision. "The superiority one has or gains in war," to quote Clausewitz again, "is only the means, not the aim, and it must be staked toward the latter."[17] Instances in which the conversion has failed, in which a sum of military victories added up to a defeat—because political victories did not follow—are legion. Germany and Japan met defeat at the end of impressive advances in World War II. "The German mistake was to think that military success would solve political problems," admitted General von Kleist.[18] The U.S. has, year after year, failed to gain political victory in Vietnam, despite an endless series of military successes. States often have "won the war and lost the peace."

Even conquest is a political problem. Unsettled territory may be conquered and controlled by force of arms. Conquest and control of inhabited regions is a task achieved only by a political victory. Military successes and occupation merely let the invader compete for the ultimate political prize. Like a gain in any qualifying round, it does not determine the outcome of the decisive political struggle. Military conquest occupies terri-

---

[15] Michael Prawdin, *Tschingiz-Chan und sein Erbe* (Stuttgart: Deutsche Verlags-Anstalt, 1938), p. 400.

[16] Clausewitz, *op. cit.*, Bk. VIII, Ch. 3.

[17] *Ibid.*, Bk. VIII, Ch. 9.

[18] Quoted in B. H. Liddell Hart, *The German Generals Talk* (New York: Berkley Publishing Corp., 1958), p. 162.

tory; only political conquest controls the population. Occupation without control is useless.

Political victory terminates resistance and establishes control. It is achieved only by persuading the people—a process quite similar to winning an election. "Public opinion decides victory," as Bülow recognized long ago, "and one governs only through public opinion." T. E. Lawrence's captures of Arab provinces were political conquests; they would be won when the rebels had persuaded the inhabitants to adopt their goals. No modern conquest succeeds without persuading the people to accept a new rule. Nor is revolution suppressed, or subversion defeated, without a political victory. Father Hoa, the Vietnamese soldier-priest counseled that "the order of importance" was "winning the people first, winning the war second." An American officer in Vietnam is quoted as saying: "Most of us are sure that this problem is only fifteen per cent military."[19] The problem is, of course, *all* political. But it is interesting to note than an expert did not believe military successes could contribute more than 15 per cent toward its solution.

When the Germans occupied Byelorussia and the Ukraine, the astute Nazi Propaganda Minister observed: "We must not only wage war in the East; we must also do a political job there." A guerrilla expert ascribed their failure to the fact that "the territory was conquered by force and strength," while "the ability to win the souls of the Slavic masses was lacking."[20] In Indochina, Colonel Geneste saw that "modern weapons can help conquer land, but Communists conquer the people."[21] A conqueror can prevail only by gaining a political victory, by persuading the population.

In military conflicts, the ultimate goals of both sides are, in a sense, symmetrical: victory for one is to vanquish the other; a stalemate serves neither side. Great-power attempts against

---

[19] *Modern Guerrilla Warfare*, p. 275.

[20] Valdis Redelis, *Partisanenkrieg* (Heidelberg: Vowinckel Verlag, 1958), p. 19.

[21] Geneste, *loc. cit.*, p. 266.

small powers can be described as aggression versus resistance. Their ultimate goals are asymmetrical: the defender does not expect to subdue the attacker, but only to defend himself. The defensive strategy is successful as long as it prevents the attacked nation from being defeated. The defender has only to frustrate the aggressor: a stalemate is a defensive victory.

What are the concrete aims of the aggressor and the defending nation in a struggle between invasion and resistance? What kind of victory are the opponents trying to achieve?

The decisive victory an invader is seeking is *to establish a new political status* in the occupied country. He wants to transform the resisting *polis* into a community under his uncontested control—to turn it into a province, a colony, or a satellite. He must conquer both the territory and its inhabitants, the land as well as the people. Land is conquered militarily and people politically; he, therefore, needs both military and political victories. He must complete five steps to establish the new status: (1) military occupation, (2) military control of the territory, (3) political victory, i.e., the elimination of resistance, then (4) political control of the population. The invader has not succeeded until steps 3 and 4 are complete. In addition, he must (5) maintain his control of land and people against any challenges if the decision is to be permanent.

The defending nation seeks to frustrate the invader's political control of the community: to maintain resistance against him and, thus, to perpetuate *a status of indecision*. National resistance and alien control are mutually exclusive—so long as the invader has not won, the resister has not lost. The great defensive advantage is the possibility of checking the aggressor at any one of the crucial steps. As long as resistance continues, this remains possible. A status of indecision is, thereby, maintained, and final victory of the invader thwarted. Napoleon recognized this possibility, saying that "great powers die of indigestion."[22] And Clausewitz wrote: "Indecision is a success for the defense."

---

[22] Octave Aubry, *Les pages immortelles de Napoléon* (Paris: Corrèa, 1941), p. 241.

The terms "opposition" and "resistance" must be understood in their broadest sense. They embrace every act or omission that perpetuates indecision and counters the invader's efforts to achieve definite control. As long as the hostile tension continues, the defender can win if his own strength increases, enemy pressure relaxes, or outside help materializes (be it only China's claim to Chenpao island in Asia). Any opposition makes a reversal possible by extending the struggle.

What is the best kind of resistance? Whatever balks enemy control will do. The form of resistance is actually irrelevant; the crucial question is not what kind of resistance, but that there is resistance. As a bare minimum, only the will to resist has to survive; even a latent opposition may be adequate. War at the frontier may be just as good as, or better or worse than, a spiritual defense of national identity, non-co-operation, or a full-scale guerrilla campaign—all according to the circumstances. The choice is a question of expediency. Battles are but one expression of an unbroken national spirit.

Political success, being the primary one, supersedes and annuls a contrary secondary success, be the latter economic, military, or other. Just as strategic maneuvers can nullify any tactical victory, thrusts against the enemy's political weaknesses can reverse military success. Military victory or superiority, no matter how massive, does not alone bring a final political decision. But political superiority often does. In short: tactics are a part of military strategy, which, in turn, is a part of politics; and a more general success supersedes a particular success. The whole, here too, is greater than its parts.

Political victories *have* often been determined by military battles, because of the mistaken belief that the two are identical. But there is absolutely no reason to assume that they *must* coincide. As a matter of fact, recent examples demonstrate that they often conflict; and where they do conflict, political victories decide, if they are correctly exploited.

The British loss of Ireland was a political, not a military, defeat. British forces easily defeated and suppressed the Easter Sunday revolt, in 1916. But the following period of persecutions aroused a strong popular sentiment against England. This resentment turned the miserable military defeat into a decisive political victory for the Irish. A national guerrilla struggle brought independence. Britain had fully intended to keep Ireland and had used military force to that end. If political factors defeated the efforts of vastly superior military forces, they must have been strategically decisive.

The French Army, in Indochina and Algeria, had as a rule nothing but military victories; in both campaigns they totaled up to unambiguous political routs. Political results alone were decisive.

The political superiority of a small nation can be exploited to defeat a militarily stronger aggressor. Such a defensive victory was won by the Poles against the Russians in October, 1956, when Russian military superiority was obvious and was not contested by the Poles. But Polish political superiority was just as complete. The one was certainly weighed against the other in the policy calculations of both sides and in the acid discussions between their representatives. Political strength prevailed: it turned out to be a quite realistic factor in a deadly serious power contest. The Poles did not risk national disaster on an illusion, nor did the Russians grant certain liberties to a subject area without a decisive defeat—in this case, a purely political one.[23] In the last seven years, Romania has achieved national independence by impressive political victories; she even felt sufficiently strong now to reduce her armed forces, despite her difficult military-strategic position. And all that was achieved without any fighting.[24]

---

[23]The events of the "Polish October" are widely known and much discussed. A good short review of the critical days is Frank Gibney, *The Frozen Revolution: Poland, a Study in Communist Decay* (New York: Farrar, Straus and Cudahy, 1959), pp. xi–xiv and 3–17; or Flora Lewis *A Case History of Hope: The Story of Poland's Peaceful Revolutions* (Garden City, N.Y.: Doubleday & Co., 1958), pp. 163–226.

[24] The story of the Romanian struggle is less well known; its episodes are only partly known. Interesting facts are described in J. F. Brown, "Romania and Bulgaria," in Adam Bromke (ed.), *The Communist States*

America's President Kennedy, no doubt with cases like Laos and Cuba in mind, told the 1962 graduates of the U.S. Military Academy of the "need to understand the limits of military power": "For the basic problems facing the world today are not susceptible of a final military solution."[25] Russians are learning this in Czechoslovakia.

Of the various ways in which a great power can assault a small nation, military invasion is used only in relatively rare cases. Most objectives of aggressive pressure—influence over a defending nation's external and internal policy, imposition of an unpopular regime, even satellitization—are beyond the limits of military power. Attack on, as well as defense of, these objectives must be political in order to succeed. They are, essentially, political contests. Military moves and countermoves are often not only ineffective but irrelevant.

The only effective defense in any case is political: a resistance based on popular help and sympathies, inside the country. This can become a true defense in depth: instead of military units thinly spread along borders and coastlines, the whole nation can oppose the aggression; instead of a mere physical struggle, the conflict embraces the various socio-political elements of the defending community.

The aggressor thus faces effective resistance operating beyond the limits of his military power. As long as opposition of any kind perpetuates a status of indecision and prevents his uncontested control, the small nation has not lost the political struggle and, therefore, remains undefeated. And absence of defeat is a victory for the defending side.

---

at the Crossroads (New York: Praeger, 1965), pp. 107-17; Stephen Fischer-Galati, "Rumania," in V. Benes, A. Gyorgy, G. Stambuk, *Eastern European Government and Politics* (New York: Harper & Row, 1966), pp. 220-39; Ghita Ionescu, *The Break-up of the Soviet Empire in Eastern Europe* (Baltimore, Md.: Penguin Books, 1965), pp. 123-49; David Binder, "Ceausescu of Rumania: Man Battering at the Kremlin Wall," *The New York Times Magazine*, May 29, 1966.

---

[25] *The New York Times*, June 7, 1962.

C. A STRATEGY OF NATIONAL RESISTANCE

A strategy of national resistance—a political defense in depth —enables small nations threatened or assaulted by great powers to defend themselves even against aggression that orthodox strategy is unable to parry.

Orthodox strategy advises either a fight or a surrender to pressure. If a small nation surrenders and accepts defeat, it is likely to lose both its spirit and its identity. It may become extinguished in the course of time, without more trace than perhaps leaving a few "historical" place names on the map of a conqueror's province—like some of the long-forgotten tribes of American Indians. A surrender, if there is no hope to resist successfully, may minimize initial physical damage, but its moral effect often spells *finis* to a nation.

The other alternative, to fight, is not very attractive either. In a military campaign the nation's economic wealth suffers; many patriots are exposed to danger and lost. Material and spiritual assets are exhausted trying to achieve the impossible. In the end, a militarily more powerful enemy occupies the country. His overwhelming capacity for violence eliminates any guerrilla groups or attempts at revolt. As the years go by, disappointing all hopes, the will to resist diminishes. A psychological defeat finally completes the physical subjugation.

In addition, modern aggressors have become expert at confronting their victims with ambiguous challenges that do not seem to warrant an armed defense, yet are likely to erode a nation's freedom gradually but surely. Often it may be quite impossible to counter such indirect, gradual, or seemingly minor attacks by military force. In these instances, the small nation, unable to defend itself by political means, may suffer decisive defeat and demoralization by default.

National resistance provides a third defensive alternative: a political opposition. French General Nemo called the war in

Vietnam "a war in the crowd."[26] In Latin America, it may take the form of urban guerrillas. A similar struggle in Europe could be defined as a war—or defense—in, and for the control of, the political community (the *polis* of the Greeks) and, in that sense, a *political* conflict. The focal point in such a struggle is the "crowd," the *polis*—the people themselves, not the military formations.

Small nations can rely on the political nature of conflicts to escape the ruinous course of military campaigns—destruction and defeat—without direct or indirect surrender. The third course is to accept a condition imposed by force (from an undue alien influence or an imposed regime, to outright satellitization or incorporation into an empire) but, with undiminished strength, to defend themselves politically. With military inequality strongly neutralized, the political advantages of small nations come into play.

Such a campaign dislocates the aggressor's strategy and secures the privilege of fighting on terms most favorable for the small nation—within its own political community, where its political strength and the aggressor's political weakness are greatest. It can succeed at any phase of the struggle, from deterrence to post-invasion resistance.

What are the fundamental objectivities of such a defense? How can it achieve them without excessive sacrifices? The fundamental objectives, stated in the order of their importance, are three:

1. To preserve national existence: This is essential; the people must survive, and they must survive as a nation. But opposition on the political level and survival can both be pursued without excessive loss of life.
2. To prevent a decisive defeat: The enemy must be frustrated by a continuous resistance.
3. To regain what was lost: In the extreme case of military occupation, to expel the invader's army and his agents. To show that the effort he must expend to maintain his regime is disproportionately high; that his best policy is to cut losses and leave the defending country alone.

---

[26] [General] Nemo, "La Guerre dans la foule," *Revue du Défense Nationale,* June, 1956, 721.

Excessive sacrifices are avoided and yet resistance is made possible because the defenders can adjust their tactics in response to varying degrees of enemy pressure. (1) Dispensing with military and quasi-military struggles, they avoid a decimation of life and wealth. Non-violent means, immune to physical force, are used to sustain national consciousness and a will to resist. As a result, risks diminish and fortitude increases. (2) The interim defensive success, the indecision, is achieved as resistance continues. Anything that counters enemy efforts contributes to resistance: the defenders have a wide choice of resistance techniques. (3) In the short run, a successful struggle can be fought even without dislodging an aggressor. Final victory can wait. The only absolute requirements are to avert irreversible defeat, and almost any resistance satisfies that requirement.

In other words: if we cannot keep the aggressor out, we must adopt a strategy that will induce him to leave, eventually. Since this may take time, the nation must remain intact and continue to resist, despite initial reverses, even under an enemy regime.

Before the Russian occupation of Czechoslovakia, this point was rarely understood. The popular assumption was that all would be lost as soon as the invader entered a small country. Comments by Eastern European refugees and other sources that "all was lost" and complete Russian triumph "assured as soon as the first Soviet soldier stepped across the border and the first tank rolled in" are typical of the obvious overstatements. Any visitor to the C.S.S.R. could find out that this was not the case. After half a year of occupation the outcome of the struggle was far from clear, the defenders were successfully holding out.

If creditable preparations for resistance and survival are made, an enemy may be deterred from attacking a small nation in the first place. But even if the deterrent should fail, there are still realistic chances of resisting a final conquest. A limited objective, and a contest fought on the political level, increase the likelihood of ultimate success.

The limited objective is to avoid defeat, not to beat the stronger enemy. Obviously, the former is an easier task, accomplished with fewer losses.

In a conflict fought on the political level, the defenders abstain from military struggles or armed risings against enemy armed forces. The positions they do contest—the political strong points—are defended on the political level, beyond the "limits of military power." A maximum of obstacles foil the intruder; a minimum of defense losses encourage resistance.

Political resistance against armed enemies can belong to one of three types: (1) *popular resistance,* where the population resists its own government; (2) *national revolt,* an intermediate type, where a population rises to throw off an established foreign rule; and (3) *national resistance,* the confrontation between an attacked nation and an alien aggressor. In the first case, the government's position is strongest; it is of the same national origin and has established itself in power. In the second case, the main strength of the government is its hold on political control; the greatest weakness, its alien nature. In national-resistance situations, both political disadvantages accrue to the aggressor: he is an intruding alien, and the established positions of political power are held by the resisting nation. All the difficulties that plague rulers in the first two cases will haunt the alien. His problem is to gain, and keep, political control by military force—a rather hopeless undertaking against a modern political strategy. In national resistance the people are, thus, in the strongest position.

The term itself indicates that national resistance has two basic characteristics. It is *resistance*—not warfare with regular or guerrilla forces, but an omniform general stand against an alien. It includes non-violent opposition (from purely spiritual self-defense to political attacks), various techniques to break down the aggressive machinery, even selected types of violence. The term "resistance" is used in its *widest* possible meaning; the scope of counter action goes beyond traditional resistance activities used in World War II and at other times. Practically everything that the people regard as resistance is in effect resistance. The prerequisite of its success is a nation undefeated in spirit and determined to resist.

It is also *national*—based on national loyalty and directed against alien aggression. It is resistance by a nation, as a nation, to preserve its national freedom, identity, its very survival, against an attack on these values. It is essentially "anti-colonialist": against all kinds of attacks aimed at *de facto* subjugation, regardless of the propagandist labels used by the intruder. "National," as used here, is a limiting term taken in its *narrowest* sense: only a nation can offer national resistance, and not every state is a nation. The prerequisites of success are unwavering loyalty to the national cause and a strong cohesion among the defenders.

Military strength is neutralized if the struggle is transferred from the battlefield, or from another arena where armed force can be applied, to levels where it cannot. If the entire contest is made to depend on a struggle in the political sphere, an army cannot win. Exactly this happens when a defending side takes up national resistance and opposes a militarily superior intruder politically.

This strategy can be summarized in Trotsky's famous call: "Neither war, nor peace!" It is not war, namely, not military fighting. Nor is it peace, not a mere passive submission. It is a determined political defense, by all available means, against assault. Neither war nor peace, but a continuing political indecision. It preserves the fluidity of the situation. It extends the period during which the tide of fortune can be reversed, the fatal indigestion takes effect on the imperialist.

National resistance satisfies the strategic requirements given at the end of Section A, above: (1) The political weakness of the attacker and the strength of the defenders are greatest when an alien enemy faces the resistance of an entire nation. (2) Fighting on the political level, the defenders gain a superiority by matching their strength against enemy weakness. And (3) they can use the resulting political superiority to annul an intruder's military advantages. Thus an ultimate political victory of the small nation becomes possible.

Political resistance is a long and complex struggle; extension and complication are among its chief advantages. It strives to preserve national existence and to avoid defeat by default. It makes great demands on the strength and endurance of the citizens. But it can succeed where orthodox defense strategy is doomed to fail.

Two main objections have been heard against it:

First, it is objected that national morale and the will to resist would weaken, were one to admit the possibility that a nation's defense forces cannot prevent enemy occupation. This may indeed be the first reaction in some cases. But people soon realize that the new strategy shows a determination to fight with every means and adds considerably to the defense potential. They are likely to become more involved in the defensive effort and increasingly confident of their ability to resist. The time when an individual patriot is likely to consider the struggle "finally and irrevocably lost" can thus be postponed almost indefinitely; and this is very important.

Second, it is objected that political resistence does not contribute to deterrence because its usefulness is not generally recognized. Even before August, 1968, it could be answered (1) that an effective defense is better than the deterrent value of an ineffective one; and (2) that the stronger strategy will prove a more convincing deterrent in the long run. It is too risky to keep useless forces hoping that someone might, mistakenly, be afraid of them. After the setbacks that the Russians suffered in the C.S.S.R. through the winter of 1968-69, the strength, and therefore the deterrent effect, of a national resistance is obvious.

Under present conditions, this is the best strategy for defending small nations. Many of them can muster the necessary loyalty and cohesion to fight a political struggle. In the hour of need, many have the spiritual strength and the will to resist that is necessary to ignite and nourish the flame of opposition throughout the conflict.

1. Political Resistance

National resistance is political. Neither its objective nor its main techniques are military. As a matter of fact, it may begin (as it did in Prague and Bratislava) after the aggressor has achieved military occupation. The chances of a political success are not seriously diminished, as we saw in August, 1968, by conceding outright military superiority to the enemy and confronting him on the political level.

The invader is militarily strong but politically weak. The defending nation, militarily inferior, is politically far superior. It cannot frustrate the enemy's military means, nor does it attempt this hopeless task; it concentrates on preventing the invader from achieving political ends. In the unlikely case in which the invasion has been repulsed or defeated by the defender's own army (or by the timely arrival of an allied force), the small state is saved, and no resistance is needed. (Except, perhaps, against the forces of a stronger ally, should the latter have the intent to abuse the small nation himself.)

On the battlefield a weak defender would have been defeated by a strong invader; on the political level a superior small nation faces a weak occupier. The relative strength is, thus, decisively reversed by the correct strategic choice. The conflict is still unequal—but now unequal in favor of the defending small nation! B. H. Liddell Hart agreed that the main aim is gaining the object of policy. Only the fact that military men have done most of the thinking about related problems explains the curious tendency to identify national objectives with military aims.[27]

Conflicts have become political in every respect: they involve the entire *polis*, the nation itself. Armies and governments are nothing but "superstructures" lacking solidity and strength, without a stable popular basis. This applies to armies of occupation and to governments imposed by force. Modern war is, indeed, "a war in the crowd." The basic aim is to win the contest for public opinion. This has changed the whole nature of the conflict. Lawrence wrote that "rebellion was not war: indeed, was more of the nature of peace—a national strike perhaps";[28]

---

[27] B. H. Liddell Hart, *Strategy* (New York: Praeger, 1954), p. 351.
[28] Lawrence, *Seven Pillars*, p. 192.

a Berber leader compared resistance to "a strike, with political demands instead of a request for a wage increase."[29] Resistance is no longer a part of war; war has become a mere part of resistance, of political struggles.

Elections, the gauge of strength, were probably first used by a shrewd tribal chief in prehistoric times as a test of his military and political chances. They let him calculate, from a show of hands, where conquest would be easy or likely, to avoid unnecessary losses and even self-destruction in hopeless campaigns in which opposition was clearly too strong. He must have been a wise, and a rather successful, conqueror.

To return to the twentieth century, the political force of public sentiment was dramatically illustrated by the peaceful developments in Scandinavia, in 1905. Norwegian nationalism prompted demands for full independence from Sweden. A plebiscite in Norway favored independence by 368,208 votes against 184.[30] Sweden acquiesced in the results immediately: after popular sentiment of such massive proportions was ascertained, there was no sense in opposing it.

All would admit that political factors decided everything in the Norwegian case, since politics alone was involved. But the same would still hold true if Sweden had sent her Royal Army to suppress Norway and had been expelled after a bloody campaign. Given such an overwhelming political sentiment, no other military result was likely. And even with an intervening war, the decisive force of the political element—the popular sentiment —would have been just as real, although not quite as obvious to observers enamored with military explanations. It would still have been the political strength that assured victory for Norwegian independence. The military campaign would have arrived at the same result by different (i.e., violent) means—that is all.

Wherever the political element is strong, it can be just as decisive. Hitler admitted as much when he remarked: "My great opportunity lies in my deliberate use of force at a time

---

[29] *The New York Times,* Nov. 17, 1964.
[30] *Svensk Uppslagsbok* (Malmö: Norden A.B., 1952), xxi, 311.

when there are still illusions abroad as to the forces that mould history."[31] And the soldier-politician de Gaulle realized that Algerian sentiment had made the French position untenable; he saw that it would be useless to continue military fighting.

National resistance aims to transform political sentiment into resistance strength, to translate political superiority into a political victory. It employs non-political (technical, quasi-military, etc.) means only to gain a political objective. It considers enemy invasion as nothing more than a dividing line between the preliminary military stage and the political-resistance stage. It ignores the main (military) forces of the enemy and concentrates the defending nation's strength against the enemy's (political) weakness.

Going against the invader's armed forces, the defenders would get only a fight. Withdrawing to the political level "where the enemy is not," certainly not at his strongest, they damage him most. They gain a strategic advantage and hold a position of strength, safe from direct enemy assault. Their political positions, organizations, and circles of patriots become fortresses of opposition. The nation exploits defensive advantages by holding only political positions.

In Czechoslovakia, the successful defense strategy turned out to be exactly of this type. The armed formations remained passive but hostile—an ambiguous strategic threat. Russian military forces were deprived of all targets. The resistance was fought with exclusively political weapons, against which the invaders could pit only a few hundred collaborators and imported agents. The Russians had planned it as an unequal military struggle with all the advantages in their favor; it turned into an unequal political struggle with all the advantages against them. . . . Other small nations, facing the mass armies of an invader, can be equally effective; they can transfer the struggle to the higher level of politics. Their strategic success is to stay above the effective range of military force and violence.

---

[31] Quoted by Stephen King-Hall, *Power Politics in the Nuclear Age* (London: V. Gollancz, 1962), pp. 33–34.

The political nature of resistance warfare renders the outcome of the political contest directly decisive. "With absolute military decision unavailable," wrote an analyst summarizing French evaluations of *revolutionary* wars, "the struggle becomes one for the allegiance and control of the population."[32] The anti-guerrilla campaign in the Philippines is said to have depended for its success "less on pure military strength and more and more on the mass support of the people, on the civilian citizens of the country itself."[33] As Lin Piao put it, "Politics is the commander, politics is the soul of everything. Political work is the lifeline of our army."[34] And Bernard B. Fall concluded: "Revolutionary wars are fought for political objectives, and big showdown battles are necessary neither for victory nor for defeat."[35] This applies fully to all modern wars; in revolutionary situations it is only more patent.

To gain a decisive victory against a national community prepared and determined to resist, the intruder is forced to go where such victory is alone possible—to the political level. The defender does not have to oppose the aggressor's military strength; the denial of political control to the alien will suffice to achieve the defensive goal of maintaining indecision. But the invader has to win political control as the only way to achieve his aims against the politically resisting nation.

An invading alien must take over or destroy the government, the administrative machinery, and the organized centers of political power in the occupied country. He must have a subservient administration and enforce obedience to his commands by political control. If this control can be secured, the conqueror has reached his goal. If not, ungovernability will result; political resistance will grow stronger; the conqueror's position in the midst of a hostile nation will become critical. Adverse as the conditions are, his only choice is between gaining political control or losing the whole contest.

---

[32] *Modern Guerrilla Warfare*, p. 429.
[33] *Ibid.*, p. 199.
[34] Lin Piao, *op. cit.*, p. 30.
[35] *New York Times Magazine*, May 10, 1963.

Control is won by persuasion. The invader has not won so long as he has not persuaded the defenders that "all is lost," that "nothing can be done" to reverse the outcome. Hitler explained to his generals in Russia that "ruling the people in the conquered regions is of course a psychological problem. One cannot rule by force alone." His judgment of the situation was correct: "They must be convinced that we are the victors; as soon as anything at all begins to waver in this conviction, some will naturally slacken in fulfilling their obligations and others will become active at once in organizing attacks, raids, etc., against us."[36]

But nothing could be more difficult for an invading alien— who oppresses freedom; imprisons, deports, and murders people; exploits the riches of the country and deprives the nation of their use; insults national pride by substituting occupation for independence of a small nation and, on top of it all, insists on the beneficial nature of his rule—than to secure a political victory in the occupied country. And political resistance prevents a final conquest so long as he has not accomplished this victory.

Where the aggressor does not resort to military invasion but chooses one of the less-extreme courses of attack, the political resentment against him may not be quite as universal. But in such cases, the defending nation is also in a stronger position: it can use its own apparatus of government. In the C.S.S.R., the top Government and Party positions remained in the hands of patriotic officials, despite occupation and Soviet subversive pressures—because of the great initial successes of resistance. Only after the Russians managed to split the Communist leadership did collaborators begin to replace patriots in Party and State apparatus. If the people, and their leaders, remain loyal and prepared for a political fight, enemy attempts at persuasion are easy to resist. If the nation refuses to give up the opposition, the intruder has lost. He will try again and again—because he must—but with every new failure his chances will diminish.

---

[36] "Auszug aus der Ansprache des Führers an die Heeresgruppen-führer am 1. 7. 43 abends," *Vierteljahrshefte für Zeitgeschichte*, 3 (1954), 309.

What has been said so far remains true, despite prevailing "illusions as to the forces that mold history." Political surrender has often resulted from the mistaken assumption that the possibilities of resistance are restricted to military means. Using a legal analogy, the military level can be compared to a lower court and the political level to a higher court. A decision below can be reversed above but not the higher decision below. A defendant, inexpertly advised, may submit needlessly to a deprivation of liberty or to a death penalty, imposed below, in the mistaken assumption that "all is lost" and that "nothing can be done," not knowing that an appeal is possible. He is imprisoned or executed although he could have won a decision on the higher level. It is the same in modern conflicts. Instances in which military victory has brought a direct political decision merely show that the nations involved either have not appreciated the decisive nature of political factors or have not known how to use them.

A party certain to lose on the lower level but to win on the higher is wise to avoid the sacrifices involved in the first instance and to appeal directly for the superior decision. A defending nation, sure to lose on the lower military level, is equally wise to forego unnecessary losses and to contest the enemy on the higher political plane from the beginning.

Hungary, in 1956, and Czechoslovakia, in 1968, illustrate the difference. Because some fighting occurred in the first week of the Hungarian revolt, both the fighters and the observers failed to recognize the purely political nature of Magyar victory. When the Russians counterattacked, they induced the Magyars to fight and defeated them with tanks. In the C.S.S.R. the entire struggle was obviously political throughout. The few days that elapsed between Hungarian political victory and military defeat made the victory appear less and the defeat more real. In Czechoslovakia, after the first week, even after the first six months of Russian occupation, the successes of resistance were undeniable.

Political opposition has many advantages over military defense for a small nation: (1) While only a fraction of the people can be soldiers, for political defense almost all patriots are available. (2) Political victories can be achieved with small losses, but they give just as valuable a lift to national morale as do military successes. (3) If the enemy has military superiority over the defenders, political setbacks are easier to reverse than military defeats. (4) Aggressive great powers are expert in the military field, where technical standards apply, but they are almost helpless in understanding the more intangible, more fluctuating political conditions and public sentiments of the defending nation. And (5) where nothing else helps, political defense may succeed.

2. *Spiritual Resistance*

The spiritually weak have no choice but to rely on their arms. Only the strong can reject the primacy of violence, conceding military superiority to the enemy, mustering sufficient endurance to fight politically. Only they can maintain a long period of indecision, and defeat an aggressor politically. Ideals and ideas cannot be shot, regardless of the caliber of weapon or warhead used.

"You can insure the safety of your defense if you hold only positions that cannot be attacked," advised the wise Sun Tzu. Spiritual positions are of this kind. *Satyagraha*, the name Gandhi gave to his campaign of non-violent resistance, means "soul-force." A militant poet spoke of "the defense of a nation's spiritual boundaries." "Force can always crush force, given sufficient superiority in strength and skill," declared Liddell Hart. "It cannot crush ideas. Being intangible they are invulnerable, save to psychological penetration, and their resilience has baffled innumerable believers in force."[37]

Spiritual strength is the only safe foundation of national strength. It is the "soul-force," the strength of hearts—a lasting, resurgent, indestructible, inner fortitude. Small states, whose material resources cannot match those of a potential aggressor,

---

[37] Liddell Hart, *Strategy*, p. 235.

have to base their defense mainly on the stout spirit of their citizens.

As spiritual strength is the core of national strength, spiritual resistance is the foundation of national resistance. Opposition requires greater fortitude than war. In the feverish atmosphere of military contest the rapid succession of electrifying events maintains morale, whereas a tenacious day-to-day political defense makes far greater demands on national morale. Orthodox war includes numerous physical elements; resistance is almost exclusively spiritual.

Spiritual resistance enters into small-nation defense in various ways and on various levels: (1) as the paramount strategic aim to preserve the nation; (2) as a strategic stronghold where resistance can survive enemy assaults; and (3) as the safest tactical weapon to be used in the struggle.

(1) The resisting nation has to insure its own existence, its physical survival, before everything else. But physical preservation alone is not enough. National existence—the survival of its traditions, language, loyalty, cohesion—is just as important. Very little has been accomplished if the national way of life does not endure. Spiritual resistance, "the defense of a nation's spiritual boundaries," is, therefore, the essential objective of national resistance.

(2) The defending nation's spirit can be "a mighty fortress," the basis without which no struggle is likely to succeed. Traditional armies need safe base areas; resistance movements need them even more. The politically-minded A.H.D. von Bülow exclaimed: "I wish every man were a fortress!" In T.E. Lawrence's résumé of political war, the first condition for success was "an unassailable base, something guarded not merely from attack, but from the fear of it: such a base we had . . . in the minds of men we converted to our creed."[38] Berber resistance leader Ait-Achmed, after the experiences of the Algerian War, advised

---

[38] T. E. Lawrence, "The Evolution of a Revolt," *The Army Quarterly* (London), No. 1 (1920), 69.

his people during an attack: "Do not hold villages but your hearts!"

Everything depends on the fortresses in the minds and hearts of the people—as long as they hold out, resistance is alive and the enemy is fighting a losing battle. Political sociologists are surprised how often tremendous violence and pressure have had very little effect on spiritually strong peoples: how completely the influence of German occupation was washed out from Norway to Greece; how, after January, 1968, hardly a trace remainded of the impressions which the Russians had tried to make on the Czech nation. The tangible strategic value of an unassailable spiritual base for resistance should not be ignored.

(3) The great tactical value of spiritual resistance lies in its remaining beyond the reach of enemy violence, even as a technique of active opposition. It provides maximum security. With an increase of difficulties and dangers, active resistance simply becomes more spiritual. It turns into a way of daily life, without losing any of its power. It can be adjusted to any kind of outside pressure—from the strongest to the weakest. Its flexibility is practically endless. Gandhi's soul-force was a spiritual defiance; and the Mahatma recognized the whole extent of "powers latent in the soul, a soul that can defy the physical combination of the whole world."[39]

Defeat grows out of the conviction that nothing can be done to resist the enemy and help the common cause. This belief can prove fatal in situations where nothing *is* done to resist, owing to a lack of adequate preparation, a high intensity of enemy violence, or any other cause. The danger of apathy can be averted if the nation undertakes something that it considers as resistance. Metaphysical opposition can save the day. It can continue regardless of outside pressures. It is a safe, and a most meaningful, contribution to the basic resistance task—to the defense of spiritual boundaries.

---

[39] M. K. Gandhi, *Non-violent Resistance: Satyagraha* (New York: Schocken, 1961), p. 134.

In ancient warfare, most of the territory of the *polis* could be abandoned to invading forces as long as the defenders were safely holding their main fortresses. In modern wars, even if the territory of a small state is overrun by an enemy, the nation is not subdued as long as its spiritual and political strongholds continue to resist.

A nation living in a country invaded by an alien enemy needs great fortitude to hold out against all pressures, to avoid defeat, to expel the invader when the opportunity presents itself. Spiritual strength alone can provide the stamina to hold out and rise again.

Communist concentration camps and Nazi ghettos provide examples of savage oppression and heroic spiritual resistance. Even if an invader applies equally savage terror, defense could safely withdraw into the unassailable fortresses in the minds of men and continue to defy the alien. The only requirement is an unyielding spirit. Even deprived of its outward manifestations, the contest goes on with undiminished intensity; psychology has demonstrated that repressed sentiments are the strongest and the most tenacious. Neither a single human being nor a whole nation is lost so long as the spirit is not dead.

The fact that the Czechs and the Slovaks did not flee their country in large numbers after the invasion was proof of their unbroken spirit and an omen boding ill for the Russians. As a matter of fact, even most of the Czechoslovaks vacationing abroad returned, instead of remaining in exile.

And a year later the number of refugees was equally low. This indication that the resistance spirit had not collapsed—although it was not flaunted as aggressively as in 1968—was confirmed both in the Czech lands and in Slovakia. Public opinion condemned the Russians and their servants, embraced nationalism and liberalism, supported the patriotic leaders with an unanimity as great as ever. The spirit of resistance was less visible but equally strong. It appeared to be there to stay for a long time.

Spiritual resistance is an essential part of the great web of national resistance. Its foundations must be developed long before the fighting starts. It is an all-embracing activity—every patriot can participate. It is the strongest—free of enemy interference. It is the least dangerous form of resistance—to escape terror and other violence opposition merely has to rise to the spiritual level, where it can go on indefinitely. It is a meaningful part of national defiance even if practiced individually. No nation is defeated so long as its spiritual strength survives.

3. The Will to Resist

The will to resist is a nation's will to live. For national resistance it is absolutely vital. When a nation is subjected to enemy pressure or occupation, as when the human body is invaded by disease, the will to resist may mean the difference between life and death. And it may help recovery in seemingly hopeless cases.

The will is the fire that ignites and maintains opposition. It is the force that sets into motion, and keeps active, the striving to defy the enemy. Resistance continues as long as there is a will to go on resisting. A determined will may find ways to express itself in action under any conditions. If the will is extinguished, resistance is dead; thereafter, the best opportunities pass unexploited.

Political opposition can be poured into any form. Whatever the techniques, however employed, the will is always the condition *sine qua non*. From the first moment of the conflict, a will to resist must ensure that the invader's initial assault does not extinguish the spark of opposition, that the decision is delayed long enough to let the defense rally. The constant will must bridge the gap of despair and lead the nation from initial setbacks to ultimate victory.

The people of the C.S.S.R. declared openly their will to resist the occupiers, signing on petitions their full names, identifying themselves to domestic and foreign reporters. Typical of the strong stand was a declaration published in the resistance newspaper *Rude Právo* on the fifth day of the occupation:

> To the occupiers: You are arresting or plan to arrest the signers of the "2000 Words." To my regret I could not sign that appeal

because I was abroad for a considerable time. Therefore I am signing it today. Yours sincerely, a former friend, LUDEK PACHMAN, international chess champion.[40]

A resistance movement, in Colonel F. O. Miksche's fine definition, is "the struggle of an unvanquished nation in a conquered country."[41] The decisive nature of a determined will is strikingly clear where the ultimate victor's troops kept running away for a good part of the fighting: Washington's militia, Spain's guerrillas, Lawrence's Arab's, and Mao's Chinese are impressive examples. The F.L.N. had won when it became clear that the resistance will of the Algerians was not broken. As long as the will remained strong, the fighters could scatter, to resist again when a new opportunity came. The Czechoslovak soldiers never left their barracks in August, 1968. The people of Prague and Bratislava went home at night during the curfew, but they were back on the streets demonstrating their defiance every day during the crucial first week of occupation. The minds decided, not the bodies.

The minimum content of a national will to resist is the resolve not to acquiesce in defeat, "to forget defeat," as Bülow advised and as the Spaniards demonstrated ten years later. Clausewitz described this response as a continued hostility:

The war—i.e., the hostile tension and the operation of hostile forces—cannot be considered finished as long as the will of the enemy is not overcome, that is, his government and allies forced to sign a peace, or the nation induced into submission; for while we are in full possession of the country, the struggle inside can ignite anew. This can happen even after the [conclusion of] peace, [which] proves that not every war brings about complete decision and settlement.[42]

The longer this determination persists, the longer extends the twilight period of indecision and the possibility of reversal.

---

[40] *East Europe,* Oct., 1968, p. 36.

[41] F. O. Miksche, *Secret Forces* (London: Faber and Faber, 1950), p. 44.

[42] Clausewitz, *op. cit.,* Bk. I, Ch. 2.

How long is the will to resist likely to survive in a given case? Predictions for the future are difficult; experience varies. Many nations lost the will to resist after a single shock attack; some succumbed to mere threats. But historical examples to the contrary are impressive: centuries without literacy or communications, without any but the most rudimentary nationalism, have seen resistance survive. Poles held out for 100 years, Algerians for 130, Norwegians for 450, Esthonians for 700, Irish for 800, Jews for 2,000, Greeks for 2,150, and Kurds even longer. The endurance of the will gives a "spring effect" to resistance: while the spring is not broken but merely compressed, it is not subdued, no matter how formidable the pressure.

The will to resist seems to provide the clue why revolutions in long-subdued nations have often succeeded, while resistance movements in newly-conquered countries have failed. The shock of recent defeat, coupled with a loss of hope, caused invaded nations to give in to a seemingly unavoidable fate. Insurgent peoples have, in a very real sense, *forgotten* their defeats: new generations grasp opportunities with new confidence and determination. Small nations must prevent a paralysis of the will at all costs.

And why do nations celebrate military defeats and the death of heroes as if they were victories: from Termopylae to the anniversaries of the Easter Sunday and the Warsaw uprising? Because, like the self-immolation of Jan Palach in Prague, they are political victories—they symbolize an upsurge of the national will to resist.

Political defense dispenses with fighting most of the time. But it can do so and still prevail only if there is an ever-present will and readiness to fight. "Once the nation grasps with full consciousness that no one may withdraw from the defense of the fatherland in the hour of danger," the Swedish poet Rydberg wrote one hundred years ago, "then even a small nation shall become invincible; then a wall is built around its national independence, as well as its internal freedom, which no enemy is able to ascend."

The aggressor knows the importance of the will. He attempts

to extinguish it by political attacks on the minds and by violence against the bodies of the defenders, before and after invasion. "Our strategy is to destroy the enemy from within," explained Hitler, "to conquer him through himself."[43] Actually, there is no other way. Stalin broke the Czech will to resist as easily in 1948 as Hitler had done in 1938. When the Russians failed to achieve the same result in 1968, failure of the invasion became distinctly possible.

Threats or violence can break the will only where the loyalities are weak or divided, where the people are irresolute. In Denmark the resistance leader Fleming Muus understood this well. For him the primary objective of the nation's fight against Hitler's expanding empire was to arouse a will to resist, to "help the Danes find their lost souls. *That* was what was needed: that was the essential thing if the Viking blood was ever to course proudly again."[44]

A strong will to resist can save a nation from despair and defeat in the darkest, most hopeless hours of its defense. The will sustains the counterpressure of opposition; compressed but not broken by superior force, yielding to pressure but rising again, resuming the struggle wherever and whenever the pressure lightens. An attacker may win battles, if the defending nation is not careful to avert them, and he may occupy the country; but there is no final victory for him against a national political resistance borne by an unyielding will to resist.

A strategy of national resistance, based on the spiritual strength of the community and carried by a strong will to resist, is an effective political defense that can, I submit, help small nations cope with the various forms of pressure available to aggressive great powers.

Do historical examples and recognized strategic authority support my conclusions?

---

[43] Hermann Rauschning, *The Voice of Destruction* (New York: G. P. Putnam's Sons, 1940), p. 8.

[44] Fleming B. Muus, *The Spark and the Flame* (London: Museum Press, 1956), p. 57.

CHAPTER IV

The Modern Era of Warfare

A look at history shows countless examples in which smaller and weaker peoples succeeded against the mighty. In ancient China, Sun Tzu advocated an irregular warfare that defeated stronger enemies. Gideon and the Maccabees scored surprising victories. Tiny Greece defeated the Emperors Darius and Xerxes. Xenophon and his ten thousand Hellenes fought their way across the realm of a mighty Persian king, overcoming countless enemies. Rome was saved from victorious Hannibal by Fabius Cunctator. Every country will find similar cases in its own history.

One may, however, question the precedent value of battles fought with the jawbone of an ass and demand more convincing parallels to our times from the campaigns of modern warfare.

The modern era of warfare—the last two centuries—provides ample practical and theoretical support for my thesis. Actual struggles and development of strategic theory at the time of the great revolutions and Napoleon's rule are especially interesting: it was not only a period of mass warfare; it was also a moment when one superpower dominated the entire continent of Europe. It was the point in history when wars became political in the modern sense of the term, involving entire communities, and when modern nationalism became an important strategic factor.

A. REVOLUTIONARY WARFARE

The American and French revolutions brought about the basic change: they involved the people directly in the struggles, gave them a sense of unity and power, injecting a strong political element into warfare and thus changing its very nature.

Friction between the English Crown and the American Colonies turned into veritable political warfare between 1763 and 1775: protests, disobedience, and riots countered all attempts to enforce England's rule. London's attempts to control the Colonies failed against the strong local sentiment.

The Revolutionary War started in 1775, and American independence was declared a year later. Fighting soon spread to such an extent that the Crown could not hope to reconquer the vast rebellious provinces by military means.

England's only hope remained to extinguish the American spirit of resistence by inflicting a series of demoralizing reverses on the troops of General Washington. The revolutionaries lacked equipment, training, and discipline; they were often defeated, and a catastrophe seemed likely on a few occasions. But clever skirmishing tactics, the able strategy and political leadership of their commander, and the aid of France prevented a decisive defeat.

England's rout was ensured when American determination did not weaken. With popular support, the revolutionaries emerged victorious.

A contemporary Prussian military analyst found the political factor decisive in bringing about the "military miracle" of American victory. He was impressed by the strategy and tactics of the colonists: "The American War is exceptionally remarkable and important as the beginning of a new political and military epoch," he wrote in 1798, "No mass battles. Only a war of light troops, the true model for all future wars."[1] In retrospect there is, of course, nothing surprising about the American victory. Startling is only the English expectation to control these vast territories, inhabited by a hostile population, with a few thousand troops.

---

[1] A. H. D. von Bülow, *Geist des Neuern Kriegssystems* (Hamburg: B. G. Hoffman, 1799), p. 268.

France had helped hasten American victory, which, in turn, accelerated the pace of events leading to the revolution in France. French soldiers and seamen returned from the New World inspired by the ideas of freedom and a spirit of revolt. Intellectuals supported the rise of revolutionary sentiment. Less than six years after the Treaty of Paris had confirmed American independence, the French capital erupted, initiating a chain reaction destined to produce an explosive blend of politics and warfare.

Revolutionary France made many dreams come true. The people won their freedom. The country was theirs; theirs was the duty to defend the new republic against the infuriated monarchies of Europe. The people even abstained from meat, on days of "revolutionary fasting," in favor of the troops; and the troops fought with a mighty enthusiasm. National defense had become a patriotic duty, a truly united effort.

The citizens' army increased national strength markedly. With inferior equipment, provisions, discipline, but with superior tactics and morale, they defeated all enemies. Where they could not hope to win regular engagements, they avoided ranged battles. Officers and men often fought as skirmishing *tirailleurs*: relying on initiative, using familiar terrain and dilatory opposition to defeat the invaders in many combined actions. Universal conscription, irregular warfare, a new quick pace, and a relative independence of supply magazines made the French superior to all opponents.

At first the revolutionary troops were considered hopeless underdogs against the united armies of the coalitions. Austrian officers on the way to France called it "humiliating" for regular soldiers to march against "such a mob"! But the conscripted citizens stopped all Allied armies, defeated them, and threw them back over the borders of France. Soon the French were fighting victoriously in Germany and Italy.

The balance of power in Europe was destroyed—before most governments grasped what was really happening.

B. NAPOLEON, THE MASTER OF EUROPE

France reached the zenith of her power under Napoleon. Led by his genius, her new armies advanced with the impact of an elemental force, crushing Europe's antiquated monarchies in their path.

Austria was defeated twice—in 1800 and in 1805. Napoleon won the second campaign with a brilliant victory over larger Russian and Austrian forces at Austerlitz. Prussia was beaten in 1806; the Russians coming to her aid were smashed early in 1807.

The advanced military power of France dominated the scene. Europe was at the mercy of Napoleon's armies. The empires of Austria and Russia—the great powers—as well as the Prussian kingdom, Holland, Spain, and Sardinia were defeated. England was expelled from the Continent and feared a landing on her home island. Far and wide, no one could challenge French supremacy. "Each new coalition against France will only increase her greatness," proclaimed Napoleon. "I never felt more powerful," he recalled later on St. Helena.[2] Europe had, in effect, lost her independence.

The year was 1808.

At this high point of his power and French invincibility, Napoleon decided to complete the blockade of England by conquering Spain and Portugal, deposing the Spanish royal house, and installing his brother Joseph on the throne in Madrid.

The Emperor had no high regard for the nations of the Iberian peninsula: "They are as cowardly as the Italians," he declared contemptuously.[3] It would suffice to show his troops in

---

[2] Comte de las Cases, *Le Mémorial de Sainte-Hélène* (Paris: Garnier Frères, 1895), p. 728.

[3] Marbot, *Mémories du Général Baron de Marbot* (Paris: E. Plon, Nourrit et Cie., 1891), p. 53.

Spain, he thought, to get all he wanted: "It will not cost us more than 12,000 men. It is child's play. The Spaniards do not know what a French army means."[4]

The Emperor's military estimate was correct. His recruits easily destroyed all Spanish regular forces. Whenever the Spaniards managed to assemble new armies, these too were crushed. Like all Napoleon's enemies, Spain seemed lost. She was a helpless conquered country—according to all accepted military standards. The Bourbons and the aristocracy meekly accepted French occupation.

The people, however, did not submit. When news reached Madrid that Napoleon had forced the Spanish king to abdicate, the city rose on May 2, 1808. Marshal Murat ruthlessly suppressed the uprising and restored order in the capital. But this was only the beginning. The spark of revolt could not be extinguished. Starting in the villages of the Asturias, the conflagration rapidly spread from province to province. By the end of May, all Spain was aflame.

The population refused to abide by the results of the regular military campaign. Unorganized, badly armed, untrained civilians without qualified leaders tenaciously fought on. Already in July, General Dupont with 20,000 French troops was forced to surrender near Bailen to scattered military units and formations of Spanish peasants. Napoleon was outraged: these "rag-clad beggars of Andalusia," this "wretched blustering *canaille*," these "troops without reputation led by commanders without name," had, with hardly a shot fired, accomplished what no coalition in Europe could—had captured one of his armies![5] All Spain was rejoicing. A bitter resistance struggle had begun.

The Emperor was still quite confident: "Spain will be reconquered in the autumn. What are a few insurgents to me when I come at the head of my dragoons? I shall finish them

---

[4] Louis Madelin, *L'Affaire d'Espagne, 1807–1809* (Paris: Hachette, 1943), pp. 94, 96.
[5] *Ibid.*, p. 235.

quickly."[6] He came with 200,000 men, destroyed another Spanish army put together in the meantime, and took Madrid in December, 1808. The regular forces of the defenders were finished. The British Corps under Moore was routed: its commander fell; its remnants fled to reach a port before the French could catch and annihilate them.

But nothing could induce the Spaniards to give up. The more desperate the situation, the more violently they fought the hated invaders. Outside Madrid and some other heavily garrisoned towns, the defiant people made French control impossible. "They are never discouraged," a French officer wrote about Spanish guerrilla tactics. "They flee, reassemble in the distance, and are back a few days later with a new confidence which, always disappointed, is never destroyed." Nostalgically he recalled: "It was fine as long as we fought among the good Germans, who never would have the idea of attacking a Frenchman who was a messenger. The Spaniards fought these couriers bitterly, and obtained information from the dispatches about troop movements. The band of fighters harassed us without interruption but could not be caught anywhere."[7] Napoleon himself called Spanish resistance *"le chancre de l'Empire."*[8]

By 1810, there were 300,000 of the best French soldiers on the Iberian peninsula. Napoleon directed the operations from Paris. But nothing could subdue a determined nation. After the French effort of 1810-12 failed, the struggle in Spain took a decisive turn in favor of the resistance. Year after year, occupation forces burned up in the consuming fires of a national war.

In Spain the master of Europe was defeated by the "wretched mob of rag-clad beggars." While most reports attribute the victory to the Expeditionary Force under Wellington; they do not explain why the Spaniards were beating the invaders even when the English were losing. Deeper analyses reveal the decisive importance of the guerrillas. Liddell Hart shows that Spanish

---

[6] Aubry, *Napoléon* (Paris: Flammarion, 1936), p. 210.

[7] Marbot, *op. cit.*, pp. 66, 482.

[8] Aubry, *Napoléon*, p. 224.

resistance had a greater impact on the war than the British campaign—that only 20 to 25 per cent of all French casualties in Spain and Portugal were suffered in action against the British. "By treating the war as a chronicle of Wellington's battles and sieges," he concludes, "it becomes meaningless."[9] T. E. Lawrence agreed that "the English forces were there only to sustain the Spaniards in their rebellion: and that the more irregular the Spanish forces the greater their effect."[10] Fighting Spain turned the tide of fortune against Napoleon.

In 1808 Napoleon's forces occupied the defenseless Papal State. To push the Pope into submission, Napoleon ordered a few regiments to take over Rome. The occupation was accomplished smoothly and peacefully. There was no open resistance.

But soon the real contest started—a non-violent struggle between the occupier's military strength and the spiritual and political power of the papacy. The Romans became hostile. Contrary to all expectations, the Imperial Forces found themselves in a steadily weakening political position. A confidential French report described papal authority in Rome as "more absolute than ever." A historian added: "Of the two governments that ruled Rome, the one more obeyed was the one having neither bayonets nor cannon; and from the Quirinal an old, almost captive monk, held in his weak hands all Rome as, may be, no pope had held it before." Napoleon's representatives had, for the first time, "come up against a moral force more powerful than the most powerful empires."[11]

The developments in Spain and in Rome were defeats for Napoleon, victories for his enemies—but surprises for everyone!

Elsewhere in Europe the Emperor had success after success until his unlimited power over lands and peoples stretched from Königsberg to beyond the Pyrenees, from Warsaw and Danzig to Naples and Brindizi, from Hamburg to Korfu. And Clause-

---

[9] Liddell Hart, *Strategy*, p. 129.

[10] B. H. Liddell Hart (ed.), *T. E. Lawrence to His Biographer Liddell Hart* (New York: Doubleday, Doran and Co., 1938), p. 14.

[11] Madelin, *op. cit.*, pp. 140–41.

witz, a determined opponent and a military philosopher careful to weigh his words, could not resist describing Napoleon as "the god of war himself"!

C. THE RISE OF NATIONALISM

(Bülow and Clausewitz)

Napoleon defeated and humiliated the kings of Europe. The nations of Europe reversed the course of events when they rose to fight his empire. The guerrillas of Spain, the mountaineers of Tyrol, the cossacks and peasants of Russia, the citizens of Holland and Prussia, symbolized the forces that brought about his downfall.

Prussia's struggle and resurgence are an instructive example of patriotism triumphant—the metamorphosis from a beaten monarchy to a victorious nation. In 1806, her old army was scattered to the winds with one blow. By 1813, her reorganized forces were among the best Allied units in the War of Liberation. At Waterloo they clinched victory.

Prussia's unexpected transformation cannot be understood without an appreciation of her national homogeneity, the forces released by an enthusiasm for freedom, and the stimulus of a lively strategic debate.

Prussian analysts of revolutionary and Napoleonic wars developed important ideas. They prepared Prussia's own political and military reforms, leading to the remarkable upsurge of her defensive strength. They also provided an insight into the nature of modern warfare. And they laid the foundations of the strategy prevalent in our times—in the East as well as in the West. Among these theorists, the most influential were Clausewitz and his predecessor Bülow.

While the revolutionary armies of France were victorious all over the Continent, the Prussian Army had been practically useless, because of an exaggerated reliance on Fredrician strategy and tactics rendered obsolete by events. Prussia was standing still militarily and politically. To suggest changes in the system inherited from the Great King was considered not only mistaken but outright blasphemous.

Adam Heinrich Dietrich Freiherr von Bülow (1757–1807) startled the complacent Germans with proposals for drastic change and provided an impetus for eventual reforms. His education and interests were wide, although not very systematic. He traveled—to America (twice: in 1791 and again in 1795–96), Belgium, England, and France—analyzing revolutionary movements, becoming increasingly convinced both of the rightness and the strength of popular causes. His writings initiated a politicizing of Prussian military thought.

In America and France Bülow recognized the emergence of new forces. "The consequences of American independence as the beginning of an antidespotic progression of things cannot even be estimated," he declared in 1797, because other colonial areas will follow the American example and become independent as soon as they feel sufficiently strong. Military factors have been far from decisive in America; but a mixture of military and political elements made, in Bülow's view, the effect of the Revolution impressive. It heralded "a new political and military epoch" and created the ideal formula "for all future wars."

Returning from his travels, Bülow despaired of a Prussia still living in her own fool's paradise. Berlin was ploying outmoded concepts, debating earnestly whether troops should march at 76 or 75 paces per minute, in the middle of a continent swept by a revolutionary torrent of change.

Bülow's first military treatise, *The Spirit of the Newer System of Warfare* (*Geist des Neuern Kriegssystems*), written in 1798, is a classic of military criticism. (Yet in the author's own development it was only the first step.) The basic Bülowian strategy is already stated in unambiguous terms:

> In the newer warfare the advantage is on the side of justice and freedom; that is, the nature of things favors defensive war and, in case of oppression, an uprising of the citizens of the state, if they have arms, against a disciplined standing army.[12]

---

[12] Bülow, *Geist des Neuern,* p. 107.

Where the population joins the struggle, victory is ensured. National power comprises all the physical, moral, and economic resources of the people. Hence, defeats will not be decisive: new forces can be raised in a short time.[13]

Bülow demanded what is now called indirect strategy and tactics: circuitous maneuvers, thrusts against the enemy's rear, flanking positions and movements. With profound insight Bülow proclaimed: "One cannot hurt the enemy more than by going where he is not!"[14]

One of Bülow's main ideas is the creation of disorder: to split, distract, isolate an attacking enemy. "Organize disorder!" he advised. Contrary to the current military opinion, he flatly declared: the new system "favors defensive war," and defense "becomes easy, when the attacker operates beyond his own borders." Beyond "natural borders" an offensive cannot succeed, if opposed.[15]

Bülow's greatest contribution to the science of war was his emphasis on political and psychological factors in his later works. Enthusiasm, patriotism, public opinion, and the fighting spirit of the nations, he realized, decide revolutionary struggles. "In the newer warfare it is not so depressing to be beaten. Indeed, it can be said that one has only to imagine that one is not beaten, and one really is not. One merely has to forget defeat!"[16] The unlimited means available to a nation, and a faith in its strength, will easily restore the situation.

Bülow's science of war is, essentially, not a military but a political science, a blend of political and military elements. Patriotism, enthusiasm, and public opinion are among the main

---

[13] *Ibid.*, pp. 118, 202.

[14] Bülow, *Der Feldzug von 1800 militärisch-politisch betrachet* (Berlin: H. Frölich, 1801), pp. 439, 568.

[15] Bülow, *Neue Taktik der Neurn wie sie seyn sollte* (Leipzig: J. A. Barth, 1805), I, 138, 169.

[16] Bülow, *Geist des Neuern*, pp. 215, 106–7. This seems to be a description of the undaunted Spanish struggle against Napoleon, but it was written a decade *before* the outbreak of the Peninsular War!

weapons. The cultivation of nationalism—"the most important of all ideas"—should be the chief aim of modern armies in time of peace. "Ideas are force; ideas rule people!"[17]

War itself has become part of a contest to persuade the public. Bülow spoke of war as a *Meinungskrieg*—"a war of public opinion"—to stress that popular sentiment was no mere side issue.[18]

In his last two books, Bülow defined the identity of politics and war (a quarter of a century before Clausewitz). He wrote that politics and war "are so closely related that it is impossible to separate them." Political factors are "the most important," political strategy is "the highest strategy."[19]

In his *Campaign of 1805, Considered Militarily-Politically,* he suggested a new scientific discipline, whose "first thesis" was to be:

> "Political relates to military strategy, as the latter does to tactics, and political strategy is the highest," because military strategy determines only the operations of a campaign or, at best, a war, while political strategy is concerned with the glory and existence of states for hundreds and thousands of years.[20]

It is a "delusion" to think that "the science of war is not, at the same time, politics." Politics and war "coincide of necessity." The science of war includes politics in both strategy and tactics. Military forces are merely an arm of the state; its strength is always guided by the intelligence of politics. War without a political aim is a senseless duel. And while duels between persons are absurd, duels between states "must be considered the silliest of all absurdities."[21]

Strategy is a part of politics; tactics are a part of strategy.

---

[17] *Feldzug von 1800,* p. 412.

[18] *Ibid.,* p. 275.

[19] The credit for demonstrating Bülow's priority belongs to Reinhard Höhn. See his *Revolution—Heer—Kriegsbild* (Darmstadt: Wittich Verlag, 1944), pp. 252 ff.; *Feldzug von 1800,* pp. 6, 258, 445.

[20] Bülow, *Feldzug von 1805 militärisch-politisch betrachet* (Berlin, 1806), pp. 150–51.

[21] *Ibid.,* pp. xiv–xv, 12, 17.

Bülow sensed the political role of small nations. The Irish were England's weakness. The Bohemians were likely to revolt at the first opportunity. The same applied to the Kalmucks, waiting to throw off Russian rule. Prussia, he asserted bluntly, could not hold her Polish provinces if their population revolted.

A state could not be militarily strong while being politically weak. The cause of victories and defeats in battle was to be sought at home. As long as popular support was not obtained, Prussia would remain powerless and be bound for collapse. Unpopular governments were useless and best done away with. He called for a revolution to abolish absolute monarchy, if necessary to save the country. "Whether A or B sleeps in the palace, *that* I do not consider important."

This was too much. All the threatened interests turned against Bülow. Three months before Jena he was arrested; his books were confiscated from the shops. In jail he heard of Prussia's catastrophic defeat. "This is inevitable," he remarked, "if the generals are locked up and incompetents allowed to command." During the retreat, he was turned over to Russia and died in a Russian prison—probably as a result of ill-treatment—in 1807.

Napoleon had a higher regard for the unfortunate writer. Immediately after the French occupied Berlin, the Emperor ordered Bülow released and cited to appear before him.[22] Too late . . .

Five years later, many of Bülow's ideas were included in the reorganization plans of the Prussian Army. And fifty years later, even an unfriendly critic—a monarchist general—had to admit that Bülow had shown "a better insight into the changed nature of wars of that time than the leaders of the [Prussian] army."[23]

The first French shot at Jena, Clausewitz wrote later, blew everything to bits "like a spark in a powder magazine." The obsolete Prussian Army collapsed. Even Napoleon, an admirer of Frederick the Great, confirmed that "at Jena the Prussians have

---

[22] Höhn, *op. cit.*, p. 271.

[23] F. von Meerheimb, "Behrenhorst und Bülow," *Historische Zeitschrift* (München-Berlin), VI (1861), 55-56.

not put up the resistance one expected from their reputation." The French triumph was complete. Napoleon thought Prussia finished.

Fortunately, the same shock shattered the old prejudices. Many patriots began to question the obsolete doctrines and to inquire into the causes of disaster. Officers, especially younger ones, rediscovered the valid criticisms of writers like Bülow. An active quest for a better system of defense developed after 1806. It was clear that political factors were decisive, that political as well as military reforms were indispensable for Prussia's recovery. This insight saved the nation.

Carl von Clausewitz (1780–1831) was the youngest member of the group that engineered the military rejuvenation; the others were Scharnhorst, Gneisenau, Bülow (Dietrich's older brother, Fredrich-Wilhelm), Boyen and Grollman. He went to Russia to participate in the campaign against Napoleon. Returning home convinced of the importance of irregular warfare, he helped persuade Scharnhorst to join Gneisenau in demanding the formation of a *Landstorm,* "to mobilize the physical and moral forces of the entire nation." Clausewitz himself wrote that "small states cannot fight wars of conquest in our time. But for defensive war even the means of small states are infinitely great."[24]

Gneisenau and Clausewitz remained in closest personal and professional contact all their lives. Between 1816 and 1830, Clausewitz wrote his book *On War,* obtaining Gneisenau's criticism for each chapter in draft; to a certain extent, it became a common effort. The work was solidly based, it was not written in the feverish atmosphere of a patriotic war but during long years of careful deliberation. Yet it repeatedly stressed national warfare. There was hardly a heading under which militias, the *Landstorm,* and national uprisings were not mentioned. Especially in Book Six, "On Defense," national warfare has a prominent place.

---

[24] Carl von Clausewitz, *Vom Kriege* (17th ed.; Bonn: F. Dümmler's Verlag, 1952), p. 974.

Clausewitz called the arming of a nation "a great strategic means of defense," one that "awakens a thousand small sources of resistance, which would remain dormant without it." A nation's strength, he said, cannot be released at will. A substantial part of it—namely, the moral element—comes into existence only when applied in this manner. To be successful in a national war, one must (1) fight in one's own country, (2) prevent a single defeat from becoming decisive, (3) obtain the support of the nation, and (4) have a large and favorable territory. National war is a "scattered resistance," dispersed over wide areas, advancing like an all-consuming fire. In the end, it either becomes extinguished or turns into a conflagration, forcing the enemy to leave the country before he is devoured by the flames.[25]

"Resistance must be everywhere and nowhere." It must, "like a foglike and cloudlike substance, never be concentrated into a solid body." Clausewitz, just as his predecessor, thought primarily of the "intermediate states" defending themselves against great powers. He was writing for Prussia. In his works, as in Bülow's, the superior strength of defense springs from the political advantages of fighting defensively in one's own country, supported by the people: "In one's own country everything is easier, assuming that the sentiment of the subjects is favorable. An understanding with the inhabitants gives the defender a general superiority." The friendly population participates in the struggle "with its physical strength, its riches, and its sympathies." Where, as in Spain, the nation itself rises and takes part in the war as the primary combatant, "one will understand that this is no mere intensification of popular assistance, but that a truly new force comes into being" (Bk. VI, Ch. 1 and 6). This expresses quite clearly the strategic value of the community.

---

[25] For the rest of this chapter, citations from Clausewitz' *Vom Kriege* (17th ed.; Bonn: F. Dümmler's Verlag, 1952), refer to *Book* and *Chapter*, rather than to the respective page. This may permit a verification of the quotes even without access to the complete original text. The translation is mine. References, if placed at the end of a paragraph, usually cover that whole paragraph. Thus, the foregoing paragraph in the text is taken from Book VI ("Defense"), Chapter 26 ("Arming the Nation").

Once a state decides not to give up but to defend itself by all available means, Clausewitz recognized, the spiritual strength of the nation, its loyalty, and its will to resist become potentially decisive. Bonaparte was "destroying states of the first order almost with one blow, yet the Spaniards demonstrated by a continuous struggle what national armings and insurrections generally can accomplish, despite their specific weakness and porosity." The Spanish example showed what a tremendous factor the courage and sentiment of the nation are in the power of a state, in its war potential and fighting strength (III, 17).

Often the loss of an important battle awakens new national strength. "I say there is only one success, the final success" (VIII, 2). Before that is secured, initial superiority and seemingly sure victory have often turned into inferiority and defeat for the invader, when he reached "the culmination point of attack and victory" (VII, 5). The point, Clausewitz wrote, will in the future come in all wars in which the destruction of the enemy cannot be the main aim, or where the attacker is unable to achieve it; and most future wars will probably be of such nature (VIII, Appendix).

Before the end of 1827 Clausewitz had fully realized, and defined, the interdependence of war and politics—of war as a political instrument—with force and clarity:

War must be considered a part of another whole—and that whole is politics. War is nothing but the continuation of political efforts with different means. This view I place at the foundation of the entire strategy and believe that whoever refuses to recognize its necessity does not yet duly realize what it is all about.

In every campaign plan, Clausewitz explained, even into its various parts, presumably even into every battle, a political element manifests itself. It is impossible to talk of a strategic situation or of a strategic plan as "purely military."[26] War is but a continuation of political intercourse with an admixture of other means. It certainly has its own grammar, but not its own

---

[26] Clausewitz, *op. cit.*, pp. 1119–20.

logics. "Once the impact of the political aim on war is admitted, there are no limits left, and even the descent to such wars must be accepted that consist of mere threats against the enemy, and of moves subsidiary to negotiations" (VIII, 6A, 6B).

Clausewitz supported these views with many examples, among them the following ones: the French Revolution and the campaign of 1812.

The tremendous effects of the French Revolution were due primarily to the changed form of State and administration, and to the new status of the nation. The twenty victorious years of the Revolution were made possible by mistaken policies of the opposing governments, who tried to oppose the new and over-powering forces by usual means. Without the political changes in France, the revolutionary intensification of warfare would have been unthinkable (VIII, 6B).

Bonaparte met with failure in Russia in 1812 because Russia could be subdued only through her own political weakness, through the consequences of her internal dissension. To hit this weak spot of the state, a shock was needed which went to the very heart of the system. Only by reaching Moscow with a strong thrust could Bonaparte hope to create such a shock. "We say: the campaign of 1812 has not succeeded because the opposing government remained unshaken, the population loyal and firm—because it thus could not succeed" (VIII, 9).

In the twentieth century, the latter insight of Clausewitz has been repeatedly confirmed. His ideas are as valid as ever.

Clausewitz strongly supported the use of national war against Napoleon and the Royal Decree of April, 1813, that provided a blueprint for making it the main form of defense. Napoleon himself turned to the idea of national war in March, 1814: he decided to raise the French people against the superior Allied Forces advancing on Paris. But his orders were intercepted by the enemy, and the plan had to be abandoned.[27]

Napoleon's empire was crushed by the buoyant national

---

[27] H. B. Liddell Hart, *Strategy* (New York: Praeger, 1954), p. 141.

strength of Europe. The main characteristic of the modern era of warfare turned out to be the ascendancy of politics over war. Bülow's and Clausewitz's works laid the theoretical foundation for this insight at a time when the practical effects of the change had already caused the defeat of the British Empire in America, the collapse of numerous coalitions in Europe, and, finally, the downfall of "the god of war"—Napoleon.

For small nations this aspect of developments in America and Europe is vitally important. Where political factors are decisive, militarily inferior defenders can save themselves by bringing their political advantages to bear on their struggles for freedom. The revolutionary struggles, the resistance of Spain and Rome, proved the point.

Today, the primacy of political factors in international conflicts has become even more pronounced. They play an essential role in the defense of small nations. Why was this important strategic insight ignored for one hundred and fifty years?

D. THE ERA OF EMPIRES

All Europe had been at the mercy of Emperor Napoleon in 1808. Eight years later the Corsican was a broken prisoner on a lonely island, trying to rationalize his stunning defeats. Europe was stronger than ever. Spain felt safe against conquest; the Pope ruled on the Quirinal; Prussia was one of the main powers of Europe. In victory they all forgot how weak they had felt before. Yet their seemingly hopeless resistance had dealt a heavy blow to the apparently invincible French Empire and helped overthrow the genius on her throne.

The old monarchies were saved, as if by miracle. The absolute rulers knew the combined strength of the people. To insure their own interests against nationalistic and democratic ideas, they banded together in the Holy Alliance.

Monarchist governments, cabinet politics, class interests, dominated the scene. States again seemed to exist only for the benefit of the royal houses and governing circles. The people?

Nations? One could, and did, ignore them; their role in subduing Napoleon was soon forgotten. Public opinion? The arming of nations? Theories of a superiority of irregulars over standing armies, of the strength of people's war? All seemed to have been a mere passing insanity, rampant while things had temporarily gotten out of hand. But now all was well: regular (armies and state administrations), orthodox (political and military theories), unchangeable—because unchanged.

Between the Congress of Vienna and the Treaty of Versailles, imperialism and great-power influence reached their zenith. Small states and nations became helpless objects of prey, able to survive only where the empires suffered temporary loss of appetite. Conquest and oppression triumphed. The great powers suppressed the Poles, the Hungarians, and the Irish. The world was theirs; their fiats remained law and Scripture for another 150 years after the strength of small nations had been impressively demonstrated.

It is true that the Belgians gained independence from Holland, the Greeks from Turkey, and the Norwegians from Sweden. But Holland, Sweden, and Turkey had ceased to be great powers. Only Turkey fought with a clumsy determination to retain her subjects, while Holland gave up after a few reverses, and Sweden bowed to the result of a plebiscite. The fact that Finland, without any outside assistance, secured her autonomy from Russia passed practically unnoticed.

The great powers returned to the prerevolutionary idea that standing armies decide wars. In all cases in which a struggle was confined to the military sphere, they enjoyed uncontestable supremacy. Their basic success was persuading everyone, including themselves, that conflicts could be decided only by armed forces. Theirs was a triumph based on a mutual mistake.

Military theory contributed to the blunder. Clausewitz's *On War*, at first well-nigh overlooked (the 1,500 copies of the first edition were not sold out in twenty years), was later consulted almost exclusively for practical advice. Its political side was either not understood or intentionally disregarded. After

1870, the work was discovered outside Prussia. But selective misreading gradually turned it into a manual of great-power mass warfare. The abstract generalities of the first five pages were accepted as dogma; the realistic limitations, which began on page six, were ignored. So were Clausewitz's ideas of the primacy of politics, of limited wars, militias, national armings, small-nation defense. Sometimes his readers were advised simply to skip over "the philosophical passages" in the book. The distorted versions have been popular ever since, notably in translation.

World War I, inspired by doctrines of mass warfare, turned into a ghastly butchery. Great-power generals staged spectacular but nonsensical battles. No imagination was needed to see how impressive huge masses looked—as marchers in parades or as corpses on the battlefields. The generals did not seem to remember that the victories of revolutionary France, and of the nations opposing Napoleon, resulted from a superior morale, a new strategy and tactics, not from superior numbers alone. It was easier to add up numbers.

After the war, historians failed to see that three out of the four defeated empires owed their downfall to their subject nations. Austria's unwilling subjects had doomed her to impotence; Russia's collapse was due to the revolutionary spirit of nations under her rule. Turkey's rout was, to a great extent, the result of the Arab Revolt.

E. T. E. LAWRENCE AND THE ARAB REVOLT

In typical World War fashion, the front in Palestine had been frozen. Britain's and Turkey's armies faced each other with horns locked. An Arab rising broke out in June, 1916. The revolt had some initial success. But Arab attacks on Medina failed, and a Turkish counteroffensive almost crushed them. Against a modern regular army the Bedouins were helpless.

Thomas Edward Lawrence (1888–1935) arrived in Arabia five months later, just in time to avert the threatening defeat.

The unknown lieutenant, an archeologist, had studied military writers from Clausewitz to Foch. But he had the sense to discard orthodox strategic principles likely to lead his forces to defeat. He invented a strategy stressing intelligence, strategic movements, the use of free space, and the individualism of his men. In short, he made Arab advantages decisive. He "combined their loose sparks into a firm flame: transformed a series of unrelated accidents into a conspicuous operation."[28]

Lawrence insisted that the smaller the Arab unit engaged, the better its performance; that individual and independent action would release their capabilities best; that "in some way it was easier to defend a range of hills against nine or ten thousand men than against nine or ten." Heavy weapons would only reduce Arab speed and efficiency. Dispersal was their strength. "The distribution of our raiding parties was unorthodox. We aimed at the widest dissipation of force; and we added fluidity to speed. In a real sense maximum disorder was our equilibrium. The efficiency of our forces was the personal efficiency of the single man." His aim was to achieve a combined impact by waging "articulate war." In irregular war, he wrote, "if two men are together, one is being wasted!"[29]

The Turks were doing well in the war; they checked the English and French landings at the Dardanelles and stalemated the British offensive in Palestine. But against Lawrence they found no defense. His campaign spread with unexpected speed

---

28 The outstanding evaluation of Lawrence's campaigns from the strategic point of view is B. H. Liddell Hart's *T. E. Lawrence in Arabia and After* (London: Jonathan Cape, 1934). T. E. Lawrence's own main writings are the classic *Seven Pillars of Wisdom* (New York: Dell Publishing Co., 1962); and the summaries "The Evolution of a Revolt," *The Army Quarterly*, No. I (1920), 55–69; and "Guerrilla Warfare, World War I," *Encyclopaedia Britannica*, X (1960), 950–950D. Liddell Hart has also published correspondence between the two men: *T. E. Lawrence to His Biographer Liddell Hart* (New York: Doubleday, Doran and Co., 1938), an interesting close look at the strategist and the man. The quote is from Liddell Hart's *Arabia*, p. 7.

29 Lawrence, *Seven Pillars*, pp. 340–41; "Evolution of a Revolt," p. 56, 68.

and force, setting into motion an avalanche of Turkish setbacks that ended with the collapse of the Ottoman Empire.

Neither Lawrence's own people nor his enemies shared his views. British officers called the Arabs simply a "rabble, a motley crew of camel stealers, no match for the well-seasoned Turk."[30] On the enemy side, similar ignorance bred by orthodoxy: "The Turks were stupid. The Germans behind them dogmatical. They would believe that rebellion was absolute, like war, and deal with it on the analogy of war." It was a false analogy—"and making war upon rebellion was messy and slow, like eating soup with a knife." For Lawrence, "rebellion was not war: indeed, was more of the nature of peace—a national strike perhaps." The population would decide the outcome "Without the friendship of the tribes the Turks own only the ground on which their soldiers stand."[31]

T. E. Lawrence defined the three basic elements of his strategy early in the campaign:[32]

First, *the algebraic element*—a territory of 140,000 square miles—favored the Arabs. How could the Turks hold it all?

No doubt by a trench line across the bottom, if we came like an army with banners; but suppose we were (as we might be) an influence, an idea, a thing intangible, invulnerable, without front or back, drifting about like gas? Armies were like plants, immobile, firm-rooted, nourished through long stems to the head. We might be a vapour, blowing where we listed. Our Kingdoms lay in each man's mind, and as we wanted nothing material to live on, so we might offer nothing material to the killing. It seemed a regular soldier might be helpless without a target, owning only what he sat on, and subjugating only what, by order, he could poke his rifle at.

The Turks would need 600,000 men "to meet the ill-wills of all the Arab peoples, combined with the active hostility of a

---

[30] Anthony Nutting, *Lawrence of Arabia* (New York: Signet Book, 1962), p. 19.

[31] Lawrence, *Seven Pillars*, p. 107, 192, 196.

[32] *Ibid.*, Ch. 33, *passim*, gives a résumé of the three elements.

few zealots." If the correct strategy of an "attack in depth" were used, sedition would be "putting up her head in every unoccupied one of those hundred thousand square miles."

Second, *the biological factor*, the breaking point, the wear and tear, in both men and material. Turkey's basic shortage was not men but things: the destruction of a bridge or rail, machinery or weapon, was more profitable than killing soldiers, of whom they had so many. The Arabs could not afford casualties, while supplies might be replaced with British assistance.

The analysis determined Lawrence's strategy: "Our cue was to destroy, not the Turk's army, but his minerals." The rebels were "to be superior in some one tangible branch; gun-cotton or machine-guns or whatever could be made decisive. For both things and men we might give the doctrine a twisted negative side, for cheapness' sake, and be weaker than the enemy everywhere except in that one point or matter. The decision of what was critical would always be ours."

To save men, the Arabs would fight a war of detachment, contain the enemy by threatening him from the desert, remaining hidden "might turn our advantage into a rule (not a law, since war was antinomian) and develop a habit of never engaging the enemy. Many Turks on our front had no chance all the war to fire on us, and we were never on the defensive except by accident and in error."

Third, *the psychological element*. Lawrence adopted Xenophon's term *diathetic*, and called modern propaganda its inadequate substitute. The struggle would be won by changing men's minds. Their military strength was small, they "could not let the metaphysical weapon rust unused."[33] "We lived by preaching to the people," Lawrence explained. He won by it.

Translated into strategic terms, the stress on the superiority of political strength opened unusual possibilities. The words *defense* and *conquest* acquired a new meaning: "A province would be won when we taught the civilians to die for our ideal of

---

[33] Lawrence, "Guerrilla Warfare," p. 950B.

freedom; the presence or absence of the enemy was a secondary matter. Final victory seemed certain, if the war lasted long enough for us to work it out."[34] This revolutionary innovation in politics and strategy was the key to victory. Correctly exploited, it turned the military campaign into a mere mop-up operation.

Arab strategy reduced the Turks to helplessness; and complete victory seemed to be in sight when the British offensive in the Palestine put an end to the war. Lawrence confessed regret that developments had not given him enough time for "following to the end the dictum of Saxe that a war might be won without fighting battles." In the end, the Arabs beat the British Army in the race for Damascus by a whole day. The Arab triumphs certainly were "a pragmatic argument that can not be wholly derided."[35]

Looking back on his experiences, T. E. Lawrence listed the conditions for success in this kind of war: (1) An unassailable base, "something guarded not merely from attack, but from the fear of it: such a base we had in the Red Sea ports, the desert, or in the minds of men we converted to our creed." (2) An alien enemy "disposed as an army of occupation in an area greater than could be dominated effectively from fortified posts." (3) A friendly population, "not actively friendly, but sympathetic to the point of not betraying rebel movements to the enemy." (4) An active striking force, not more than 2 per cent of the population. (5) This force must have the virtues of secrecy and self-control; the qualities of speed and endurance, ubiquity, and independence of supply arteries. (6) "They must have technical equipment to destroy or paralyze the enemy's organized communications, for irregular war is 'the study of communications' in its extreme degree, of attack where the enemy is not."[36]

"With 2,000 years of examples behind us we have no excuse,

---

[34] Lawrence, *Seven Pillars*, p. 200.
[35] Lawrence, "Evolution of a Revolt," 68–69.
[36] *Ibid.*, 69.

when fighting, for not fighting well," Lawrence of Arabia wrote
to Liddell Hart.[37] He had fought splendidly. Lord Wawel called
his deeds "a spiritual even more than a physical exploit. He had
read more and thought more on military history and military art
than probably any other Great Commander."[38]

Lawrence's main achievement is to have modernized political
and military strategy. He brought the identity between politics
and war to its logical conclusion, and he proved the paramountcy
of political factors in war.

---

[37] In Liddell Hart, *To His Biographer,* p. 75.
[38] Lord Wawel's tribute is quoted in David Garnett (ed.), *The Essential T. E. Lawrence* (London: Jonathan Cape, 1951), p. 19.

CHAPTER V

Violence and Political Control

International aggression has so far defied all attempts at a legal or political definition. The reason is simple: aggression can manifest itself in a practically unlimited variety of ways. It may suffice here to describe it as an act calculated to deprive, in whole or in part, a nation of its independence, national identity, or physical existence. Aggression is such a serious menace to small nations because it is, as a rule, supported by an express or implied threat of force.

The specific objective of an aggressive great power can vary from a mere attempt to influence a small nation's foreign policy to its very incorporation into the empire. But behind every aggressive move lurks a superior capacity for violence. And this violence may be used at any time either to threaten or to invade the defending small nation.

If, however, violence can coerce obedience, then there is not much sense in considering political defense against an aggressor who can threaten to use this capacity for violence.

Although military invasion and terror are applied only in comparatively rare cases, the events in Europe in the summer of 1968 proved that they may indeed be used by an aggressor. The ability of a small nation to deny control to an invading enemy remains the acid test of the political strategy for small-nation defense.

Si vis pacem, para bellum applies fully to the political defense: the best way to deter an invasion is to know how, and to prepare, to deal with it. As a matter of fact, many instances of political pressure are intended primarily to test the determination of small nations to face this ultimate threat. Finland,

for instance, has been able to defend her independence only because the Finnish nation defied the threatened and actual Russian
invasion for a quarter of a century—from 1937 to 1961.[1] Switzerland (1939-44), Yugoslavia (1948-52), Poland (1956), and
Romania (1961-70) are other examples of small states able to
resist, despite a threat of military invasion.

Invasion, although not the only, is the most oppressive form
of military intervention. (The next most oppressive is the Russian
invention called "allied maneuvers.") Its discussion, therefore,
covers cases of less direct enemy pressure, by analogy. Wherever
the threat, or likelihood, of invasion is the ultimate foundation
of an imposed regime or another encroachment on national
independence, similar conditions apply, *mutatis mutandis*. And
in all such cases, a possible enemy invasion with its consequences
must be a part of strategic calculations.

This chapter examines violence and political control, as the
means and the end.

A.   INVASION AND ITS WEAKNESSES

If military invasion can secure political control, political defense of small nations may be doomed to fail. Stalin, the master
of *Realpolitik*, pointed this out to the Finnish representatives
before his attack on the small nation: "Finland is small and
weak. You are not in a position, even if you wished, to prevent
a great-power army from invading Finland. A great power could
land [anywhere on your coastline] and continue to march without

---

[1] The twenty-five years of Finland's heroic political defense are vividly
described in Austin Goodrich, *Study in Sisu: Finland's Fight for Independence* (New York: Ballantine Books, 1960), pp. 39 ff.; its last
ten years are reviewed by Katarina Brodin in *Finland, 1956–1966* (Stockholm: Utrikespolitiska institutet, 1966). Descriptions of some of the fierce
political conflicts can be found in the reminiscences of the participants:
Väinö Tanner, *The Winter War* (Stanford, Calif.: Stanford University
Press, 1957); Arvo Tuominen, *Kremls Klockor* (Stockholm, 1958); S.
Hjalmar Rantanen, *Som Politruk i Finland* (Stockholm: Natur och Kultur,
1958); to name a few.

worrying about your protests."[2] What are the chances for a small nation to defend itself politically even if, unlike Finland in 1939 and 1944, it cannot defeat the attempt of military invasion?

National resistance begins when an alien power invades a small country. Unable to defeat the aggressor militarily, the defending nation refuses to fight "to the bitter end" on the battlefields. Since its greatest strength is political, it rallies to defeat the invader politically.

Orthodox strategy claims that armed force decides all, that military occupation, minus a counterattack, equals final victory. It asserts that the invader *has won* when occupation is accomplished: that political control flows directly from military superiority, that one must cede control to the occupier. Military occupation, thus, marks the end in orthodox strategy.

A strategy of resistance recognizes only political victory as decisive. Military invasion may be one means to approach that end, but it is not decisive of itself. A political opposition, using various defensive techniques, can reduce the significance of occupation to a minimum. According to this theory, the invader *has not won*. Despite a preliminary success, the aggressor can be prevented from gaining a victory. In national resistance, invasion is only the starting signal for the decisive contest.

The decisive contest is the struggle for political control of the population: the attacker tries to establish and maintain it; the defender tries to preserve his own control, or at least frustrate that of the invader. In this crucial struggle the invader's chief weapon is his military presence. The resisting nation's main weapon is its political strength—the support of the people and the strong points they hold.

Every contest is an interplay of rival forces. National resistance can be described, in a polemologic sense (the sense of conflict analysis), as a conflict of influences or controls—the invader's military versus the defenders' political control. The two have to clash; both have the same objective. The resisters act

---

[2] Goodrich, *op. cit.*, p. 49.

in the presence of, and in opposition to, enemy military forces. They hold political control, which is the enemy's objective: the enemy must seize it or fail. Military invasion can succeed only if it leads to political victory. National resistance can succeed only if it can withstand invasion. The victory of one rival equals the defeat of the other.

Military occupation has always been a popular means of enlarging empires and chastising unruly satellites. The evaluation of this practice in military theory, international law, and international politics has not varied appreciably for centuries: they assume that nations expire when their territory is occupied by an outside power.

But when are definite areas occupied? And how occupied are "occupied areas"? What is the political situation of influence and control in such areas?

There are no accurate instruments or tests to diagnose *occupation*, but there is usually a lot of information. Unfortunately, modern reporting, statistics, and maps are too complete—far more complete than reality. They mislead rather than inform about the actual state of things.

In many cases reports create an impression directly contrary to the facts, sometimes intentionally. In 1944, German occupation authorities had disbanded Danish police, but a few criminals were apprehended, nevertheless. Copenhagen newspapers reported such cases extensively; they misled both the public and the criminal elements into believing that law enforcement continued almost normally.[3] On April 10, 1940, a few German troop units landed in Oslo, the capital of Norway. Since the Norwegian forces were not resisting in the city, it was said that the Germans "occupied" Oslo, that they "controlled" it. In actual fact, the few ostentatiously displayed companies could neither occupy nor control the extensive community. Nor, for that matter, could the hundreds of thousands of Russian troops control the invaded Czech capital in 1968—despite repeated insistence of

---

[3] Jørgen Trolle, *Syv Maaneder uden Politi* (København: Nyt Nordisk Førlag, 1945), p. 207.

foreign news media that they "ruled" Prague and that the resistance was being suppressed.

Maps can be equally misleading. They tend to show a line connecting the points of an attacker's furthest advance with everything behind it as "occupied and controlled." They mislead —an invader holds nothing besides some main routes, certain road junctions, a few strong points, and parts of the more important towns and cities. And even there his hold may be more illusory than real.

Pictures of Russian troops with machine guns in front of a printing office keeping everyone out looked impressive only so long as we did not know that ingenious people were printing resistance newspapers in the basement and distributing them over the back fence to delivery vans. General Pavlovsky's threats to send Russian troops into Czech schools was equally impressive. But what would the soldiers do when they got there? They would either do nothing or make themselves ridiculous. . . .

Modern warfare is one of thrusts, not of a general advance along an uninterrupted front. In countries of extensive size—like Sweden or Romania—only a fraction of the territory could be dominated by any occupier, even less against resistance. Invaded areas should be called by some other name—"penetrated," for instance, or "overrun"—but not "occupied."

As a matter of fact, an entire territory is never occupied: some points within it are held in the hope of radiating influence and maintaining a limited control from such points. And people are never "occupied" at all: military invasion is only a step preliminary to an attempt at establishing political control over them.

A country should not be considered occupied and controlled, or not. Just as, in medicine, the only distinction is not between someone dead or someone in perfect health, in political science the main task is not to diagnose one of two extremes. In both sciences, the most significant contribution is to recognize the degree of affliction and the ability to resist, combined with efforts to improve this balance.

The real task of military and political leadership is to cope with various kinds and degrees of danger and opportunity when a nation is invaded by hostile forces. A resistance struggle—between alien army, administration, and a resisting nation—is an interplay of opposed pressures. Tensions and advantages keep fluctuating between both ends of a polemometric scale (a measure of conflict-intensity). The country is "controlled" by both opponents, more or less. This is true not only as to the entire political community, but to any one of its components as well—even the individuals. The true picture is extremely complicated at all times. And, correctly exploited, this complication becomes a strategic asset of resistance.

The complicated power relationships in a territory where opposing forces contend should not be described as possession and control but, more precisely, as a conflict of possessions and a conflict of controls. These power relationships are further confused by the various forces active throughout the contested country; the four types of places where different control predominates; and the endless variety of the relative degree of competing occupations and controls.

The possession of an invaded country is divided between the occupier (the foreign troops) and the occupant (the people living on the spot). Both have a kind of possession in all inhabited resistance areas. The situation is best described as a *conflict of possessions* (or occupations).

Each of the possessions rests on a different type of strength or control: the invader's, on military control; the defenders', on political control. This is another dimension of the struggle: a *conflict of controls* (or influences). In addition, there are differences of *degree* of the relative controls: the military control of an alien invader over newly-taken territory usually lacks the degree of perfection or effectiveness typical of the resisting nation's political control over its own citizens. The defenders exploit this advantage.

National resistance is a contest to resolve the conflicts of possessions and controls, one way or another. At the end, as Clausewitz explained, either resistance is extinguished or it destroys the foundations of enemy rule "like an all-consuming fire."

Four forces participate in this contest, which goes on in four different areas. The *four participating forces* are (1) the invader's troops and agents, (2) the national leadership, (3) the active resisters, and (4) the population. Depending on which of the forces is predominant at a certain place, the invaded country falls into *four areas:*

1. *Invader-dominated areas*: If accurately shown on a map, these areas will consist of hair-thin main roads and small, solidly-held points, surrounded by large spaces beyond the invader's grasp. Obviously, no nation is controlled from this fraction of its territory.
2. *Resistance-dominated areas.*
3. *Population-dominated areas*: These include practically every point outside the invader's reach. The people are the most widely present of all the forces. In the long run, they are the decisive ones. Small nation defense must exploit the people's ubiquity. (See Chapter VIII, B, below.)
4. *Contested areas,* where the influences interact to create somewhat of a balance, without the enemy, the resistance forces, or the population having a clear predominance.

In the situation just described, the invader's political domination is a distant goal, one he may never reach against determined resistance.

The situations are, in addition, neither entirely clear nor static: (*a*) A country falls into the four types named not definately, but only more or less. (*b*) The exact limits of the areas can hardly ever be determined. (*c*) Even if the degree of control and the limits were ascertained, they could not be kept constant; they keep fluctuating with time and place. A map of the struggle for control will, as a consequence, look more like a meterological map than like a geographical one. And it will always be dated.

Dominating a territory, although simplest to describe, is only one of the invader's control problems. In political contests it is not even the most important. But that does indicate the profound complexity of a resistance struggle waged on many levels.

Let us keep in mind that resistance is both multiform and

multidimensional. It is just as impossible to describe as is international aggression because it too manifests itself in an endless variety of ways. Everything that contributes to resistance is part of the total resistance picture. (The Russian tank, for instance, driving around in Prague with Czech resistance slogans painted on it was part of the national resistance.)

The operation of resistance forces in, and among, the various components of the political life is far more intricate. Organizations, groups, activities, and individuals are more vital for political control than mere points of the terrain. Nor does the control of them coincide. The interplay of the four forces results in a varying degree of relative controls they hold over each component of national life, over practically every relationship in the country that can be broadly described as political. In the last analysis, it includes the minds of individual citizens—each of them another problem. And the more elements are added to the volatile polemic mixture, the less able is the occupier to control all possible reactions.

In the past, a nation was called conclusively defeated when either its armed forces ceased to exist, or its state was destroyed. But military fighting is only one, dispensable, form of resistance. Neither its presence nor its absence is conclusive proof of national survival or demise. And the administrative machinery, called the State, is nothing but a superstructure: neither its inability to function, nor its destruction or take-over by the enemy, signifies the end of a nation and national resistance. The German state was smashed in 1945, but the existence of a German nation was never it doubt. And the Polish nation has undeniably survived the consecutive demise of half a dozen Polish States. The only true test is the national spirit and the will to resist. Unless they are extinguished, the invader has not achieved his objective. A nation given up for lost earlier is buried alive.

Where occupation did mean decisive defeat it was often due to a series of prefabricated misconceptions about the nature of modern conflict. One is reminded of a tale by H. C. Andersen: "The Emperor's New Clothes" were as illusory as an invading empire's political strength. By a similar technique as in the Danish fairy tale, people convinced themselves that an aggressor was omnipotent, that a tank, a bayonet, a rocket, give political power. And men who believe that they are defeated are in fact defeated: the belief induces the paralysis.

If national resistance is to succeed against enemy military power, the people must realize the invader's political nakedness. His domination extends only to a small part of the invaded territory. His control of organizations and political activities is minimal; many of the activities are outside his reach. His domination can be effective only at the times and places where his army and agents can be present, supervise the activities, discover and correct disobedience. Characteristic of the intelligent Czech resistance was the reply of a television technician broadcasting secretly when warned that a Soviet tank was posted in front of the house: "I know, but tanks are not equipped to detect TV broadcasts." If resistance operates outside the grasp of military forces, an army cannot check it effectively.

Rather than improve an alien's political chances, invasion creates political disadvantages and hostility. In a hostile country military gains are diminished, and the weaknesses of occupation forces is increased. The attitude of the omnipresent population has a double effect: friendship for the resisters and antagonism toward the intruders simultaneously strengthen the defending side and weaken the aggressor. National resistance can exploit popular animosity against an invader. Stalin spoke of the "oppressed peoples, who remain silent, but whose very silence exerts pressure and decides much." He called "this tacit sympathy which nobody hears or sees" one of the "factors which, although they are obscured by the victories of our armies, in the long run decide everything."[4] Stalin did not forget that of the two equally disliked alien powers, the burden of resistance

---

[4] C. Aubrey Dixon and Otto Heilbrun, *Communist Guerrilla Warfare* (London: Allen & Unwin, 1954), p. 24; quoting his "Report on National Factors in Party and State Development," at the XII Congress of the Russian Communist Party, April 23, 1923.

falls on the one who occupies a hostile territory. That is why he adroitly left to Hitler the occupation of Warsaw, and the costly task of fighting the main Polish resistance forces, in the late summer of 1944.

Bülow's natural borders, beyond which an aggressor cannot succeed, if opposed, are on the hostile territories of resisting nations. And Clausewitz's culmination point of attack and victory is reached when the impact of a resisting nation's hostility becomes strong enough to tip the scales against a victorious invader.

Aware of the decisive contribution of national ill-will in political war, Lawrence listed "an alien enemy" as a condition of success. King-Hall suggested that, in order to exploit fully the defending side's political strength in case of a conflict between Britain and Russia, "we should do our best to force the Soviet Union to undertake an occupation."[5] Analyzing the anti-guerrilla campaign in the Philippines, Lieutenant Colonel Villa-Real wrote: "It would be rare, indeed, if the use of foreign troops would not of itself doom to failure an anti-guerrilla campaign."[6] He meant friendly foreign troops, invited by the national Government. Invasion forces, entering the country in anger, may turn out to be an even greater political liability: their presence may activate and unify resistance, it may render impossible the political persuasion of a hostile people.

Military difficulties in a hostile country are many. Strategy has spent centuries looking for ways to gain the enemy's rear, where he can be hit with the greatest impact; the invader exposes his own rear to the defender. The invader's communications and supply lines are highly vulnerable targets, never safe from sabotage and commando raids. Efforts to protect them scatter invasion forces. Their burden is heavier yet if troops have to carry out the policing of the country—a task for which they

---

[5] Stephen King-Hall, *Defence in the Nuclear Age* (London: V. Gollancz, 1958), p. 155.

[6] Louis A. Villa-Real, "Huk Hunting," *The Army Combat Forces Journal* (Washington, D.C.), 5 (1954), 36.

are badly suited. Lin Piao was very emphatic: "It is only after letting the enemy in that he can be compelled to divide his forces, take on heavy burdens and commit mistakes."[7]

But popular hostility hits the invader hardest on the political level. Russian Premier Khrushchev, with his noted gift for vivid expression, admirably described the predicament. In 1958, long after fighting had stopped in Hungary, he described that country as "a dead rat" in Russia's throat. And in the summer of 1962, he called Berlin "a bad tooth that must be extracted to ease the pain" in Germany.[8] He failed to add, although probably not to realize, that the discomfort had been caused by Russia's inability to resist the sweet temptation of trying to swallow Hungary and half of Germany. . . .

The only way to success for an invader is through a political victory. Military invasion and superiority do not guarantee him political control.

B. POLITICAL CONTROL AND RESISTANCE

1. *Political Control—the End*

An anecdote, popular in Eastern Europe, tells why Stalin was a far greater statesman than Hitler: "For years Hitler tried to make us hate the Russians—without success. Stalin accomplished that very result in a matter of days, after his troops marched in!" This saw suggests how hard it is for an invader to dispose the population favorably, and how easily the mere arrival of alien troops can lead to his political defeat.

The invader has strengthened himself militarily and weakened himself politically. The armed forces of the defender are defeated, or at least scattered. Regardless of a temporary dislocation, exhaustion, or possible overextension, the presence of oc-

---

[7] Lin Piao, *Long Live the Victory of People's War!* (Peking: Foreign Languages Press, 1965), p. 35.

[8] *New York Times,* July 17, 1968.

cupation troops on the spot is a great military advantage. Politically the aggressor's position is far worse. While absent, he could have relied on the sympathies, or at least the indifference, of certain population groups—be it only the admirers of ballet or jazz. Invasion antagonizes almost everyone. Enemy pressure ends all good will and leaves only animosity; none but traitors and collaborators remain favorably disposed. The invader has conquered the territory and lost the population of the occupied country. Occupation crushes military defense, but multiplies political opposition.

At this point of the conflict, the aggressor has not won and the defending nation has not lost. The invader cannot accept such a state of indecision—with resistance holding the political positions. To tolerate it would mean disaster. He must attack politically to establish control and end all defiance; as long as opposition continues, no invader is safe.

Political power over human beings has not been sufficiently explained. But one thing is clear: they are not "conquered" like trees and rocks by stationing some troops with rockets and tanks around the countryside. To control them one needs, if not their loyalty, at least their habitual obedience. Only by transforming military domination into political victory can a conqueror reach his goal: a general acquiescence in his rule. Without the acquiescence, his rule is not secure; without political control, there is no final success for him.

The invader must achieve military domination as well as political control. He needs both, while the defender can prevail by defeating him at either step. Orthodox strategy fought him for the military means; national resistance tries to deny him the political goal.

One may say that a ruler controls his subjects either (1) directly, through their loyalty to him personally or to the office he legitimately claims; or (2) indirectly, through a control apparatus the different levels of which—national, provincial, and local administrations—can be called links in his chain of power. In the first case, the control apparatus is used chiefly for reasons of expendiency. In the second case, it is the indispensable means of control: through the administrative chain or machinery the ruler's orders pass down and the subjects' obedience, in whatever form, passes back up.

This description is highly simplified, reduced to the three basic administrative links—national, provincial, and local. It suffices only where the internal structure of "the chain" is not the point at issue and the machinery is treated as a whole. Complexity is, however, one of the ever-present characteristics of such systems. And side by side with the Government machinery, various public and private organizations are similar and, equally important, *parallel control apparatus* in their own fields.

"Control" may be the name given to a routine functioning of the system. What is usually called the "power" of a ruler is actually his ability to control his subjects' efforts (physical, economic, intellectual), and to apply them according to his wishes. In a totalitarian society rulers hold the administrative chain as well as other means of control—the apparatus of trade unions and professional associations; organizations devoted to sports, education, arts, commerce, travel, etc. Through them all, a ruler controls his own country more or less completely.

A conqueror (the ruler of a state that occupies the territory of another nation) finds similar systems of control in the invaded country. But with two essential differences: he holds neither (1) the loyalty of the hostile population nor (2) any of the apparatus forming the chains of control. Naturally, his primary endeavor is to get these apparatus.

Resistance opposes his efforts by all available means. It contests the control of the apparatus and his influence inside them; it attempts to recapture the lost links and to activate systems rivaling the ones that the conqueror has secured for himself. The chain of control can be broken at any point. Once broken, the conqueror's rule does not work beyond the point of breach. To prevent or break enemy control becomes the main part of the struggle on the political level.

Before he can consider himself in full political control, the invader must secure the controls of the occupied country's (1) government, (2) administrative machinery, (3) organizations, (4) informal circles and groups, and (5) individuals.

The ultimate success is the control of individual citizens. A conqueror, unable to win their loyalty, will try to secure their obedience through the apparatus of control. His first targets will, therefore, be the Government, the administrations, and the organizations. He will try various techniques: to (1) take over and use, (2) infiltrate and influence, (3) outlaw, or (4) physically destroy them and create new institutions to exercise their functions, where necessary or advantageous.

Each of these attempts faces different problems; each of the targets can resist in its own way. It is usually easiest to take over the Government itself, but individuals are hardly ever brought under direct control. The further down into the political community the process of take-over descends (from the governing top toward the level of the individual), the more difficult it is to overcome resistance, to establish and maintain control.

Government buildings can be occupied immediately; the top Government positions may also be taken over without much delay. Infiltrating the administrative machinery takes considerable time; in the face of resistance it may take years. Other organizations are even less easy to subdue. The occupier may seize their offices, may even go through the motions of outlawing them. But if they submerge underground and continue to function covertly, very little has been done. If they decentralize into small, clandestine groups and remain active locally, they are withdrawing into an area safe from control. Circles such as families and informal friendships cannot be abolished. Only a few can be physically destroyed. They cannot be taken over; hardly ever can they be infiltrated. And although individuals may be induced to obey specific orders, outside of a jail or concentration camp they can never be effectively controlled.

In Czechoslovakia all the Russians could accomplish in 1968

was to occupy the buildings of the Government, the central Party offices, and a few of the more important ministries. But they could not prevent the country's leadership from protesting the occupation, rallying the citizens, and directing the activities of state and party organs. While the defending nation holds the state apparatus, the enemy cannot secure control over the people.

In the two years after the occupation of Czechoslovakia the occupiers and their agents—the present leadership—have repeatedly failed in their attempts to take over or infiltrate and direct many organizations, including unions, associations of students and intellectuals, even cells of the Communist Party. They have been forced to deprive these groups of their income and jurisdiction, to declare many "dissolved." It cannot be ascertained to what extent each of the affected organizations has been neutralized. Some of them have disappeared from view, while others are still continuing variform resistance.

So far I have discussed political control as if it were an undivided whole. Actually, as can be seen in the preceding analysis, it is a sum total of an infinite number of partial controls, or control fragments. If not every individual, at least each of the formal and informal circles of a few individuals, capable of purposeful activity, are such fragments. In a resisting pluralistic society, the invader must control them all if his political control is to be fully effective.

The multiple nature of political control multiplies his difficulties. It also helps resistance, which holds the political positions and is not defeated as long as it has *some* tools of control in its possession.

The occupier has no choice but to push his attempts to deprive the defenders of *all* apparatus that could conceivably direct and control resistance. (Among these must be included broadcasting stations and newspapers, even underground publications, not only formal Government or Party apparatus. He has to take, and hold, the higher levels before he can capture the next-lower links in the chain of control. But every new acquisition requires further effort. Even if he had taken over the

Government—the national, provincial, and local administrations
—disbanded or dominated every organization (a truly Herculean
task, not easily achieved by the most expert and politically
astute alien), he would merely hold additional means of control,
not the final objective. Active, organized resistance of small
groups and circles would still be very much alive. The aggressor's control would still be incomplete, and in danger. To
pursue it, he must attack local groups, most of which cannot
even be found.

It is almost impossible to dominate closely-knit small groups,
extended families, and people at the same place of work. But
all of them contribute to national resistance whenever they
oppose the enemy. The cumulative effect of their opposition can
be considerable. Such resistance has been effective before. Norwegian teachers, Dutch physicians, Belgian railroadmen, defied
the Germans who had defeated their armies and chased their
Governments into exile with incredible speed and ease.
Hungarian workers continued opposition for weeks after the
Russians had taken over their country in November, 1956.[9]
Greek Cypriotes resisted the British, as Algerians did the
French, until their combined loyalties—not military battles—
decided both conflicts. These examples show that resistance is
possible on every level: from the governmental to the individual; that no one is hopelessly conquered unless all are
subdued. And that all are important.

In their attempts to control individuals the invaders proclaim
laws and orders; use the control apparatus that they have taken
over; and apply the stick of violence and the carrot of reward
directly. They try to create a habit of obedience.

Generous doses of propaganda and ideology are, as a rule,
dispensed in the occupied country. This will not suffice to
establish a general loyalty to the alien, but it may confuse the
loyalties of some people and induce them to become collaborators

---

[9] George Mikes, *The Hungarian Revolution* (London: André Deutsch,
1957), pp. 165–66; Karl Heinz Hoffmann and Otto Mayr-Arnold, *Okänd
Armé* (Stockholm: Hörsta Förlag, 1959), pp. 140 (Norway), 149 (Holland), 178 (Belgium).

against their own nation. And it may help confuse the population as to the real issues involved—national independence and freedom versus alien oppression and colonialism. Gaining even one of these aims can be a great success for the invader and a blow to resistance. But a well-prepared nation is almost impossible to deceive. In the Czech and Slovak lands all the extensive propaganda efforts of the invaders were nullified by the invasion itself. The national information media kept clear the distinction between friend and enemy, between the legal representatives of the people and the alien agents. The resistance success was so great that even confirmed collaborators were deterred from open betrayal. Only in the following year did the Russians manage to split the Communist leadership and impose a docile regime.

Loyalty is the only safe foundation of control, and loyalty is given, not taken. It can be neither conquered nor enforced. Obedience can be given voluntarily and taken by force. Usually the invader settles even for the most grudging obedience, especially in the first stages of an invasion. But enforced obedience is reversible: nothing is decided so long as the basic loyalty of the citizens—be it the President of the Republic, a local leader, or the cleaning woman of an office—belongs to their nation. Voluntary obedience, in accord with loyalty, is stable and reliable. Coerced obedience, against loyalty, is unstable and unreliable: it lasts as long as the pressure; it disintegrates when direct pressure weakens. The last decade in Russian-Romanian relations is a classic example: after Soviet occupation troops were withdrawn, a determined national leadership easily rallied the Romanians and restored the independence of the country.

2. Resistance and Ungovernability

If wars and resistance are seen as primarily physical phenomena, the only meaningful distinction is between obedience and disobedience. Open defiance of enemy orders or pressure is the core of opposition. People conditioned to think along these lines regard resistance crushed once they are coerced to obey.

In cases of outside pressure, one concession to threats of violence almost automatically tends to lead to another. There is no clear second line of defense where the retreats can be stopped. A continued retreat may well lead to a general collapse.

In political resistance, however, a military retreat does not have to lead to a political surrender. Nor does enforced obedience have to bring about loyalty to the invader.

Small nations must strengthen their defense by stressing the spiritual element in political resistance and recognizing the primacy of loyalty. Obedience may have to be conceded on a case-by-case basis. But such *ad hoc* yielding, far from being decisive, merely reflects the degree of pressure. (The national Dubcek leadership of Czechoslovakia displayed a real genius for not cooperating more than absolutely necessary due to the exact amount of Soviet pressure at any time.) And it may permit many citizens to survive. Only loyalty must be denied the invader—always and at all costs. Even temporary co-operation may be permissible if there is no other way to achieve vital results, and if national loyalty stays constant. Widening the range of available responses makes political resistance less dangerous and more effective. It becomes almost impossible for an invader to secure control against a loyal, intelligent resistance. The best advice one can give a defending nation is the one painted on a wall in Prague: "Hate intelligently!"

Based on a strong loyalty, national resistance is flexible, enduring, and extensive. No single defeat, whatever its nature, decides the fate of an all-embracing struggle. Military setbacks are not fatal. And no one success of the invader's secures him victory in the fight for political control. General control of a political community is the sum total of countless specific controls; to establish it is a complex process. Some objectives are easily captured. But all can resist, and many will defeat attempts to control them.

No loss should be considered final. Temporary yielding to enemy pressure does not preclude renewed opposition. Where the invader has established control, he must struggle to maintain it against the defenders' attempts to reassert themselves. Attempts to reduce, neutralize, and break down his control continue at all times. And the struggle for the administration, the organizations, and the population is likely to range on all levels, outside as well as inside the apparatus. Pressures and counterpressures can hamper the invader's control or hurt it beyond salvage. There is always a possibility of turning the tide against him.

Under no conditions should the defenders fail to use counterpressures. Often they will succeed. Even where they do not, they at least divert enemy forces, easing his pressure at other points.

In the political struggle the invader attempts to establish and maintain control over the nation. The nation fights to preserve and reassert its own. The invader's goal is not achieved until he has eliminated the defending side's control and prevented its restoration. To secure a decisive political victory, he must do four things:

1. Eliminate national control.
2. Establish his own control.
3. Maintain his control against attempts to break it.
4. Prevent a re-emergence of national control of the people.

His task was considered easy as long as only the first step was held essential; the rest was to follow as a natural consequence of invasion. A closer look at resistance confirms that all four are necessary if the aggressor is not to lose the whole contest.

A mere listing of the various steps in the process points to more difficulties for the occupier and to new opportunities to check his attempts. All four steps are essential; the whole effort can be thwarted by preventing any one of them. Resistance can choose the targets; it can decide what is to be critical. The invader has no choice but to take and hold all of them; if one is omitted, his rule is incomplete. If he cannot rule the country, he has failed. Resistance can prevail despite invasion.

"The art of governing men," said Clemanceau, "is infinitely more complex than the art of massacring them."[10] Great-power strategy provided for the invader the opportunity to massacre

---

[10] Cited in King-Hall, *Defence*, p. 29.

the people. National resistance would force on him the difficult task of governing the defending nation and deprive him of the luxury of an easy and conclusive massacre. Even an invader without scruples about killing liberally is never sure to have eliminated the right people. Faced with political opposition, the alien must shoulder the burden of obtaining popular consent. Their minimal participation in, and co-operation with, the system is indispensable.

The people can defeat the conqueror's rule if they maintain *ungovernability*—a situation in which his regime, its laws and orders, are not obeyed because they violate the interests of the nation and exploit it for his benefit. Gandhi saw this clearly: "I believe, and everybody must grant, that no government can exist for a single moment without the cooperation of the people, willing or forced, and if the people suddenly withdraw their cooperation in every detail, the government will come to a stand-still."[11] A revolution withdraws co-operation. Resistance withholds it. In both cases the result is complete or partial ungovernability: in a revolution against the established ruler, in national resistance against the alien invader.

The Russians broke Hungarian armed resistance in a few days. But their hold on the country was insecure for weeks thereafter because Hungary was ungovernable: strikes, demonstrations, clashes, boycotts, civil disobedience, showed how little had been achieved by an overwhelming and conclusive military victory. When the stick and the carrot failed to gain popular consent and co-operation, political control for a time eluded the occupier. This was an instructive development (although merely temporary and little noticed); it proved that military strength does not necessarily generate political power. Napoleon's difficulties in Rome, British frustrations on Cyprus, United States' troubles in Latin America, and the Sisyphean predicament of the Russians in Prague are cases in point. The Czechoslovaks provided a classic example in 1968: the national

---

11 M. K. Gandhi, *Non-Violent Resistance: Satyagraha* (N. Y.: Schocken, 1961), p. 157.

leaders—destined to be executed—had to be restored to their positions. The situation in the C.S.S.R. can still be described as a partial ungovernability, two years after the invasion.

Political boycott can be a strong weapon. It contributes to ungovernability. The people refuse to recognize the alien as their government; they do not co-operate with his agents or collaborators; and most important of all, they do not recognize an invasion regime as an arbiter of their internal problems. They unite and "freeze out" the enemy. Such a course of action effectively reduces the influence of enemy political efforts to divide the people; it crushes the morale of his soldiers left without public contacts or assistance.

Another resistance tactic is to *ignore the enemy*. During the Second World War, under German occupation, Norwegian organizations—the Church, the schools, professional and sports organizations—in effect ignored the presence of occupation forces and the acts of the Quisling government on various occasions. Despite confiscation of buildings and other material possessions, they often continued to function as if nothing had changed.[12] To act as if the enemy were not present strengthens the will to resist, and the effectiveness of opposition, in various ways. Bülow's advice to ignore defeat aimed at a similar result.

When the defenders ignore enemy presence, they are ignorant neither of it nor of the dangers and difficulties created by the invasion. They do not intend to escape from reality, but to appreciate better their political weapons. It is a psychological device to substitute a cool, objective estimate of the situation for awesome timidity. Ignoring the display of enemy violence reduces the shock value of his ostentation. Ignoring enemy boasts of "unlimited power" helps recognize the blind spots of his supervision, the loopholes in his control. It makes the practical limits of his rule stand out more, not less, clearly. Mao tried to achieve a similar effect when he called on his partisans to "despise the enemy strategically and take full account of him tactically."[13]

---

[12] King-Hall, *Defence,* p. 188.
[13] Lin Piao, *op. cit.,* p. 46.

The Czechoslovaks understood the strength of such tactics from the very beginning. Leaflets and broadcasts repeatedly called on the people: "Ignore the occupiers!"

To prevent the unwelcome results of ungovernability, the enemy claims *legitimacy* (by right of conquest, if not otherwise) for his regime, and binding force for the laws it proclaims. Observers of occupation policies have repeatedly marveled at the length to which invaders go with seemingly useless and needless moves: Why all the laughable routines of faked democracy? Why the transparent pretense that persuades nobody, when the conqueror can take over everything directly by force? are the recurring questions. The answer is that he cannot subdue and expect to hold a country successfully without political persuasion. Naked force alone does not give control. Not every rape generates affection. . . .

Propaganda, straw-men governments, faked coalitions, fraudulent or *pro forma* elections and referenda—every means is used to convince the people that the conqueror, no matter how despised, is the proper successor to the national Government. All are attempts to cover the emperor's nakedness with at least a minimal fig leaf of legitimacy.

The defending nation must resolutely reject enemy claims of legitimacy. The sociologist Philip Selznick explains that legitimacy is needed "in order to reduce dependence on naked power," and that "the striving for power must also be justified no less than power already held." To speak of a rule as moral or immoral in this particular sense, he points out, "implies no moral judgment. It is merely an assertion that certain types of power will be effectively maintained or easily overthrown."[14] His analysis reveals the practical value of legitimacy: it affects the survival of a new regime, and the impact of resistance on it.

In the first phase of the invasion Czechoslovak resistance

---

[14] Philip Selznick, *The Organizational Weapon: A Study of Bolshevik Strategy and Tactics* (New York: McGraw-Hill, 1952), pp. 242–44, *passim.* See also the subchapters on the Search of Legitimacy (242–52), and the Denial of Legitimacy (327–32).

stressed the legitimacy of their own institutions and the illegal nature of the occupation, its measures, the acts of its agents. All the news media drew a distinct line between the legitimate national efforts and the illegalities of the invaders. The whole nation followed this resolute stand. The inability to obtain even the slightest color of legitimacy was one of the main reasons why no right collaborator government could be formed after the occupation of Prague. People did not deal directly with the invader's agents. They could be reached only through their own legal leaders, if at all.

As a part of the effort against ungovernability, the invader tries to vest in himself, his orders, and agents what Aristotle called "the *habit of obedience*, for law has no power to command obedience except that of habit." To preserve a regime, "there is nothing which should be more jealously maintained than the spirit of obedience to law; especially in small matters," he wrote, dealing with revolutions, "for transgression creeps in unperceived and at last ruins the state. But if the people are always kept under, they will learn to be humble."[15] That is why the invader tries to popularize law-abiding behavior among the people. He marks all opposition "illegal" and "criminal" as if nothing had changed; as if the nation owed the same obedience to his laws, made to suppress and exploit the people, as it did to laws promulgated by its own Government for public benefit. But the defenders do not have to believe him.

Denying legitimacy, habitual obedience, and consent, boycotting the conqueror's rule, ignoring it, and many other techniques help defeat his attempts to control a country. Each one creates added difficulties for the invader. Combined, they go a long way toward ungovernability. All of these techniques are important, and they reinforce each other, achieving a cumulative effect.

A parallel with internal power struggles deserves mention:

---

[15] Aristotle, *Politics* ii. 9; v. 8, 11.

the little-noticed fact that in many European nations, it has become impossible to seize and hold power against the will of the population, that an unpopular *coup d'état* cannot succeed. King-Hall asserted that "no man or group of men have much chance of seizing power in Britain because of their ability to use violence and win a civil war."[16] This is equally true for Switzerland, the Scandinavian countries, and others. In Switzerland unpopular forces could not even win a civil war, because the men in the country have arms, including tanks and artillery. Without the people's consent Britain, Scandinavia, and Switzerland would remain ungovernable. The internal aggressors could not establish control; their rule would collapse in a short time.

An external aggressor—an invader—is no stronger politically than a militarily dominant domestic clique. Actually, the alien is even weaker because he aims not only at unpopular autocracy, but at national subjugation as well. Divested of the myth of invincibility, he becomes politically helpless. Unable to have his forces present at all times and places—and thus in no position to command directly—he needs political control in order to rule. Ungovernability can, therefore, be achieved merely by frustrating his control.

The ultimate test for coups and invasions is the ability to achieve and maintain political control of the *polis*. The same applies to all other forms of aggression, and to deterrence as well. Whatever form of pressure a great power applies against a small nation, the aggressor as well as the defender has to calculate how likely it is that a possible invasion can secure political control. Where the alien cannot expect to maintain control, invasion is useless.

In a struggle on the political level to prevent the invader's control of a community, the advantages are on the side of the ubiquitous defenders. As long as at least a partial ungovernability continues, the alien has failed to reach his objective.

---

[16] Stephen King-Hall, *Power Politics in the Nuclear Age* (London: V. Gollancz, 1962), p. 12.

C.   VIOLENCE AS A MEANS OF CONTROL

Political power does not grow out of the barrel of a gun, nor out of the nuclear warhead of an intercontinental missile. Ideas and loyalties cannot be shot. Control is necessary because the stick and the carrot are not effective at all times and places. Even where they are, a coerced performance may be defective or worthless because of non-co-operation or resistance; where they do not motivate adequately, no control exists. Where imposed control fails, national loyalty prevails.

An invader's means to achieve political control are mainly his occupation forces. Are these means well suited to achieve that end? They are not: against a clever resistance they are not likely to succeed.

Only in two cases does occupation by military force extinguish opposition and achieve the end of political conquest: first, where the shock of a surprising military defeat numbs an invaded nation's spirit and apparent futility paralyzes its will to resist; second, where the antagonists agree, expressly or impliedly, to abide by the outcome of the military campaign and to concede, without further contest, political victory to the side whose armies are stronger. The second includes the practice described earlier as orthodox strategy. Although, strictly speaking, the results of military battles are just as irrelevant in a political struggle as the outcome of beauty contests or football games, everything is conclusive that is accepted as such without challenge.

Political resistance should accept as final only a conclusive political decision. Since the invader's objective is usually not to destroy but to control, he has no military way to his goal against such resistance. Soldiers with machine guns and tanks standing on street corners look dangerous. But in political contests, decided not on the battlefields but in the quite different environment of politics, where different rules apply, an occupation army and military police are ineffective. They can fight their way into the small country. But neither by training and equipment nor by the choice of their rank-and-file personnel are they qualified to secure and maintain political control. Clausewitz wrote: "An army, advancing in enemy country, lacks all the instruments of obedience. It must establish its own administrative organization by the authority of armed might. This it cannot achieve everywhere, not without sacrifices and difficulties, not at once."[17] A modern invasion army has to supervise local activities, eliminate opposition, secure obedience and control. But most political activities are outside the effective reach of military violence.

The occupation forces in a strange country are, actually, a rather helpless lot: unacquainted with the locality; unable to communicate with, and hated by, the population; ignorant of its psychological and political peculiarities; without means to administer the captured areas. They cannot so much as find their way to places of drinking and ill repute without the help of the local people.

Gandhi firmly believed that armed forces could not achieve political victory. During World War II, he seriously advised Englishmen to "lay down their arms, let the Nazis overrun Britain if they dare, but develop internal strength to refuse to sell themselves to the Nazis."[18] The results of such an action will remain a subject of conjecture forever. England, unprepared for political resistance, fortunately had other means of victory. (But many small states today have no ways of defending themselves against strong military forces; they would do well to reflect on the method suggested by the sage of Indian resistance.) Military occupation itself would certainly not have brought about German domination of the island, nor a Germanization of the people. A minimal opposition would have foiled all invader's attempts to gain political control of the British.

Control is not simple to maintain. New York City police are certainly better able to combat crime in their own city than invasion armies are to rule a foreign country. But the police can do little against crime in certain Negro and Puerto Rican

---

[17] Carl von Clausewitz, *Vom Kriege* (17th ed.; Bonn: F. Dümmler's Verlag, 1952), Bk. V. Ch. 16.
[18] Gandhi, *Satyagraha*, p. 309.

neighborhoods, still less against Mafia crimes, where the communities in question simply refuse to co-operate.

In Algeria, after a century of fairly undisturbed rule, the French had a well-established, experienced government. Their own one million loyal nationals were a substantial part of the inhabitants, eager to help. France had gained resistance experience against German occupation. Her army knew Algeria well. It had many veteran soldiers and officers familiar with the irregular warfare of the Second World War and of Indochina, many leaders informed of political and subversive tactics. A number of gifted young officers had analyzed resistance war, were willing to experiment and learn, showed imagination coupled with an instinct for psychological warfare. Nor did they lack determination to use any means, including terror, if necessary. Both the stick and the carrot were applied, often intelligently, to keep or regain control over the native population (an easier task than a foreign invader's, who must build from scratch), by supervision and indoctrination, in accordance with the lessons of China and Vietnam. With all these advantages on her side, France seemed sure to win. Her failure showed the strict limits to what an army can accomplish. The French fiasco in Algeria makes it clear, *a fortiori*, that an alien invader unfamiliar with the country and its people, without numerous nationals and supporters of his own there, and without either an established control machinery or the habitual obedience of a defending nation, will hardly get better results against determined resistance.

An invader uses *terror* at least temporarily. Its aim is to impress everyone with the "unlimited" power of the new regime able to disregard norms of civilized behavior; to spread panic and paralyze opposition; to convince the reluctant that safety from indiscriminate violence can be bought only with submissiveness. Military terror—shootings, bombings, etc.—may be used as a first step of invasion. But small nations may also be subjected to terror campaigns of subversive agents in the deterrence stage, or to secret police terror—after invasion. All, except bombing, were used in Czechoslovakia.

The use of terror, actually the dread of it, is a controversial topic. Essentially, terror is but a political attack aimed at breaking the spirit through fear of discomfort and suffering. Despite a general awe on the part of the public, experts of political warfare seem to agree that terror is ineffective in suppressing resistance, that it may boomerang to damage the invader himself.[19] Terror often stimulates the will to resist and releases a hostility that sustains defiance for decades, even centuries. It can strengthen existing opposition, and it can arouse new forces. Where this happens, the aggressor has insured his own defeat.

British political defeat in Ireland was traced to the sharp practices employed against the rebels of Easter Sunday. Hitler's extermination camps and countries under Stalin are much more impressive examples of terror, but even there it had only limited effectiveness as a means of political victory. Resistance continued within the ghettos, the concentration camps, and the small countries. Many were, admittedly, demoralized and ready to accept tyranny, to do anything to save their skins. But the majorities often maintained an inner resistance against the inquisitors.

Military shock attacks have been politically ineffective, despite numerous casualties. A British military critic called the destruction caused by Allied "strategic bombing" in Berlin and other cities "inconceivable." Contrary to expectations, the bombed city functioned well. "As for the theory that German war industry could be destroyed by the demoralization of the workers, it failed because, as a general rule, the workers refused to be demoralized."[20]

---

19 It is not possible to discuss the varied significance and implications of terror here, but it may be useful to mention its place in the struggle for political control. A documented study of terror from one invader's viewpoint is part of Hans Luther's *Der französische Widerstand gegen die deutsche Besatzungsmacht und seine Bekämpfung* (Tübingen: Institut für Besatzungsfragen, 1957).

20 Cyril Falls, *The Art of War From the Age of Napoleon to the Present Day* (New York: Oxford University Press, 1961), p. 173.

Stalin and Hitler attempted to shoot the conquered people's will to resist. The Allies tried to bomb German determination. The Russians tried to frighten it out of the Czechs and the Slovaks. All should have noticed that the weapons selected were not really suited for the specific purpose. At least one should understand it now and not unduly exaggerate the advantages, nor depreciate the disadvantages, accruing to aggressors from the use of terror. The will to resist decides, and violence can attack the decisive national will only indirectly. "We sincerely believe," admitted Guevara, "that terror is a negative weapon which in no way produces the desired results."[21] Spiritual strength can withstand physical violence.

The successful imperialists become increasingly aware of the limitations of terror, and the unsuccessful have been put out of business. General, long-term terror is, therefore, less likely in the future; although short, furious applications, intended to produce temporary shock and to lame resistance during crucial periods, cannot be discounted. The favorite technique will be to threaten rather than to apply terror.

Understanding the limitations of terror helps the defenders evade violence and remain firm against it. Fearlessness defeats the effect of threats; evasiveness reduces the impact of violence. Threats are ineffective when they do not induce fear; calm determination preserves the will to resist even in times of pressure. After the first assaults, it becomes evident that terroristic violence is a sign of the invader's insecurity, not of his strength—and that it can be treated accordingly.

Resistance often survives and prevails against alien terror. A nation well prepared to understand and avoid the dangers will be able to resist with small losses. According to Jørgen Haestrup, a Danish resistance expert, German oppressive measures rose in direct proportion to Danish resistance successes, and in an inverse proportion to resistance losses. When the actual terror applied was greatest, so was resistance and its success!

---

[21] Ernesto Che Guevara, "La Guerra de Guerrillas," *Modern Guerrilla Warfare*, 371.

This can mean only that some other factors were decisive. In the Danish case these factors were a strengthened will to resist, and learning to damage the invader most with the least risk. Both factors showed a steady increase from near-zero in 1940 to a peak in 1945.

Stalin probably understood this when, even enraged, he did not invade Yugoslavia. Both she and Finland were practically safe from Russian attack during the last years of the conqueror's life. Despite threatening noises from Moscow, their only real danger is internal subversion.

Recognition of the political nature of "small wars" has contributed to the understanding of all contests. The insights of T. E. Lawrence are confirmed in the writings by and about guerrilla leaders (Mao, Giap, Guevara, Grivas) and by experts of their opponents (French, British, American, Greek, etc.). Numerous analyses explain the nature of revolutionary war. The lesson is clear: they are political conflicts; they cannot be won by military forces alone.

All wars and conquests are political. In guerrilla and resistance struggles the political factors are only more obvious because there often is no continuous military activity, and because victory is won frequently by the side that is militarily so clearly inferior that a tenable explanation of the outcome in military terms is impossible. Again, Czechoslovakia is a case in point: from Eger to Košice a purely political resistance defeated, in 1968, the invading army of a superpower.

Struggles between national resistance and occupation forces are political contests *par excellence.* Arms have practically no value in these struggles in the political community. Political superiority at home is a strategic advantage that small nations can exploit to defend themselves successfully not only against subversion and intimidation, but even against invading armies.

Military invasion, just as subversion, is a mere preliminary to a decisive political contest. It does not directly decide victory. It does not bring about political control. It is not even a very effective means of achieving either political victory or control. In resistance struggles its role is, at best, secondary. To strive for political victory by means of an invasion is, to quote Lawrence, "messy and slow like eating soup with a knife."

Where political defense is strong, the aggressor acquires nothing but difficulties by invading a defending state. The hostile country may well become a "chancre" of his empire, as Spain became of Napoleon's. The conqueror swallows something he cannot digest. He must, in the end, disgorge it or risk even greater complications.

About the Author

V. V. ŠVEICS, an Assistant Professor of Political Sociology, was born and raised in Europe and has traveled there extensively. He has studied at the universities of Heidelberg, Stockholm and Warsaw. The author has also served in the U.S. Army. He holds the degree of *Juris Doctor* from Columbia Law School and a Ph.D. from New York University.

CHAPTER VI

Marshaling National Strength

A. THE NATIONAL BROTHERHOOD

National resistance uses the nation's strength in political contests. It is national, and it is resistance. Its resistance aspect was sketched above. This chapter outlines its national character.

National resistance defends the nation's freedom, its way of life, and independence. It is fought *by* the nation itself (by its members individually or in an organized manner); *as* a nation (a common effort for a common cause); against an *alien*,

Loyalty consolidates individuals into a nation; cohesion unites them. Loyalty and cohesion create a national brotherhood, on which a strong defense can be built. Resistance may, indeed, be successful in some cases where loyalty or cohesion are missing. But there it must be a different kind of struggle, using different techniques and facing difficulties that do not plague a truly national enterprise.

It has long been known that cohesive minorities, with an intense common loyalty, possess a strength far in excess of their numbers. They are recognized as a significant, at times decisive, force. Suppressing these groups has proved a difficult political task. Military and political experts acknowledge them as an important factor.

The defensive strength of majorities has been practically ignored. In international politics their potential is overlooked by some, discounted by others. This neglect may be in order where apathetic, satiated majorities inertly enjoy their rights and freedoms, while persecuted or disaffected minorities militantly exert their strength. It is absolutely wrong to disregard the power of suppressed majorities resolved to defend themselves.

An outside attack on a small nation is likely to create a hostile majority against the alien. (An invader occupying another nation's territory faces a hostile majority there, and imports a hostile minority into his empire as a whole: he thus assumes a double political handicap.) This hostile force may be sufficiently strong in loyalty, cohesion, and determination to defy the aggessor.

Nationalism has become an expression of the dignity of peoples. The great revolutions restored a feeling of solidarity, of a need for a common defense to protect everyone's interests simultaneously with the freedom of the Fatherland. No longer do men go into battle to defend merely class interests and the rule of absolute monarchs. The modern democratic nation-state is a synthesis of individualism and nationalism: no nation is stronger than the united fortitude of its citizens, and as the revolutionary poet Schiller wrote, "No man prospers without a Fatherland." As in the ancient *polis* and under a commonwealth, foreign interference is again a real threat to the freedom, rights, and property of the individuals as well as to the independence and welfare of the whole, the nation. Every citizen has again a stake to defend.

A united effort is the strongest defense of the commonwealth. Self-interest, if nothing else, dictates that citizens protect the success of the joint venture. The opposite view is based on thinking in terms of pharaohs and slaves, of a Hobbesian world, of irreconcilable conflicts of interests, or of class struggles. In the small European nations today this does not apply—securing their welfare and defending their independence is everyone's concern. In times of crisis the common cause is an especially potent reality, and conflicts of interest yield to an overriding concord of purpose.

A nation united in spirit and effort is the decisive force in modern conflicts. It is not an amorphous mass with the characterless features of a mob or a crowd but, in the face of danger, a conscious, closely-knit brotherhood, an organization with a common purpose. It fights with all its strength to defend itself against an alien bent on doing it harm. Not only is victory proclaimed by public opinion; it is fought for, and won, by the whole people.

To have this unity and strength, the community in question must be able to act as a true nation. Nationhood is an absolute requirement. But not every state with its inhabitants constitutes a nation, nor even a part of a nation. Some states are administrative units embracing two or more nations; others are a collection of many nations or national fragments; still others have no distinct national character at all. (Outside Europe, there are many states of this last type.)

In theory, countless distinctions have been drawn, some degenerating into outright hair-splitting or acid debates, about which are and are not, should and should not be, nations. It is not necessary for me to contribute to the ventilation of such captious subtleties. If a working definition is needed, J. S. Mill's is a good starting point:

> A portion of mankind may be said to constitute a nationality if they are united among themselves by common sympathies which do not exist between them and any others—which make them co-operate with each other more willingly than with other people, desire to be under the same government, and desire that it should be government by themselves, or a portion of themselves, exclusively. This feeling of nationality may have been generated by various causes.[1]

Resistance is a practical policy. Whether the people are a nation capable to defend themselves as a nation is determined pragmatically, not by dogmatic speculation. Whether a small state could defend itself should be decided, in each case, in the light of available facts. Formal characteristics—a common ancestry, language, race, history, geography, tradition, etc.—are useful evidence but not absolute criteria. "The nation is today

---

[1] John Stuart Mill, *Considerations on Representative Government* (New York: Harper and Brothers, Publishers, 1867), Ch. XVI.

the largest community which, when the chips are down, effectively commands men's loyalty, overriding claims of lesser communities within it and those which cut across it or potentially enfold it within a still greater society."[2]

One should try to judge how the people will act when the chips are down. If they would act as a nation, they are one for the purposes of their defense strategy. Politics being the art of calculated guessing, this is a political decision quite appropriately reached by a guess.

In the case of Czechoslovakia it was rather difficult to guess the outcome; both the Western experts and the militant faction in Moscow must be forgiven for having made the wrong prediction. There are *two* leading nations in the C.S.S.R., the Czechs and the Slovaks, disagreeing as often as agreeing with each other. What is more, *four* sizable national minorities—Germans and Poles in the Czech lands, Hungarians and Ruthenians in Slovakia—have, not without justification at times, felt unfairly treated. On the available historical and other evidence one could expect no resistance, at least no unified resistance against a massive military invasion. Actually the Czechs and the Slovaks displayed a unique will to resist, realizing that they could survive only together; the Hungarians and the Germans joined in opposing the invasion; the Poles and the Ruthenians remained loyal. As a result, an undivided and sustained defiance emerged spontaneously in a few hours and surprised almost everyone.

In most cases the problem is not as difficult as it may seem. Sweden, Holland, and Hungary are nation-states beyond a shadow of doubt. So are many others. Elaborate and sophisticated definitions are useless. The decisive elements are feeling like a nation, being ready and able to defend themselves as a nation, and having the necessary loyalty and cohesion.

Lack of a strong loyalty and cohesion is the main reason why new or synthetic entities, mislabeled "nations," are unable

---

[2] Rupert Emerson, *From Empire to Nation* (Cambridge: Harvard University Press, 1960), pp. 95–96.

to defend themselves against internal and external attacks. They cannot, in all fairness, be expected to duplicate the mature firmness of historic European nations. One cannot draw an analogy between Finland and Laos or South Vietnam; to do so would be utter political puerility.

Aristotle knew the character and strength of cohesive societies similar to the nations of our times: "A *polis* is not the growth of a day any more than it grows out of a multitude brought together by accident." He recognized "the difference of races which do not at once acquire a common spirit [as] another cause of revolutions."[3] The modern sage Gandhi understood the political strength of national unity. In his estimate, "complete unity would bring freedom for the asking,"[4] although in India it remained a mere ideal. Many a small European nation can achieve near-perfect unity; it may be a natural reaction to outside pressure.

The Czechoslovak example shows that more than one nation can act with sufficient unity to defeat an aggressor alien to all of them. This unity is a hopeful sign for such other multinational and multilingual small states as Switzerland, Yugoslavia, or Romania.

In a resistance struggle a clear line must be drawn between friend and foe: the nation versus the alien invader. The defenders must react as a team. In a political opposition, everyone is needed as an active or sympathetic participant. The common effort itself—embracing the whole scale of individual and common activities—reinforces common ties and brings the people closer to unity. Traitors and collaborators, who break this solidarity, are the most dangerous enemies of resistance because their acts tend to poison the nation with mutual suspicion and mistrust. People have sensed this danger time and again: popular hatred of the Quislings and the Ulbrichts is often stronger than that of the alien powers who would not succeed without them.

---

[3] Aristotle, *Politics* viii. 9.

[4] Gandhi, *Non-Violent Resistance: Satyagraha* (N. Y.: Schocken, 1961) p. 362.

A loyal and cohesive nation can be relied on to recognize and defend its interests. One need not worry even if the alien replaces holders of administrative positions or arms a part of the people as his auxiliaries, police, etc. When an opportunity arises, these citizens will use their positions and fire their weapons against the enemy. (The Army and police forces armed to protect a dictatorial regime in the C.S.S.R., leftist organizations such as the League of Anti-Fascist Fighters—or for that matter the Communist Party itself—all supported the national fight for freedom.) Meanwhile every rifle, every administrative position, every technical bottleneck in the hands of a patriot, is a political weapon of defiance, a potential threat for invaders and unpopular dictators.

National brotherhoods have matured through centuries. They are united by scores of bonds, reinforced by a common history of good and bad times. It would be inexcusable waste to leave this strength unmobilized, not to make political resistance truly nationwide, when every ounce of strength is needed for national defense.

B. SOURCES OF RESISTANCE

National resistance is political; its forum—the *polis*—is a nation. It can be both constant and flexible because national loyalty holds the people together even where opposition consists of a sum of individual small-group actions. In political defense the strongest action is co-ordinated action. In national defense every group can operate independently. yet in concert with others, because a common idea guides them toward the same objective—national freedom. Everyone can fight for the common cause in his own ways. And everyone can lead the national struggle, from practically any formal or informal political position or any place in the country, because the popular leader only translates into action an already-existing national sentiment. To the strength inherent in unity this adds the equally formidable strength of co-ordinated diversity.

Nationalism is the main source of resistance and the uniting loyalty. But it is by no means the only one. Many other loyalties do exist. They can strengthen opposition; diversify it; extend it to all fields of activities, including political and individual relations. The aim of a truly nationwide resistance is to release as many of the energies slumbering within a nation as possible, to make it a struggle waged by the overwhelming majority of the people against the minority of the aggressor's own forces and collaborators. The best policy is to tap all available sources of resistance.

1. Nationalism

Nationalism—a product of patriotic loyalty and uniting cohesion—is the main source of resistance. Neither local interests, ideologies, nor international causes can generate similar strength. Nationalism strengthens, unifies, and guides the opposition. If sufficiently virile, it can sustain the entire defensive effort. In 1967, a leading Soviet politician confessed that it had been a cause of many Russian reverses: "We simply underestimated its force. We underestimated it in Europe, in Eastern Europe, for example. And we did not begin to understand its force in Asia. Or in China, for that matter."[5] This is impressive testimony from an expert. In 1968, they underrated it again.

Nationalism is a fact, a real force, not a myth. Many small nations are distinct national entities, not mere fragments in the great power systems of alliances and satellites. To deny the existence of Finnish, Polish, Irish, Slovak, or Romanian nationalism would be ridiculous. Its significance is increasing, not decreasing.

To describe resistance as national resistance is to show *who* is fighting, *why* and *how*. The term itself fixes the basic loyalty; the political objective; the strategy, and many techniques, of a struggle—its form as well as its contents.

The United States and the Soviet Union have great difficulties when opposed by nationalism. The three words "Yankee, go home!" have caused unpleasantness to Americans for a long

---

[5] Quoted by Harrison E. Salisbury, *New York Times*, Nov. 3, 1967.

time. Where the majority of people picks up this call, hardly anything is left but to accept the invitation to leave. It is a formidable weapon, indeed, if it can "invite out" the world's leading
power. The simple call "If you are a Magyar, come with us!"
started the Hungarian revolution of 1956. In 1968, the expression
"This is our country!" aroused the most spectacular resistance
movement of this century in the Czech lands and in Slovakia. A
floodtide of nationalism washed away Russian political domination and rendered their military might irrelevant, a thing held
impossible by all political and military experts, Eastern and
Western.

Great powers like to condemn nationalism when it frustrates
their advances, and when it makes swallowing and digesting
small nations more difficult. Why they are, at times, supported
by a chorus of small-nation sycophants is surprising. Small nations would do well to disregard such voices.

There is absolutely no need to argue the abstract merits of
nationalism against its accusers. Great powers know that it is a
basic element of national strength. It is interesting to note that
shortly before the Cuban crisis of 1962 and after the Chen Pao
crisis of 1969 Soviet news media suddenly began to praise
Russian nationalism.

The claim that nationalism is a source of aggression or an obstacle to international co-operation is unfounded. In fact, mature
nationalism is the very enemy of aggression and imperialism—the
logical tool of defense when a nation has to defend itself. It is
most effective *for* a nation and *within* a nation. The Swedes and
the Norwegians are very nationalistic peoples, but there is little
likelihood of their engaging in aggression for that reason. And
the fiercely nationalistic Swiss have not fought a single offensive
battle since 1515. Czech nationalism would not achieve anything
outside the country. To call expansionist ideas like Pan-Ger-
manism and Pan-Slavism "nationalism" is a mere confusion of
terms: they are its very opposites—typical imperialism. One
cannot blame nationalism for their sins. Men and nations proud
of their own independence actually have more respect for the
freedom of others, since freedom, like charity, begins at home.

Slaves are usually the most obedient tools of enslavement. Freedom is contageous.

Nor do international co-operation and nationalism contradict each other. The feeling of humanism does not necessarily dampen the ardors of religion and love, nor does regard for the individuals extinguish feelings for the human race. National loyalty and pride do not exclude internationalism.

Being an idea, nationalism is immune to physical violence. It is a very strong idea, generally immune to ideological attacks in the name of alien dogmas.

Hardly any other force can replace it; one cannot plant foreign nationalism in any nation as long as its own loyalty survives. And alternatives like the Nazis' "New Europe," or the Communists' "Soviet patriotism" have proved ineffective. Ideologies have had as little success in their attempts to suppress and eliminate nationalism. Socialists, Communists, Nazis, and Fascists —all have seen their doctrines fail repeatedly when confronted by it. Cruelly, the long list of Communist fiascoes was extended by one ultimate irony: the co-operation of the two major deniers of nationalism—Marxist Russia and Marxist China—has foundered on the very cliffs they claim do not exist.

Khrushchev attacked nationalism at the XXII Soviet Communist Congress, in 1961. A commentator, echoing the Premier's words in a typical article on "Internationalism and Soviet Patriotism," admitted

. . . that bourgeois nationalism and chauvinism are among the most tenacious survivals in the people's minds. That is why these disappear more slowly than other survivals of Capitalism and recur more easily. Hence nationalism can be dangerous even after the victory of Socialism in the field of economic and social relations has been achieved. A relaxation of the struggle against nationalism may enable it to develop to such an extent as to endanger the Socialist gains of the people. We know, for example, what a pernicious role nationalism played in Yugoslavia. It caused Yugoslavia to break away from the Socialist camp. We may also recall that the nationalist fever which for a time affected the minds of a part of the youth and intellectuals in Hungary created conditions which made possible the [revolt] in that country.

And Albania, he wrote, has been "slipping into the morass of nationalism.[6] This explains why "the Marxist-Leninist parties devote such attention to combatting nationalism," despite disappointingly meager results. It also explains why, in times of danger (the Cuban crisis, for one), they stress Russian nationalism for their own people.

This excellent description of the tremendous resistance force of nationalism bears restating: In countries tens of years under Russian domination, nationalism tenaciously survived in the minds of the people, holding out longer, reasserting itself, more easily than other ideas—with a force capable of endangering Russian rule. It is credited with the independence and revolt in Yugoslavia, Albania, and Hungary. In 1968 nationalism threatened to break apart the whole satellite system.

What could any resistance strategy possibly invent, or undertake, to bring about equally impressive results! Nationalism appears to be an almost invincible force.

Adequately mobilized, nationalism enhances resistance strength in many ways: it strengthens and intensifies opposition, unifies national efforts, clarifies the issues involved, and guides the resistance activities.

THE STRENGTHENING AND UNIFYING FUNCTION.—Outside pressure usually rallies national forces. An attack on the independence of a state and a threat to the freedom of its citizens produce a determined effort to protect these values. Nationalism injects into the struggle an emotional element adequately strong and lasting to sustain the flame of resistance, despite difficulties and setbacks, where ordinary opposition would collapse.

This increased strength and intensity can be called a new strategic factor. The dormant national power released by this enthusiasm has often astounded the world.

The French armies swept like a cyclone over Europe, after 1789, carried by their *patriotisme;* the Spaniards, the Germans, the Russians, destroyed Napoleon's empire fighting for freedom.

---

6 Sh. Sanakoyev, "Internationalism and Soviet Patriotism," *International Affairs* (Moscow), 12 (1961), 15.

Lawrence stated, in 1916, that the release of Arab national sentiments "has harmed Turkey more than it will be harmed elsewhere until Constantinople is captured."[7] Mao gained unexpected victories against the Japanese by basing his fight on Chinese nationalism: "The pivot for winning victory lies in a resistance by the whole nation. Only through such a resistance," he reminded his followers, "can victory be won."[8] Before the Second World War, Ewald Banse insisted: "We must make the idea of nation the pivot on which all our thinking turns."[9] After the war, in a general résumé of European resistance from 1939 to 1945, Henri Michel stated that it had been "first of all a reflex of patriotism."[10] It is logical, therefore, to make the idea of nationalism the mainstay of opposition.

Pressure can both destroy and solidify. Where internal cohesion is weak, enemy blows scatter the fragments and prevent organized resistance. Where nationalism is strong, foreign pressure, and invasion, call forth a vigorous defiance and increase unity.

Nationalism may be the only idea able to unite all patriots. Ideologies and special interests, favoring certain groups, create divisive side effects by preferring some people to others. The result may be split loyalties and internal contradictions. But nationalism is only one; its sole aim is to defy alien pressure. It *unifies* all forces. In addition, it is sufficiently strong to *divide* the loyalties of collaborators and exert a considerable pull on them to rejoin their own people.

Czech leader V. Silhan recognized on the fourth day of the invasion that an important new force had emerged in the crucible of the struggle: "We have lost a great deal, but at the

---

[7] David Garnett (ed.), *The Essential T. E. Lawrence* (London: Jonathan Cape, 1951), p. 90.

[8] Mao Tse-tung, *On Protracted War* (Peking: Foreign Languages Press, 1954), p. 15.

[9] Ewald Banse, *Germany Prepares for War* (New York: Harcourt, Brace and Co., 1934), p. xvi.

[10] Henri Michel (ed.), *European Resistance Movements, 1939–1945* (London, 1960), 28.

same time we have gained something—the patriotism of the people." The divisive pull of nationalism on actual and potential traitors became apparent at the same time. President Svoboda's delegation to Moscow that resisted Russian efforts within the limits of the possible counted among the members six patriots and nine collaborators. The numerical preponderance of the collaborators did not lead to surrender.

The defending forces are not physically concentrated; individuals and groups resist while engaged in widely scattered and varied activities. Their spiritual unity must, therefore, be especially intense. Nationalism provides the common purpose and the solid unity for an extended resistance.

In many instances, or in most, the nation will not be sufficiently organized and prepared at the moment of attack, despite previous warnings. A threat is likely to come as a surprise, before the foundations for opposition are laid. In such emergencies nationalism, built on tradition and education, will be the only readily available source of strength and unity. (This was exactly the thing that saved the Czechs and the Slovaks.) It can make the difference between a potent and impotent community.

CLARIFYING ISSUES AND GUIDING ACTION.—Resistance is a struggle of ideas as well as a clash of activities. Its political attitudes and efforts need a common direction as well. There must be an effective system of guidance, a simple and workable yardstick to avoid indecision and missteps.

Not only does national strength have to be released and united; it also has to be directed against the common target—the enemy. But in an emergency the usual channels of information and guidance may not be available. Uninterrupted direction by the leadership under ground or by resistance headquarters outside the country cannot be assured at all times. Groups and individuals will lack instructions for long periods when important developments call for changed reactions. While some variations of response are harmless, or even beneficial, a concerted general attitude is required.

The enemies will employ all means of political warfare to confuse the basic issues; to obscure the distinction between friend and foe; to create indecision at critical moments, hoping for a paralysis of resistance will and action. The Russians did indeed increase the psychological pressure and their propaganda efforts to confuse the people of the C.S.S.R. and thus cut the ground from under the national leadership during the Moscow negotiations in August, 1968. They have been trying ever since to confuse the issues, so far with only limited success.

To compensate for the absence of direct leadership there must be an inner guiding philosophy, a rough compass and radar to navigate resistance through the confusion of the struggle. Nationalism is the safest guide: familiar and close to all, constant as only a sentiment matured through centuries can be. It is directed to one's own nation and, therefore, almost immune against outside tampering. Its interests and values are those of the nation itself—neither subservient to, nor subject to interference by, Moscow, Peking, or Washington . . . Rome, Cairo, or Tel Aviv.

National survival and independence are the only goal. The means to reach that are clear: to resist enemy attempts to control and subdue the nation and, ultimately, to recover the lost positions. The alien cannot sidestep the impact of nationalism by any irrelevant concessions: a slight raising of the living standard, a greater leniency in matters of religion, the adoption of pseudo-democratic practices, or increased liquor rations will not do. Were resistance directed by other motives, it could be eliminated or confused through conceding what does not endanger the intruder's gains. Opposition based on nationalism can be reduced only to the extent to which he yields to it—to which his invasion itself is weakened or annulled.

National survival, freedom, and dispossession of the intruder as the leading issues and aims are clear to every citizen. Once its direction is fixed, the common effort can go on for years. Increased oppression will only generate more friction. Partial yielding by the enemy may temporarily ease counteraction, but it does not bring a balance that can be maintained: the patriots' demands will rise again. There is no way to satisfy them, short of the intruder's departure.

Nationalism immunizes the defenders against enemy propaganda and eases their tasks in psychological warfare. Without this constant strength, resistance might collapse after any successful political or technical breakthrough of the enemy. No amount of previous organization, training, or foresight can cover all contingencies.

The effect of nationalism on resistance can be compared to that of a lens on the rays of light: it collects and focuses them, with multiplied force, on the point of impact. It directs a unified opposition against the alien enemy.

Security considerations demand that a nation distinguish between friend and foe, that it band together and keep out possible infiltrators. Where the people close ranks and "freeze out" the aliens, one of the main purposes is achieved. National characteristics, physical and psychological, are the safest test. Beliefs and ideologies leave a much wider scope for error and uncertainty: for centuries honest men have tried and failed to determine what a faithful Christian can or cannot do; armies of ideologues struggle without success to decide who is a true Marxist. It is much easier to see who is or is not a compatriot, and what serves the interests of a resisting nation.

The national way of doing things is safest, as a rule. National psychology is difficult for the foreigner to fathom; planning and action based on it will seldom be anticipated. "The more unorthodox and Arab your proceeding," advised T. E. Lawrence, "the more likely you are to have the Turks cold."[11] In Czechoslovakia, for one, among the Russians' main difficulties is their inability to understand the European mentality of the resisting patriots. In any country, the national language is actually a code, incomprehensible to most of the enemy personnel; even more difficult are provincial and local dialects, or special terms of reference used by different professions, interest groups, generations, and other circles.

Examples show that nationalism guides resistance activities well and gives the people a keen sense of what steps to take

---

11 Garnett, *op. cit.*, p. 141.

against an alien. The Spanish nation won its struggle against Napoleon almost on its own. The Irish, the Jews, and the Arabs have been deeply conscious of what their interests dictated. Slovaks, Ukrainians, and Kurds preserved a national spirit and purpose. National sentiment safely guided many peoples through centuries of oppression, when conditions for their survival were far more difficult than they are now.

The lack of national strength and unity is the decisive weakness of many African and Asian countries. It is easy to see what a big difference a transcending nationalism would make, say, in South Vietnam. A vain hope: a *polis* is not the growth of a day, nor of ten or twenty years. . . .

Small states that do possess the precious inheritance of historical nationalism should recognize its value as a foundation of national defense. They should build their strategy on it.

2. Religion

"What is your religion?" "Polish."
"Then what about your nationality?" "Catholic."
A simple farmhand gave these answers with conviction. His profession expressed the close ties between national and religious feelings in many nations. The ties are a result partly of a historical development, partly of simultaneous pressures against both. Religion and nationalism make common cause in an adversity.

Religion has been intimately tied to political conflicts all through history. Luther's struggle against Rome contained both religious and national elements. A master of spiritual resistance, he wrote the hymn "A mighty fortress is our God!" as an affirmation of faith; but it was equally valid as an expression of opposition, as tactical advice, and as a weapon of political warfare. For some Protestant nations it is still a song of resistance, practically a second national anthem in times of struggle. Gustavus II Adolf of Sweden and Cromwell of England, explains Liddell Hart, "mixed prayer and gun-powder into an explosive compound that would shatter all resistance."[12] The successful opposition to Napoleon in papal Rome was sustained for years by the spiritual and political power of the Catholic Church. The spiritual opposition of the Jews has emerged victorious after thousands of years, their religious and political strivings intermixed to such an extent that they seem indistinguishable. Only thus could the Jews preserve, without force of arms, their identity and survive as the unique living monument of resistance triumphant that they are today. The Irish and the Spaniards provide other instances in Europe of religion as a strong source of defiance. Obviously impressed with the significance of the spiritual element in modern conflicts, General Nemo asserted: "There is no true war except religious war."[13]

Religion and nationalism increase national strength: national loyalty is supplemented by religion, and expresses itself in religious activities. In most invaded countries religion is a pillar of resistance. It is hardly possible to subdue nations without treading down their faith. During World War II, with the people of Eastern Europe searching for "a third solution—neither Soviet nor German—the church, whatever its denomination, was bound to be the focus of allegiance."[14] After the war, in the same parts of Europe, nationalism and religion are almost identical; the fight against religion is indistinguishably linked with a fight against national culture and national traditions. In today's Poland the church is, beyond any doubt, the last barrier and obstacle to foreign domination. In Lithuania, the Catholic Church is a unifying force for the people of all religious beliefs; "to attend church services has the same value as to protest. It is the only means left to the Baltic peoples to show that they do not accept Russian rule." Almost thirty years after the occupation of the tiny country, an official has publicly expressed fears that the Church

---

[12] H. B. Liddell Hart, *Great Captains Unveiled* (Boston: Little, Brown and Co., 1928), p. 110.

[13] [Gen.] Nemo, "La guerre dans le milieu social," *Révue du Défense Nationale* (1956), 611.

[14] Alexander Dallin, *German Rule in Russia, 1941–1945* (London: Macmillan and Co., 1957), p. 489.

is "stirring up religious and nationalist activities, the nationalistic sentiments of believers, in Lithuania." This is quite a significant admission of the combined strength of the two loyalties.[15]

The main contributions of religion to national resistance are its spiritual character and its organization.

Experience shows that all national institutions of a country may be taken over or destroyed by an imposed regime. The Church often remains the sole organized forum where compatriots can meet openly. Religious communion is the only organized activity possible. National and religious feelings thus reinforce each other; they become the expression of each other when people assemble to show their loyalty to one God—and to one nation.

Conquerors supervise the physical organization and the functions of churches too thoroughly to permit revolutionary activities. But they are not necessary. The essential strength of religion as a source of opposition is the feeling of common loyalty that it generates. Being spiritual and intangible, it is unconquerable and indestructible: therefore lasting and able to uphold the people's spirits for a long time.

Religious organizations—this is another important point—may be the only ones able to maintain some sort of contact with the outside world. International connections, and the feeling of international solidarity of fellow believers, are inestimable psychological supports. And they may enlist world opinion against oppression. It is often due to a deference to international sentiment that organized religion is not directly attacked by the occupiers.

There was a considerable religious ingredient in the Czech and Slovak resistance. A century before Luther, the Czech reformer Jan Hus lead a struggle for national and religious emancipation. After he was burned alive as a heretic his ideas inspired a gallant national effort. More than 550 years later, after January, 1968, the Czechs recalled the Hussite legacy. One of the main reasons for the resistance was the vivid memory of relgious oppression under Stalinism.

---

[15] K. V. Tauras, *Guerrilla Warfare on the Amber Coast* (New York: Voyages Press, 1962), p. 100; *New York Times*, March 8, 1970.

Religion should never be discounted as a part of national opposition. Even in countries where it is not a dominant force, it may come to play a role, possibly an increasing one, under enemy occupation. Small nations must utilize the force of religious loyalty and the strength of the Church, both as a national and an international organization, in the struggle for survival. As a spiritual element of strength, it is especially well suited to contribute to political defense. In *The Suppliants,* Aeschylos told us that

> An altar is stronger than a fortress,
> An impenetrable shield.

Religious and national loyalties are not contradictory but complementary; ofttimes they are almost identical: religion supports national strength; nationalism helps religion survive. Care must be taken to rely on the combined strength of both.

3. *Other Sources*

Multiplicity and diversity add to the strength of resistance. The more sources of loyalty to the nation, or of animosity against the enemy, are tapped, the stronger grows opposition. Fortunately, the widest variety of means is available to a small nation. Many are at the command of an intelligent resistance leadership.

Nationalism and religion are by far not the only ones. Others can, and they definitely should, be utilized as elements of a political defense struggle. The Ruthenian minority in Slovakia belongs to the Ukrainian nation and is quite conscious of the national bond. They also have religious ties with their compatriots in the Ukrainian Soviet Republic. The invaders knew of these ties—had secured the services of a Ruthenian leader of the Slovak Communist Party—and hoped to use them as a solid minority of 55,000 collaborators. The plan failed because the Ruthenians had visited their own people on the other side of the border; they knew very well that the living standard was much lower and that there was less cultural freedom under the Soviet system. They knew equally well that their national brothers in the Ukraine were no masters of their own fate but were ruled by Russians. It was a choice between two foreign governments, and they chose the one that offered better economic and cultural conditions. Mere national kinship was outweighed by other factors.

Modern conflicts are multiform, almost omniform. Far from limiting them to military strength alone, a truly nationwide opposition embraces every type of defiance or adverse sentiment that can frustrate an opponent to sustain resistance and indecision.

An enumeration is neither possible nor necessary here. More important than any listing is to state, and restate, that there are no clear limits between aspects of national life inside and outside the scope of opposition. Excluding any one of them, *a priori*, would only correspondingly limit the defense potential of a small state.

All of them are closely intertwined; they cannot fail to affect each other. It is quite wrong to dismiss anything as *purely* economical, social, cultural, etc. In fact, economic and cultural disobedience in any form may easily turn into a seed of general rebelliousness. (See Chapter VII, B, below.) The connection of various factors should be discovered and brought into play.

National traditions—history, culture, customs, language—have increasing significance under enemy pressure. With a natural insight that their own superiority is in the spiritual sphere, oppressed peoples turn for inspiration to their traditions. Folk songs and dances, folk arts and crafts, gain a surprising new meaning, as do other things.

Political ideologies, economic hardships—all of them have their place, defensive as well as offensive, in the common effort. Social factors, likewise, can nourish the spirit of resistance. Changes tend to dislocate the social structure and bring to the surface a lot of sediment. The invader has to dredge the society for people willing to collaborate in imposing his rule on their own nation. But favoring this new class of collaborators and incompetents with extra privileges only antagonizes the people. Much that was forgiven one's own government causes bitterness and resentment against the alien's regime.

Crimes committed by, or attributed to, soldiers of the invading army arouse popular indignation. Rapes, murders, assaults, and robberies are especially likely to stir the people's wrath. Voluntary fraternization of the soldiers with local women can provoke lasting ill-will. Cultural and religious *faux pas* cause serious misunderstandings. Good-natured mistakes invite ridicule and contempt. Even concessions or improvements made by the conqueror are derided and attributed to selfishness or fear. The mere sight of personnel wearing enemy uniform has caused unrest and forced withdrawal of his troops to military reservations outside population centers, in order to avoid an eruption. All this, in turn, weakens his control, multiplying complications and ineffectiveness.

The opposition of a nation determined not to accept servitude receives new sustenance from all sides. An endless number of political advantages accrues to the defending side. Leaders of the national struggle can use any of these to strengthen the common loyalty and to focus accumulated ill-will against the alien intruder.

C. THE EXTENT OF NATIONAL STRENGTH

What does national resistance include? How extensive is it? Generally speaking, national resistance includes everything; it is multiform and nationwide. The national resolve to resist must be shared by the majority. Opposition cannot succeed as the concern of a handful of people, no matter how dedicated. The whole population must be of "the high-spirited kind"—a term used by Aristotle—and they must be ready to express their sympathies in action.

One may well speak of a great web of national struggle. Every activity and emotion bearing on the life of the political community can become part of the defiance. With imagination new elements can be added to cover practically the whole range of a dictionary. The chances are endless. "The science of national defense," wrote Banse, "is the systematic application of every branch of human thought and human endeavor to the end of increasing the defensive strength of our nation."[16]

The aggressor's predicament is of nightmarish extent. Resistance against him can spring from so many sources, express itself in so many ways, at so many places, and on so many levels that it is impossible to neutralize its various incidents. He cannot expect to master their interwoven consequences.

From historical research, teaching, and technical expertise to the ambushing of enemy forces—everything is a part of the common effort. Every active participant helps keep alive the national spirit and the will to resist. Every act of defiance expands the whole contest.

And the complexity of the contest helps resistance and weakens the alien intruder. It reduces his ability to supervise and control the defending country. The patriots, bound by a common loyalty, can preserve the necessary minimum hold on the situation (1) because nationalism is a reliable guide, (2) because their mutual contacts inform and orient them, and (3) because most opposition takes place on the local level. Local political resistance is autonomous: unlike military organization, it needs no detailed, central direction because it draws its strength directly from the people.

National resistance is as strong and extensive as its supporting public sympathy and public action. Can a sufficiently solid unity of the people be achieved to make it truly nationwide? After having observed the American, French, and Belgian revolutions, Bülow was convinced that it could be done. Spain and Rome achieved it against Napoleon. So did the Arabs against the Turks and the Irish against England. Under German occupation in World War II 90 per cent of Norwegian teachers signed an open protest against an order requiring them to join a Nazi organization.[17] The Norwegian plebiscite of 1905 had documented an adequate unity of spirit. The Finns maintained a

---

[16] Banse, *op. cit.*, p. 406.
[17] *European Resistance Movements, 1939-1945*, p. 23.

solid unity against an alien enemy, despite numerous internal squabbles, to defend their independence for the last thirty years. The Hungarian revolt of 1956 and the Romanian developments since 1961 provide similar examples.

The Czechs and the Slovaks proved that not only can one nation muster the necessary unity, but that two rivaling small nations can jointly oppose an invading great power. The extent of national unity was shown by the unanimous protest resolutions of the workers (of the 4,000 men at the Auto Praha factory 99 published a pro-Soviet letter in July, but even the 99 joined the workers' protest against invasion and occupation, reducing to zero the 2.5 per cent of support the Russians had had before the attack) and by the Communist Party Congress (its declaration condemning the intervention in sharpest terms was approved by 1,094 votes for, none against, and 1 abstaining).[18]

No traitors came openly out in support of the Russians during 1968. In a few days before the Cierna Conference about 1,000,000 people had signed a letter supporting the leadership. And in the first day of the occupation, 16,000 citizens signed a petition against invasion and arrests of leaders in a single borough of Prague.[19] One month after the invasion a public-opinion survey of the Public Opinion Research Institute at the Academy of Sciences confirmed the high degree of unity throughout the country.[20] The best evidence available to me a year after the occupation, months after the removal of the liberal leadership, was that neither the unity nor the popularity of liberal leaders

---

[18] R. Littell (ed.), *The Czech Black Book* (New York: Praeger, 1969), p. 116; *Dagens Nyheter*, Aug. 23, 1968.

[19] *East Europe* (No. 9, 1968), 7; *The Czech Black Book*, p. 230.

[20] *1918–1968: Vztah Čechů a Slováků Dějinám* (Praha: Ústav Pro Výzkum Věrejneho Minēni CSAV, 1968). The resistance leaders Dubcek, Svoboda, Smrkovsky, are named as Greatest Personalities in Our History by Czechs and Slovaks; known colloborators score zero among both nations (pp. 15–17). The Most Inglorious Time in Our History is for both nations the Stalinist period of the nineteen fifties and the invasion of 1968 (pp. 10–11).

was substantially reduced. The Czechs had indeed achieved almost complete unity.

In times of peace, it is usual and wise to limit political activities. When national existence is in danger, it may prove suicidal to keep any effort from contributing to its defense. This does not mean that a resistance struggle should be total. Quite the contrary, it is best to exclude wide areas of community life from the impact of the conflict. When opposition is raised to the political level, most of it is withdrawn from the physical reach of the enemy. But the limitation of defense should result from careful planning, a weighing of the advantages against the handicaps involved, in each specific instance. It should not result from a failure to appreciate the *ubiquity* of the extended struggle or the *basic oneness* of its various elements.

The strength of the national struggle and the oneness permit great flexibility and cause a basic inequality in favor of the defending nation.

1. Flexibility

A nation united in sympathies and action can turn anything into resistance. Its defiance can express itself in various ways; it can spring from various sources. It can be rallied by any national organization. And it can be translated into action by any patriot who assumes the role of a leader.

The resisters are not tied to any tactics or techniques, to any particular people or institutions. Everything can be adapted to the needs of the situation. And there is wide room for new methods. Czechs and Slovaks excelled in flexibility and inventiveness. "Even in the present grim situation, we are not without weapons," wrote resistance newspaper *Literarni Listy.* "The seven days of occupation have shown that our nations are capable of inventing, in the most difficult circumstances, new ways of resistance, dissent, and protest.[21]

Resistance based on the foundation of national support can

---

[21] Quoted in *The Czech Black Book,* p. 291.

shift and yet maintain its strength. If the support is nationwide, opposition is adequately based throughout the country. National leaders can effectively rally and direct popular defiance whenever they express national sentiment and tap national strength.

2. Superior Effectiveness of Resistance

The ubiquitous presence and involvement of the defiant population entails a basic inequality between the defending nation and the aggressor. It increases the effectiveness of the popular cause and reduces the impact of enemy endeavors.

In war the reduced effectiveness of foreign forces on hostile territory has long been apparent. Whether a Free French division got behind the German lines in France during World War II or a German division behind the French lines, the Germans would be cut off in any case. In the same situations on German territory the result would have been exactly the opposite. Obviously then, the country was the decisive factor, not the positions held by the respective military units. Or, to be more precise, it was the local population, its sympathies and antipathies, that mattered.

Bülow recognized 165 years ago that war itself was becoming a contest to persuade the public. He spoke of war as *Meinungskrieg* —"a war of public opinion"—to stress that popular sentiment was not a mere side issue. Persuasion he considered as "a part of the art of war." The setbacks of the monarchies in their struggle against revolutionary France were, according to Bülow, due to their fighting against national sentiments, since "one governs only through public opinion." His views were stated rather unequivocally: "In all events in the world it is important to win public opinion; the wish of the nations usually proclaims victory."

"In one's own country," wrote Clausewitz, "everything is easier, assuming that the sentiment of the subjects is not unfavorable. An understanding with the inhabitants gives the defender a general superiority." Where the nation itself rises and takes part as the primary combattant, "one will understand that this is no mere intensification of popular assistance, but that a truly new force comes into being." This expresses quite clearly the strategic value of community support.

The further we move from a primarily military battle to a political contest, the more decisive becomes the political contribution of community support. In modern complex societies the impact of a politically aroused nation's assistance or opposition is multiplied: with the people everything is easier; against them everything is more difficult.

As a rule, an invader can take over by force only physical objects that matter little in a political struggle. The occupation forces can seize and use the bridges and roads, but only in a politically irrelevant manner: the captured roads do not lead to political control; the bridges do not span the abyss of hostility created by the invasion.

The invader's forces can loot banks, but not operate them efficiently. He can take over editorial offices and radio buildings for his own publications and broadcasts; but he can hardly compel the citizens to read and listen to his views—and he cannot force them to believe his propaganda. But ignored and disbelieved news media are useless.

Where a nation is determined to defend itself, political-leadership positions, organizations, and the news media are much more effective in the hands of resistance than they are when taken over by the invader. With the good will and aid of the people, resistance enjoys a maximum of advantages. Against the ill will and obstruction of the people the alien and his collaborators draw only a minimum of use from their possession. The attitude of the people can render leadership positions, organizations, and the news media highly effective or practically useless in a political struggle. Active public sympathies can make all the difference, even against the armies of a superpower, as we saw in 1968.

Where national involvement and readiness to act are sufficiently general—approaching the degree of Swiss militarism but on the political level—resistance gains *qualitative* superiority. As a result, the same political position in enemy hands is not nearly as strong as it is in the hands of resistance: (*a*) Resistance enjoys the positive (or maximal) and active (rallying and directing) use of a position. (*b*) The invader gets no more than a negative (or minimal) and passive value (depriving resistance of it). In other words: the invader takes over only a possible outlet of national strength but does not reach the strength itself; resistance benefits directly from national strength. Their own compatriots can tap the strength at almost any place; the aliens and collaborators cannot succeed unless they block all of its outlets.

The patriots are much stronger even where equal political facilities are available to the invader's agents. In the C.S.S.R. the Russians distributed about as much printed matter and broadcast as long from their radio stations as the resistance did during the crucial first week of the invasion; while the national press and radio aroused the defiance of the entire population, the occupiers' media aroused only resentment. The patriots are often stronger even though the facilities available to them are quite inferior. If the invaders' stations had been broadcasting twenty-four hours a day and the resistance stations only fifteen minutes, the national broadcasts would still have had a stronger total effect!

An increased use of violence is unlikely to increase the political effectiveness of the alien. Often resistance increases as the invader turns to harsher methods; this was the case with Roman defiance of Napoleon and Danish defiance of Hitler. Nor does time work for the occupier, it did not in either of the cases just mentioned. The detested intruder may flood the small country with propaganda and use indoctrination for years without convincing the people; one strong appeal by the resistance leaders can win back their loyalty.

National leaders are equally superior to enemy agents or collaborators. Political control—an intangible relationship between leaders and followers—cannot be maintained by simply holding the offices from which the national or local leadership exercised it. Unless the population is thoroughly apathetic, a new political control can only be slowly and carefully cultivated. And the invader's control will, as a rule, be effective only to the extent to which the control of the national leaders is uprooted and wiped out. Yet even if this were accomplished, new leaders could tap national strength by sounding the call to resistance at any time, place, level, or activity. The control exercised by disliked leaders is *quantitatively inferior* (less obedience); often it is *qualitatively* inferior (no real obedience at all).

The political strength of a leader is directly proportionate to how well he translates public opinion into action, not to what formal position he occupies: the most successful Arab leader in modern times was T. E. Lawrence, not an Arab at all; and the man who inspired Czech resistance was the Slovak Dubček. The power a true leader has is not his own power but the power of the community: he may awaken it, he marshals and directs it; but he cannot create it. The "power" of leaders dwindles rapidly if they act contrary to the basic predispositions or strongly held opinions of the nation. Championing the cause of Polish independence in 1956, Gomulka became a popular hero, able to withstand Russian pressure; twelve years later as a servant of Russian interests he had become merely a bureaucrat able to keep his position only with the aid of the Soviet Army. The Romanian Communist leaders, on the contrary, turned from disliked bureaucrats into respected national leaders when they adopted a policy in accord with national sentiments. Followers create leaders; without popular support someone who clings to a leadership position is only an impostor.

The same principle applies to organizations: their strength is their members' strength, translated into action. Undoubtedly this includes the super-organization of a country—the government and all its branches. Dozens of exile governments have had no power at all; many others that were supported by the nation have effectively commanded the loyalties in their home country. A government inside the country is just as dependent on popular opinion and support. "Opinion, queen of the world," wrote Rousseau, "is in no wise subject to the power of kings; they themselves are her first slaves."

Organizations held by the agents or collaborators of an alien suffer the same quantitative and qualitative inferiority as compared to their effectiveness in the hands of national resistance. The nation *lends* its full strength to its own organizations. When given orders by hostile organizations, the people "hear nothing, see nothing, know nothing, and say nothing." It is, thus, not so important if the invader takes over a leadership position or an entire organization: he gets no more than partial advantage from it.

Even informal organizations in the hands of patriots can be more effective than formal ones in enemy hands. A stronger support of the members is decisive. The committees of correspondence were sufficient to direct American sentiment against the agents of the English Crown. Informal committees of coordination effectively guided many actions of Czechoslovak resistance in 1968-69.

The superior political effectiveness of resistance in leadership positions, in organizations, and in the field of the news media is but a part of the over-all political superiority of a nationwide opposition. It can be safely said that Russian propaganda in the C.S.S.R. was less than one-tenth as effective as the information and encouragement disseminated by resistance media. It can also be assumed that one national broadcast lasting only fifteen minutes a day could annul the results of twenty-four hours of enemy broadcasts, indicating a disproportion of strength almost 100:1 in favor of the defending nation. It is pointed out below (Chapter VIII, B2), that continuing resistance may be ensured and enemy control frustrated even if opposition forces take over an occupied locality for as little as two days each year, a ratio of better than 180:1 in terms of time. The exact quantities named here are not important. But it is extremely important to note the overwhelming political strength on the defending side. This strength can more than compensate for the military superiority of the invader.

In certain situations this superiority of a nation renders the presence of an enemy force rather irrelevant. The controversial proposals of Dr. Barzel, the German Minister for All-German Affairs, in his New York speech in June, 1966, were sound: if the Soviet Union agreed to German reunification, its soldiers could stay. "In fact, in a reunited Germany and in the framework of a European security system there might even be room for Soviet troops. The Red Army on German soil is a subject of discussion." The Germans would also guarantee freedom of Communist agitation in their reunited country. And the arrangements for Russian economic exploitation of the eastern parts "shall continue for another twenty years with an annual increment of 5 per cent, if it helps achieve German reunification."

There was certainly no real danger in having a few hundred thousand Russian troops on the territory of a nation of more than sixty million. Or, if there was something to worry about in such a situation, it was for Soviet concern: how to keep their men from yielding to the temptation of the high living standard and the free life, from deserting to the West in droves. Military garrisoning, economic exploitation, and political propaganda are three of the four advantages an invader gets by occupying a country (the fourth being an opportunity to terrorize some of the people). But the three concessions would certainly not have resulted in any Russian control of Germany. (Even adding the fourth would not bring an invader's political control any closer to achievement).

Supported by active popular sympathies, resistance becomes truly nationwide. Based on the entire population, defiance can be flexible and can exploit its political superiority over the alien invader. After Serbia gained *de facto* independence in 1806, the Turkish empire kept military garrisons in the small country for more than seventy years. As far as Serbia was concerned, the presence of alien troops was of no great importance even a century ago when military strength appeared almighty. In our times it is much easier to see the political irrelevance of such occupation garrisons. With growing political awareness, the nations will realize the superiority of their own strength.

D. THE ACTIVE FIGHTERS AND LEADERS

National resistance is nationwide: all groups and organizations participate in it; its leaders come from all strata of the population. The crucial question is not who expresses the feelings of the people but how well those feelings are expressed.

By disposition or experience, however, certain groups are more likely than others to provide the active resisters. They deserve the special attention of resistance planners. So do certain organizations because they are as a rule closer to, and have a natural propensity for, opposition; because they have the experience with political-warfare-type or resistance-type activities; or because they command the loyalties of people who usually are ready to defend their ideals and their nation. These groups and organizations are the cornerstones of defense.

1. Active Fighters

INTELLECTUALS.—In the beginning is the idea: sentiment has to be defined, the direction indicated in which its realization must be sought. This is a task of the nation's intellectuals. Among them it is the more spiritual—poets, preachers, philosophers—who inspire and guide the contest between the national spirit of resistance and the force of alien arms. The idealistic and the imaginative can best show the goal; the eloquent and enthusiastic provide the noblest inspiration; the original and independent of thought see a way where dull servants of routine despair.

It may be one extraordinary man—a Xenophon, a Lawrence, a Gandhi—or an entire calling—the priests of the Papal State, the poets of Ireland, the teachers of Norway, the journalists and academicians of Czechoslovakia. They are the quick match of resistance that ignites the spirits; they formulate the defiance. In a political struggle ideas, poems, and news are more valuable than the output of atom reactors or tank factories. The spiritual elites supply attitudes and values that remain beyond the reach of physical force, are hence indestructible.

Invasion troops in Czechoslovakia considered it among their first tasks to occupy the offices of Czechoslovak newspapers, radio and television stations, universities, the buildings of the writers' union, the journalists' union, and the Academy of Sciences. Only after cowing the intellectuals could they hope to subdue the nation. On the third day of the occupation the Czechoslovak National Assembly honored newspaper, radio, and TV personnel in an official proclamation: "Thanks to you, a mighty patriotic movement is spreading; our backbones are being straightened; our determination to resist occupation and to face up to the traps laid by traitors and cowards is getting a firm hold."[22] More than a year and a half after the invasion, the professional associations of authors, newsmen, and artists were continuing to resist, despite oppression.[23]

YOUTH.—Youth is not merely the hope of the future; it is also the active strength of the present. Besides bodily capacity, spiritual vitality is at its peak in them. The young people of a nation are the bearers of its enthusiasm, its idealism, its faith; they are the part of the people most sensitive to outrage and injustice. Unless the younger generation is on the side of the defenders, no success can be expected. Once the youth of a nation is corrupted, there is little hope for the future—or for the present.

Fears are widespread that the young would be helpless against indoctrination and controlled education equipped with all the modern facilities of propaganda and brainwashing. But they have preserved a remarkable spirit of resistance and a yearning for freedom, even where older generations have burned out or succumbed to a combination of terror and bribery. Actually, conquerors' ideologies, be they Fascism, Nazism, or Communism, have singularly failed, despite serious and long attempts to indoctrinate. This was frequenty apparent during World War II. Since then, the steadfastness of youth has been proven anew in many hopeless situations. In this respect, as in others, the resistance potential of a nation has been underestimated.

Czech and Slovak youth were, together with the intellectuals, the main leaders and simultaneously the main fighters of the political resistance. The young people fought, many of them died, with greatest courage. From the first day they demon-

---

[22] *The Czech Black Book*, p. 113.
[23] *New York Times*, March 13, 1970.

strated, talked with Russian soldiers, collected signatures supporting the national leaders, denounced the collaborators. Some youths were shot while painting slogans or distributing leaflets; others immediately thereafter refused to yield even with machine guns firing over their heads and carried on their backs signs with the license numbers of secret-police cars making arrests. "The longhaired youths performed the hardest tasks of passive resistance during the occupation," reported a foreign observer.[24]

And the young demonstrated great discipline. When clashes with the invaders were feared, they helped the police to persuade the people to disperse. The nationwide student strike in November, 1968, supporting the leaders of the country was peaceful. Even the funeral of Jan Palach was conducted with disciplined restraint, although half a million people participated in the demonstration. It was quite impressive to observe how Czech youths informed the public of the latest political events and how they watched over the shrines of resistance, even in 1969.

Their perseverance and nationwide participation were equally impressive. The young people actively expressed defiance throughout the country; their opposition never stopped. And from all the age groups of the population, those under twenty-five were the strongest supporters of Dubcek in the public-opinion survey under occupation and considered the Russian invasion of 1968 the most inglorious period in the history of the nation.[25] The future of the country seems to be in good hands.

Youth Organizations, throughout the C.S.S.R., carried more than their share of the resistance. Student groups and organizations, central and local units of the Czechoslovak Youth League, the newspapers of the youth organizations, all were in the forefront of defiance. Neither their determination nor their effectiveness was reduced in any way when the foreign troops occupied the editorial offices of the papers and the headquarters of the Youth League, or when they surrounded the universities. They have remained the most outspoken opposition. Ten months after

24 *Svenska Dagbladet* (Stockholm), Aug. 28, 1968.
25 *Vztah Čechů a Slováků* . . . , pp. 10, 16.

the invasion, the regime, unable either to convince or control them, dissolved student organizations. Three months later it even had to dissolve Communist Party groups at Czech and Slovak universities.

From Ireland to Cyprus youth has fought valliantly. Youth organizations are important for resistance because they serve a group with a great capacity for defiance. Through these organizations the young can be prepared, trained, guided; they can be predisposed to patriotic thought and action. National resistance depends greatly on the spirit and the active exertions of the young generation.

WORKERS.—Workers are the solid core of the fighters. Writers and students ignited the opposition in Hungary, in 1956, but workers joined unreservedly on the first day. They continued to fight and to resist without weapons, keeping the regime in a position of practical impotence, well into 1957.

Marx, Engels, and Lenin recognized the fighting spirit of the working class; so did most other radicals. As time passed, some people assumed that the workers would always fight on the side of radicalism and Communism, even against their compatriots and national interests. Examples to the contrary were explained away, saying that ideologies had laid no claim on their loyalties before our days. Berlin in 1953, Poznan and Budapest in 1956, Prague and Bratislava in 1968–69, restored the true picture—that workers do consider national freedom the highest value and defend it faithfully, despite attempts to mislead them with alien ideologies. Their constant loyalty has decided many national struggles.

Throughout, Czech and Slovak workers were unequivocally on the side of national freedom and liberty. They eagerly took sides themselves and openly supported the resistance of others. The absolute unanimity, the political maturity, and their clear stands on the crucial issues are among the outstanding features of the national struggle. "Rather frightening," commented the humor magazine *Dikobraz*, "how the working class turns out to be a concealed intelligentsia!" It was much more frightening for the invaders that the first instance where the workers in effect became a dominant force in a country, they unequivocally supported national resistance. . . .

Workers' organizations are in contact with, they are the leadership of, the potentially strongest resistance group in a nation. Hence, they have great importance in all phases of national defense.

From their very beginnings, unions have been fighting for social justice and welfare, resisting oppressive exploitation by employers and governments. They have successfully united, organized, guided the people, leading thousands in economic and political resistance campaigns. Their control over the fighting muscle of the nation, no less than their sensitivity to popular psychology, gives them great power in politically unstable situations. The experience gained by labor leaders and organizers in domestic conflicts makes them invaluable in opposing an alien who attacks the country to exploit and oppress everyone. As fighters and leaders they are familiar with strikes, slowdowns, demonstrations, propaganda, boycotts—many important resistance techniques.

The Revolutionary Trade Union Movement in the C.S.S.R., and every one of the trade unions, appealed to world opinion; addressed the soldiers and organizations of the invading countries; supported and physically protected their political leadership; organized and led strikes, demonstrations; informed their own members and the general public; supported the struggle through their newspapers; demanded the immediate withdrawal of occupation troops. Their resistance was open and outspoken, but they were ready at all times to go underground if necessary. In March, 1969, they chose a new leadership in free elections and proclaimed a program fully supporting the demands for national freedom. After a year of occupation, they were far from subdued.

The workers' organizations went through a remarkable metamorphosis after the invasion of the C.S.S.R.: developed for twenty years as transmission belts enabling the rulers to oppress the people, they suddenly became transmission belts enabling national sentiment to influence the rulers.

Nations will do well, as a rule, to rely unreservedly on the patriotism of the working people and their organizations.

WOMEN.—The role of women is extremely important, impossible to pass over without mention. In a national struggle they must not be excluded from the ranks of participants. Antigone and Elektra are classic symbols of loyalty and resistance since the times of ancient Greece. From Ireland to India they have actively participated in the fight for independence. Gandhi repeatedly stressed how important women were for the disobedience campaign; he took great pains to ensure their fullest participation. During the Algerian revolution a reporter wrote that "even if the men were disposed to give in, the women would drive them back to their duty with a strong hand. There is an Antigone in every one of them."[26] The various psychological advantages women bring to resistance must be exploited wherever possible. The obsolete notions that women should not, could not, or would not take part in this vital national effort are best discarded. Political defense can hardly succeed if the defending nation excludes half of its citizens from participating in it!

2. Leaders and Cadres

The defense of small nations depends on the quality of leaders on all levels; the lower levels being by no means the least important. Selection, assignment, and training of the people who are to translate national sentiment into purposeful action are among the main tasks of political defense.

To begin with, the new nature of political struggle dictates new strategic rules. This is true of national defense generally; it applies especially to resistance under enemy occupation. When the legal leadership is supplanted, partly or completely, by an invading enemy or by an imposed regime, the problem of leadership and cadres is much more serious. A few points must be stressed here.

The old practice expected military forces to stand and fight, while the political leadership and the elites of the nation left

---

[26] *Dagens Nyheter*, March 9, 1961.

the country to go into exile. The new defense strategy tells the armed fighters to "go where the enemy is not," but it expects the citizens and the leaders to stay and fight with political weapons.

A nation cannot expect to win a difficult campaign if the political resisters disappear and the military defenders are forced to offer themselves to be massacred by the invader. As long as military fighting was thought essential, and political warfare barely of secondary, if any, importance, it was logical to demand maximum sacrifices in battle, but to forego additional trouble once nothing more could be salvaged. It is just as logical now, when political opposition is recognized as decisive, to demand that everything be mobilized for it. The secondary military joust should not be allowed to consume the youth of a nation when no victory can reasonably be expected to result from such human sacrifice. The soldiers may simply disperse to take up their various resistance tasks. The citizens are spared the destruction of life, limb, and home; but they are summoned to fight the political struggle for their freedom and possessions.

POLITICAL LEADERS.—Political leaders must be in the forefront of the nation. People with experience, with the richest store of enterprise, should stay in the country and provide the necessary guidance. They should not scatter into emigration and leave the body of the nation decapitated and hardly able to act until a new generation can provide new leadership (if the struggle is not hopelessly lost before).

General Marbot, evaluating Napoleon's defeat in Spain, called it "a misfortune for France" that the Spanish Government had not left for South America, as the Portuguese rulers did, "because the Spanish nation, abandoned by its princes, would have at least offered Napoleon's armies a less lively resistance."[27] In 1939, the Chinese government ordered that the people were not to depart from the war areas. The officers of local forces, the chiefs of police, and other essential local administrators did not retreat with their forces but remained at their stations and resisted.

---

[27] Marbot, *Mémoires du Général Baron de Marbot* (Paris: E. Plon, Nourrit et Cie., 1891) p. 10.

As the occupation troops rolled into Czechoslovakia, State, Party, and administrative leadership was instructed to "remain in their functions as the legal elected representatives" of the people. The Government, though decimated by arrests, continued to function; the National Assembly convened and remained in session during the first phase of the invasion; the leading organs of the Communist Party remained active throughout; they even successfully convened the Extraordinary XIV Party Congress. The ability of the regular leadership to function under occupation turned out to be an unexpected political strength.

One cannot deny an element of fairness to the new system, whereby people enjoying the greatest privileges, the benefits and honors of position, bear the main responsibility for restoring national independence and their own prerogatives. People who are not ready to fight for their country should not be in the Government. It is not fair to apply Frederick the Great's famous reproach "Dogs, would you live forever?" to the common soldiers alone.

An intense political struggle will involve a high turnover of leaders and cadres. It will demand replacements prepared to step forward and lead. Most losses are due to psychological emasculation and collapse as the peacetime patronage appointee, who chose a career with an easy income, a routine life, and occasions to exhibit himself in public from time to time, faces enemy invasion. Many idealistic leaders as well are broken by terror; others are put out of action by physical means.

Leadership losses must be replaced with men whose fitness has been ascertained before the need arises. National resistance is most effective as a prepared resistance; its leaders need special preparation. Four groups of potential leaders require special comment.

Political parties are the main target of dictators and conquerors. The reason is clear: "They are in fact bodies engaged in a form of political warfare with each other in a battle of the brains for the allegiance of the minds of the electorate."[28]

---

[28] Stephen King-Hall, *Defence in the Nuclear Age* (London: V. Gollancz, 1958), pp. 215–16.

They have, in addition, an organized network covering the entire country—a perfect resistance apparatus, a parallel control system. On all levels they can supply the necessary leaders.

Washington has been described as "the city where political backstabbing was developed into a 20th-century art form."[29] The definition fits any capital city with vital political parties. The parties are the reservoirs of people experienced in resistance tactics. They are schools of non-violent throat-cutting and quasi-conspiratorial activities. They specialize in influencing, directing, and exploiting public sentiment openly as well as covertly. Once outside pressure eliminates the usual intra-party and inter-party fighting, a force is freed to resist the invader.

Experience shows that absence of vigorous partisan politics in a country frequently goes hand in hand with the inability to maintain an adequate resistance after invasion, while a certain internal pugnacity (Ireland, Finland), when focused on the alien, is a formidable weapon. Political parties teach and lead national opposition.

(*Organizations of students and workers* were discussed above.)

NATIONAL ARMY.—Military personnel have experience and training useful in resistance. Since most armies of small states acquire full significance only after the invader has occupied the country, a correct defensive strategy would assign to them a double role: including a full participation of the military in resistance, once the army is dissolved or disintegrates in the course of a conflict.

The main need is to assure that the second task can be fulfilled. Preparation for resistance should, therefore, be a substantial part of the training of all military and police forces. And a thorough resistance consciousness should be awakened in the officers and men.

The orders given to the Czechoslovak Army were to avoid fighting, to prevent any armed confrontations. This armed force, one of the largest in the world in proportion to the size of the country's population, was militarily practically useless. Yet as

---

29 William Haddad, *New York Herald Tribune*, Dec. 14, 1963.

a political weapon it was useful: the Russians were undoubtedly impressed by the soldiers' expressions of support for the national leadership; they were even more impressed when certain Slovak units got ready to go into the mountains with their weapons for guerrilla warfare. There can be no doubt that the mere existence of such an armed force urged on the Kremlin a certain caution and prevented Moscow from taking even more drastic steps. Some political price had to be paid for the inactivity of the armed forces of the C.S.S.R.

POLICE.—The police forces are in a somewhat similar position. They should, in the interests of opposition, continue to function as long as possible. They are not to fight the invader openly. But police machinery and operations should be kept in the hands of the patriots.

When the invader excludes nationalists from the force, they can join resistance. Their expertise with the limits of supervision and enforcement, with the weaknesses of a control system, with the importance of popular co-operation and defiance, enhances their value as resistance advisers and cadres.

The Czechoslovak police forces remained strongly loyal to the legitimate leadership, except for some units of the political police. Merely to look at the regular activities of the policemen—and then to imagine how enemy personnel or agents would have performed the very same tasks—in occupied Czechoslovakia brought to mind countless advantages of having their own people do the job. A patriot can devote much more of his energies to resistance activities if he does not have to be on guard against police terror.

This short mention of some of the groups and organizations is not intended to suggest that they are the only significant ones. On the contrary, *all* organized circles are potentially important; *none* should be disregarded or neglected. And *all* leaders are important; in the higher, as well as in the intermediate and the lower positions. Each one has a vital task. The entire nation is part of a national resistance. National strength should be marshaled as fully as possible.

CHAPTER VII

Predisposition and Political Attack

A. DIATHETICS: THE PREDISPOSITION

The entire nation has to be prepared for the decisive political contest. In this kind of struggle, with spiritual strength the crucial factor, preparation must necessarily be spiritual and political. In 400 B.C., Xenophon told Greek officers that

> . . . if someone could turn the soldiers' minds from wondering what will happen to them, and make them wonder what they could do, they will be in much better spirits. You know, I am sure, that not numbers or strength brings victory in war; but whichever side goes into battle stronger in soul, their enemies generally cannot withstand them.[1]

He went on to prove it: he saved the Hellenes in a seemingly hopeless situation. Based on spiritual strength, his became one of history's great military exploits.

Exaltation was, in Bülow's system of warfare, the spiritual strength able to develop unheard-of energies in battle. It was used to move, hold together, bring into action, and control the fighters. The task of the officers was to kindle enthusiasm and to maintain it by steady care. Bülow hoped for a moral rebirth of the nation. Instead of just dispensing drill and exercises, he wrote, army camps should become moving universities: "I wish every man were a fortress." Clausewitz stressed the psychologi-

---

[1] Xenophon, *Anabasis* iii. 1.

cal element and public opinion as "the center of gravity" in national struggles.

Twenty-three hundred years after Xenophon, on the other side of the Arabian desert, T. E. Lawrence faced a similarly critical situation. The Arab cause seemed lost. Neither the revolutionaries themselves nor their British allies believed in success. But he soon recognized that the force of the spirit was decisive, that it was to bring victory. He adopted Xenophon's term "diathetics"—predisposition—to describe the process of spiritual guidance. It was the psychological element in his winning strategy.

"It was the pathic, almost the ethical in war. Of this our propaganda was the stained, ignoble offspring." Diathetics concerned itself, first of all, with the crowd to adjust its spirit "to the point where it became useful to exploit in action, and the predirection of this changing spirit to a certain end." Its main concern, however, was the individual,

> . . . the mood of our men, [and] the cultivation of whatever in them promised to profit our intentions. We had to arrange their minds in order of battle just as carefully and as formally as other officers would arrange their bodies. . . . As we seldom had to concern ourselves with what our men did, but always with what they thought, the diathetic for us would be more than half the command. . . . In Asia the regular elements were so weak that irregulars could not let the metaphysical weapon rust unused. On it we should mainly rely for the means of victory on the Arab front.[2]

Lawrence called this preaching. The predisposition for him included everyone concerned—in addition to his own men, the enemy, the Arab nation, the enemy population, and neutrals as well. The decision was arrived at by diathetics, which was the basic stuggle, spanning every aspect of the contest: "The preaching was victory and the fighting a delusion. We lived by preaching." Predisposition, not fighting, determined the issue in Lawrence's strategy. Fighting only clarified the result.

---

[2] T. E. Lawrence, *Seven Pillars of Wisdom* (New York: Dell Publishing Co., 1962), p. 198.

Political defense within the political community depends on the spiritual strength of the nation. Diathetics must develop and sustain the spirit. It must arouse the combined national strength.

National growth is a historical process achieved during, and measured by, long periods of time: tens, hundreds, thousands of years. "For a *polis* is not the growth of a day," wrote Aristotle. And the familiar saying that Rome was not built in a day applies equally to the origin of her glory, the Roman spirit. Fortresses in men's minds rise slowly; they need solid foundations.

For political strategy the significance of the national spirit is its ability to resist ephemeral influences. Its solid foundations cannot be easily destroyed by processes of short historical duration, like wars and invasions, lasting only a few years or decades.

A nation's strength matures long before the actual fighting starts. The outcome of a given struggle is, thus, in a very real sense decided in the past. Without Greek victories over the Persian kings Darius and Xerxes, there would probably have been no Greek nation to resist Hitler's occupation in the Second World War, and Stalin's attempts to take over Greece in the late 1940's. For the latter struggle the sea battle in the narrow waters between the island of Salamis and the mainland of Attica, in 480 B.C., was as important as the mountain warfare in the Vitsi and the Grammos near Albania, A.D. 1949.

For the Swiss militiaman today a diathetic tradition is ever present. The *Soldiers' Handbook*[3] has a chapter entitled "The Confederates [of 1291]—our Contemporaries." Fleming Muus, the organizer of Danish resistance in World War II, invoked the Vikings, "the Viking blood," and "the Viking spirit"; he appealed to "the Spirit of 1864" and achieved surprising results, in 1944.[4] His prognosis of Danish resistance potential, expressed in such "romantic" terms, was confirmed as more accurate than that of more realistic observers, who failed to take into account the forces rooted in long forgotten history. Just as unexpectedly the

---

[3] *Soldatenbuch: Auf Dich kommt es an!* (Bern: Eidgenössische Drucksachen- und Materialzentrale, 1959).

[4] Fleming B. Muus, *The Spark and the Flame* (London: Museum Press, 1956), pp. 56, 87, 89, 103.

traditions of Hus and Žižka, after more than five and a half centuries, inspired and sustained Czech resistance of 1968. The growth of spiritual strength continues from the past, through the present, into the future. In this sphere, the contest for a nation's survival goes on at all times: whether a future struggle for freedom can be won is determined by what was in the past and what is in the present. Diathetics, in its transitory form, blends with this historical process. It contributes to the growth of spiritual strength in its own way—often imperceptibly, but never insignificantly.

Diathetic preparation is one reason for tiny Switzerland's considerable defensive capability. "Education on all levels," writes a member of the Government, "is not an indirect, but a direct element of our defense policy."[5] The inscription on a Swiss village schoolhouse reads: "National education is national liberation." And the military writer Captain H.-R. Monfort assigns a direct military importance to tradition, stating that a militia system was worth as much as its traditions. It could not be copied abroad where the century-long history of the Bund was lacking: "It needs time to realize its potentialities. It cannot form in a few months, nor in a few years. It acquires its full value only after the entire population identifies with it, and this fusion will occur only with time."[6]

As a part of national defense, diathetics has three short-range functions: (1) to release the dormant national strength, and to kindle the will to resist; (2) to focus all available opposition strength against the alien invader; and (3) to guide the day-by-day resistance, to maintain the people's spirit, to inform them of the opportunities and the techniques of the struggle.

Diathetics can be used defensively and offensively: its ideas and information strengthen political defense, and are a weapon of political attack against the enemy. The better nations understand political defense as a means of resisting force, the more

---

5 Peter Dürenmatt, "Wehrpolitik in der Demokratie," *Die Schweizer Armee Heute*, p. 205.

6 Captain H. R. Monfort, "Force et Faiblesse des Armées de Milice," *Révue Militaire Générale*, 1959, 471.

the role of violence will diminish and that of spiritual strength increase. In the future, the significance of diathetics in activating and guiding national defense will continue to grow.

1. Preparing the Nation

The first task of diathetics is defense. The first need is to prepare the nation to defend itself. For political defense the predisposition of the people is, together with planning and preparation, the most important step. Diathetics can make the nations strong and keep them free.

Diathetic preparation is the best means to increase the deterrence effect against aggression. And it helps fight successfully if an attack should come.

World War II revealed a surprising lack of planning or preparation for political defense. Even small nations having no realistic hope for outside assistance inertly succumbed, thinking that "all is lost" once a great power decided to become aggressive. The people paid dearly for the omission of their governments.

There is no sign of adequate resistance planning even at the present time. The state of affairs is not a satisfactory one.

Diathetics is both a historical and a day-to-day process. The spiritual fortresses have been built in the course of centuries; the short-range activities of predisposition are the actual manning of the ramparts. The nation's leaders, preachers, and teachers— everyone concerned with public opinion—have a responsibility to prepare the common defense as part of their daily work. The best strongholds are useless if they remain unmanned in the hour of danger. Hitler was alluding to this possibility when he enunciated: "Our real wars will in fact all be fought before military operations begin."[7]

German behavior in World War II showed the significance of predisposition. The same nation that supinely accepted occupation without resistance of any kind had firmly withstood

---

[7] Hermann Rausching, *The Voice of Destruction* (New York: G. P. Putnam's Sons, 1940), p. 4.

heaviest setbacks at the fronts and ceaseless bombings at home. The military blows did not shatter their morale because they were ready and simply refused to be demoralized. Occupation found them on their knees, and on their backs, when, according to the familiar military rules, "nothing could be done." Consequently nothing was tried, and their morale collapsed completely. The surprising political resistance of Berlin may be due to the fact that its two postwar mayors were experienced resistance fighters who understood the spirit of defiance and managed to instill it into the Berliners. In the critical postwar crises these people seemed to have forgotten how to be afraid.

The role of the people in great power strategy was the same as in "The Charge of the Light Brigade": "Theirs not to reason why, Theirs but to do and die." No more. The duty of the modern *polis,* as well as of its individual members, is to fight and live, not to die. And to reason—their initiative and intelligence are invaluable in political contests.

The nation needs a basic understanding of resistance, of its principles and techniques. Diathetics must cultivate the understanding. If this can be achieved, if the people are able to oppose threats and subjugation, national defense will have a new strength.

Small states, relying on political defense, need a strongly committed population. Gandhi taught that "one must first mobilize public opinion against the evil one is to eradicate, that an awakened and intelligent public opinion is the most potent weapon."[8] Mao agreed: "Political mobilization is the most fundamental condition of winning the war."[9] Muus stressed, in retrospect, that his main task had been "to build up a resistance consciousness" in Denmark, "a will to defy the Germans."[10]

A nation must understand the political forces. If knowledge

---

[8] M. K. Gandhi, *Non-Violent Resistance: Satyagraha* (N. Y.: Schocken, 1961), p. 77.

[9] Mao Tse-tung, *On Protracted War* (Peking: Foreign Languages Press, 1954), p. 137.

[10] Muus, *op. cit.,* p. 56.

is power, the cognizance of one's own strength is the greatest power of all. The difference between impotence and invincibility may depend on a recognition of our own abilities. Seeming helplessness harms as much as actual weakness. The people must realize not only that the national community influences the political contest, but that the whole outcome of the struggle—defeat or victory—depends on their participation.

The nation must also know the difference between orthodox strategy and political defense. Diathetics must demolish the current superstitions that military force alone decides, that "all is lost" once the country is invaded, or when it is merely threatened. It must explain the political nature of modern conflicts, the primacy of political strength. It must show that aggressive enemy pressure does not end the conflict, but merely begins the decisive political phase. Examples from recent history are valuable diathetic material.

The people must know that resistance, although based on intangible spiritual and political strength (or exactly because it is so based), is a sound and practical strategy. Only where the fighters believe that their risks and sacrifices shall not be in vain are they going to make resolute efforts. A vague sentiment becomes a firm determination as soon as a successful outcome is anticipated.

Diathetics can rely on the enemy himself to arouse opposition. Aggression is the most effective motivation, an impetus sufficiently strong to arouse patriots. They feel that there must be a way of counteracting alien oppression; they look eagerly for ways to resist. Diathetics has only to inform them how they can help the national cause.

Technical resistance information and training to cope with the difficulties and dangers of a struggle (the blows to be expected, the ways of evasion, and the counterblows to be dealt) strengthen the will and the ability to fight. Possible enemy attempts to use terror and to paralyze resistance should be discussed as part of defense training.

Anticipated crises are easier to cope with. Shock and terror can be psychological weapons deliberately used by the invader to induce fear and break the attacked nation's will to resist. The speed, noise, and apparent efficiency of an invasion may numb the senses. An invading army rolling into town with its tanks rattling, its planes swooping overhead, its troops intoxicated with the speed of advance and with booty liquor, letting their weapons rain fire on anything that moves, may create the illusion of majestic strength. Unprepared for this, the people may forget that what they see is not the strength that decides the contest in the end, but a mere preliminary spectacle.

The irrational response may be one of uncontrolled fear; it may cripple the mental as well as the physical capacities. An intelligent estimate will show how limited the danger actually is. The irrational response of the uninformed can be turned into intelligent behavior simply by informing the people in advance. Unknown danger disables. A known danger defines the limits of safe action and may, thus, increase both safety and efficiency of opposition.

Predisposition, even if it is only partly successful, adds greatly to the resistance potential of a nation. Prepared defiance becomes a purposeful struggle, and not a mere clinging to a lost cause. The spiritual and political strength of nationalism under alien invasion does not have to be only a brake applied to delay the people's deserting to the enemy or bowing under an inevitable yoke. It can become the moving force of a defensive, and offensive, opposition. Adequately prepared, political defense can start any time and continue without interruption.

2. *Diathetics in the Resistance Struggle*

Political conflicts can include (1) the deterrence phase, (2) the military interlude, if any, and (3) a resistance struggle after enemy invasion. Hitler's saying that the real wars would be fought before military operations began was only partly correct; actually, the real struggle continues after the military interlude is over. (There can, of course, be many politically decisive conflicts without any use of military force.) Ultimate victory and defeat is the outcome of the political stage of any conflict. Before that has been fought out, only conjectures are possible about the defensive strength of a nation, and about the effectiveness of its spiritual preparations.

In many political conflicts, the potential threat of enemy invasion cannot be discounted. That is why the defenders should be ready for the invasion phase. And that is why the function of diathetics in the stage of resistance against invasion forces must be discussed here at some length.

Before the real contest starts, the most dangerous moves of the invader aim at confusing and discouraging resistance, at preventing its crystallization. All diathetic means must be mobilized to proclaim and constantly reaffirm, for all people to hear an absolute, unconditional determination to defend freedom and independence—to resist as long as necessary to restore both. Anticipating enemy attempts to create confusion, the Government of Sweden circulated an official pamphlet to every home in the country, in 1952, affirming that if war comes resistance will be made everywhere, that all orders to the contrary be ignored, regardless on what purported authority they are issued. The Swiss population was informed in 1940 that "all news questioning the will of the Government or army leadership to resist are to be considered enemy propaganda."[11]

The first days and weeks under invasion have their own problems. Psychologically the initial period is the most difficult, although the practical conditions are very favorable. Regardless of the demonstrations that the invader makes to impress the people, his ability to control fluctuates around the zero point for a considerable time if he meets any disobedience. Diathetics has the task of bridging the initial spiritual dislocation. It must let the people change from peace to resistance footing, grasp the initial advantages, before the enemy has secured a firmer hold on the country. Resistance may last a long time—nations have

---

[11] *Soldatenbuch*, p. 79. A second edition, of the Swedish pamphlet *Om kriget kommer* (Stockholm: Kungl. inrikes-departementet, 1952), is distributed now as *A Guideline for Sweden's Citizens*. Note, however, that both Sweden and Switzerland concentrate mainly on military resistance; neither is preparing for an adequate political defense.

been known to defend themselves for centuries—but the failure, if not the success, of opposition is usually decided at the very beginning.

The nation must maintain resistance and frustrate the political measures of the invader. Both tasks are closely interwoven and are pursued simultaneously. But at the outset of the conflict, when national morale and will to resist must be guarded jealously, the main task is the first. An apparently conclusive defeat must be prevented at all costs; any advances of the occupier must be contrasted with resistance gains before the people despair. Initial setbacks weigh more heavily than far graver reverses later in the struggle, after men have adjusted to the changing fortunes and know that the main purpose is to go on resisting. A long indecision demonstrates the weakness of the invader and the power of the defenders. This insight, more than anything else, fans the will and defiance. Final victory, men will come to understand, can be won despite numerous partial defeats. But the impact of initial reverses wants careful cushioning.

At this point, with most significant positions and facilities still in the hands of the defending nation, many preparatory gains can be scored: strategic sabotage completed, essential stores destroyed or hidden, organizations prepared for independent functioning underground, etc. Political countermeasures are easy—"shadow" organizations and control apparatus (prepared to emerge in the later stages of the coming struggle) formed, leader and cadre replacements alerted, groups and networks of fighters formed or activated, contacts and communications arranged, planning adjusted to unexpected developments. Neither defensive nor offensive moves are difficult at first.

In the course of the struggle, diathetics, like resistance itself, enters all places, all types of activities, every aspect of the nation's life, every political relationship in the country.

The nation must share a sense of purpose to succeed. Diathetics expresses the common feeling and strengthens national cohesion against enemy attempts to divide, confuse, infiltrate the community, and to pit the patriots against their own countrymen. If security becomes difficult and persecution extreme, it is best to deal only with local people known to each other, speaking the same dialect, and the like. Cohesion increases resistance strength.

Communication between like-minded fighters raises their morale and effectiveness. Regular contacts are a source of inspiration, coordination, and information. Once the contacts spread beyond the narrowest circles, they become a danger to enemy control. As soon as *three or more* patriots act in concert, opposition has, in a sense, become aggressive already.

The people must be provided with information: including world events relevant to the nation's struggle; activities of their compatriots abroad; the extent and nature of resistance in the country. News is definitely a weapon of political warfare. Items suppressed by the invader's censorship, resistance experiences and ideas (they learn by doing, teach by communicating), reports about such dangers as enemy secret agents, planned provocations or attacks—all should have the widest circulation. The strengthening effect on German-invaded nations, during World War II, of news about their representatives abroad active for the cause, and beyond the reach of the powerful conqueror, is well known. So is the influence that events in Poland and Hungary, in 1956, had on each other. Prepared and imaginatively used techniques can make this information constantly available.

The Czechs and the Slovaks taught us that resistance must be everywhere, but that violence is not necessary for success. The more extensive is political defiance, so we learned, the less fighting is needed to defend the nation politically. But there must be resistance (almost any kind will do), and there must be adequate information about it to show the limits of alien rule and to encourage further disobedience.

Press, radio, other information media—all must become a part of the diathetic effort. News, rumors, and ridicule can be spread by everyone in contact with the public. The main communication, however, is the routine contact of individuals with each other: these contacts are the safest, the most influential, and they permit the widest participation.

Lawrence stressed the value of information: "The printing press is the greatest weapon in the armory of the modern commander. The printing press and each newly-discovered method of communication favoured the intellectual above the physical."[12] Dutch resistance published 1,193 different titles during World War II. A number of the publications came out for long periods, distributing as many as 45,000, even 100,000 copies; the paper *Vrij Nederland* is said to have put into circulation almost half a million copies, despite energetic German attempts at eliminating the active underground press. A Belgian expert concluded: "It seems to be possible to print anything, at any time at a risk which is not great, even in a country as severely occupied as Belgium was."[13] In Czechoslovakia, under an equally severe Russian invasion, millions of copies were published and distributed in the first week after invasion. A single newspaper, the *Rude Pravo* came to have a daily circulation of 200,000 copies at that time.[14]

The use of radio is spreading in political conflicts. In the Czechoslovak resistance the extensive participation of the national radio network astounded the whole world. Their exploits are truly legendary and are hardly likely to be surpassed. Press, radio, and television showed how much national information media can accomplish. Their achievements are a real breakthrough in the theory and practice of resistance.

Anecdotes, painted slogans, caricatures, jokes, are as impossible to stop or control as radio waves; they spread the word almost as fast and as widely. The desperate measures the Russians took to stop these activities indicate that they were succeeding well. On the very first day TASS was complaining bitterly against "expression of hostile moods, circulation of rumors, distribution

12 T. E. Lawrence, "The Evolution of a Revolt," *The Army Quarterly* (London), No. 1 (1920), 62.

13 Karl Heinz Hoffmann and Otto Mayr-Arnold, *Okänd Armé* (Stockholm: Hörsta Förlag, 1959), p. 155; M. Ugeux, "Quelques Considérations, Techniques et Morales sur l'Expérience de Guerre Psychologique," in Henri Michel (ed.), *European Resistance Movements, 1939–1945*, p. 174.

14 *Expressen* (Stockholm), Aug. 28, 1968.

of leaflets, incendiary statements on the radio, on television, and in the press."[15] Young people were forced to remove posters and wash off slogans under threats of execution. Youths distributing leaflets and newspapers were killed; transistor radios were forcibly taken from the people by Soviet troops. Offices of radio, television, newspapers were occupied; all broadcasting and publication without Russian permission was prohibited.[16] Efforts to stop them failed miserably.

Enemy propaganda may for many nations be a serious problem. But nationalism usually immunizes the defenders against enemy psychological warfare. If, in addition, the people get information contradicting the invader's propaganda, that propaganda is not very dangerous.

Inherent weaknesses are sure to render enemy efforts at persuasion ineffective. First, in Europe an aggressor can hardly claim cultural superiority, as the white man could do in Africa and Asia at the height of colonialism or the French still could in Algeria a few years ago. If the invader makes this claim in Europe, he merely exposes himself to ridicule not consistent with a healthy respect for his regime. Second, it is difficult for an alien to understand the psychology of the resisting nation. Propaganda spread by opposed foreigners remains unsuccessful, at times self-defeating. The most elaborate efforts of this kind were in vain during World War II. Third, the enemy's propaganda is doomed essentially because he is an invader; his deeds benefit aliens and harm the interests of the attacked country, contradicting the shrewdest dissimulation. Whatever the first impact, the diathetic tide will soon turn, with a vengeance: people disbelieve many things for the sole reason that the conqueror affirms them.

In the C.S.S.R. the invader's propaganda was not only ineffective, but very counterproductive indeed. Their radio and television broadcasts and the tons of printed matter they dropped from cars and helicopters aroused resentment much

---

[15] R. Littell (ed.), *The Czech Black Book* (New York: Praeger, 1969), p. 59.
[16] *Ibid.*, pp. 171, 184, 225, 229, *et al.*

more than they weakened resistance. Russian as well as collaborator propaganda was disregarded, disbelieved, and despised.

Diathetics must contribute to ungovernability: show the limits of the invader's control and how to disregard it safely. People must deny the legitimacy of the alien's regime, reject him and his agents as arbiters of intra-national differences. They must understand the tactics of ignoring enemy presence. Preventing habitual obedience and fostering disobedience are also the province of diathetics.

The rule by laws and orders is one area in which the invader's attempts to enforce obedience and impose his will can succeed only partially. As soon as his forces are on the spot, they issue orders to the population. Obedience to them, it is generally believed, can always be compelled and should therefore be conceded.

Not true: Aristotle knew more than two thousand years ago that a law is valid only to the extent to which it is obeyed. This still applies. Were it otherwise, any regime could be secured by issuing a single fiat: "You shall obey everything I order!" and all rule would continue safely forever.

Few laws can be fully enforced, for various reasons: (1) violations sometimes cannot be ascertained; or (2) violators cannot be found; or (3) there may simply be a shortage of supervisors. Yet a mere fragmentary enforcement does not change the habit of disobedience.

Law enforcement, like all means of political control, rests on the consent of the people, on co-operation. Against disobedience, any law remains a failure. There are laws against adultery and homosexuality in the United States and Britain. But both are just as ineffective in these two countries, where courts openly admit their unenforceability, as are laws against economic crimes in the Soviet Union, where vigorous enforcement is proclaimed and the death penalty meted out as punishment.[17]

---

[17] Two hundred executions for economic crimes in four years are reported in the *New York Times Magazine,* May 2, 1965.

The prohibition laws in America not only lessened respect for, but also stimulated contemptuous disregard of, the law.

Since law enforcement is an integral part of political control, frustrating the former goes a long way toward negating the latter. Defiance of the oppressive weapon of legalism is a proper task of political opposition. Resistance analysts must search for the limits of enforcing an invader's ukases. Diathetics must show the limits to everyone; they are an inherent defect of enemy rule, and another way to defeat his control. Forbidden radio and newspapers are more effective, for instance, because the prohibition guarantees that they do not express the views of the occupiers.

Opposition can be offered in every field. I shall mention here only the schools, but there are, of course, similar opportunities for defiance in other areas.

Schools in an occupied country will remain open. The invader wants to keep the young busy—in places where their activities are easy to supervise, away from nationalistic home and family influence. He hopes to turn the schools into instruments of control of, and dispensers of his ideology to, youth. The resisting nation wants to educate and inspire its developing generation—to keep them in daily contact with companions and teachers of their own, especially at such a critical time. The conflicting aims soon lead to a political struggle for the control of schools—the strategic positions of access to the minds of the young—the "commanding heights" of diathetics.

At first, the situation favors the defending nation: patriots hold the decisive posts; they have the training, experience, and tools needed. The invader must conquer these positions. He must find a somewhat adequate number of experts (teachers, instructors, administrators) to man them. And he must produce new technical tools—textbooks and teaching aids. One does not have to be an educator to see the many opportunities these problems give for resistance.

During the first school year under occupation, the invader tries more to impress than to supervise—mainly to deter teachers and students from contagious overt defiance of his regime. The value of his informers remains limited, since a closed community like a school soon discovers their identity. Actual enemy control is low in the first year. Schools are able to operate almost as before, all but ignoring his rule. His agents and collaborators may take over the Ministry of Education, but in the beginning they cannot adequately supervise how their orders are obeyed.

National textbooks may be outlawed. But they will be the only ones available and, therefore, the ones actually perused. New texts take time to write, censor, and publish; to issue a complete set may take a decade.

Obviously, this is a political struggle *par excellence*: fought, with textbooks as weapons, in the classrooms of primary and secondary schools. Yet, no invader can secure his conquest without winning this very battle. He cannot win it by military force, no matter how powerful. Texts are more than tanks in this campaign; a woman teaching first grade, even if confined to a wheelchair, often decides more than a regiment, or a division, of paratroopers. (What could possibly be better proof of the political nature of the struggle!)

From the second year on, the struggle for control intensifies. Some teachers can be dismissed: to get rid of the more independent minds and, more important, to intimidate the rest. But the vacancies have to be filled—mainly with former public servants and those thrown out of other jobs, because the number of people qualified and willing to teach is limited in any country, regardless of its level of education. And creating a friendly specialized elite in a hostile foreign country—one of the major problems for the alien enemy (see Chapter IX, A-B, below)—is difficult and time-consuming. Reliable substitutes are hard to come by; never can an adequate number of them be mustered to replace more than a part of the former teachers.

Conscious of their importance and indispensability, teachers can continue opposition for many years, increasing the fortitude of the young generation. In Norway, the Nazis ruled five full years and were greatly plagued by the resistance of the teachers; yet they could not even begin replacing the patriotic educators.[18]

---

[18] Hoffmann and Mayr-Arnold, *op. cit.*, p. 140.

And in Lithuania, teachers guilty of "nationalist tendencies" and "ideological errors" are known to have held their jobs for more than fifteen years, under severe Russian rule.[19]

Every year, every month, the young spend in national schools learning from devoted teachers strengthens their determination. The older generations, including the teachers themselves, are often encouraged by the patriotism of the younger; thus one strand supports the other in a national struggle. Some of the most admirable episodes of defiance are always fought in a nation's schools and youth organizations.

The country-wide student strike of November, 1968, showed the strength of national resistance among the young Czechoslovaks and the importance of this strength in the political struggle. Soviet inability to control them became clear with their commander's empty threat to send Russian soldiers into Czech schools. The national discipline of the young people was exemplary throughout. The hero-martyr Jan Palach is a symbol of their defiance.

Families and groups of friends can help: these circles, safe from enemy penetration, can teach the young what teachers are not free to expound. Such an interwoven spiritual and diathetic opposition can be very effective.

Education of the young is only one phase of diathetics, albeit a very rewarding one. Similar opportunities for resistance will be found by a perceptive observer in every field of specialization.

The general task of diathetic defense is the education and information of the whole community. Predisposition of the people for national resistance is the daily responsibility of teachers and leaders. National education *is* national liberation. No small nation can afford to neglect it.

B. POLITICAL ATTACK

Pure defense is pure nonsense. A totally defensive national resistance would lead to certain failure. Offensive is the only

---

[19] K. V. Tauras, *Guerrilla Warfare on the Amber Coast* (New York: Voyages Press, 1962), p. 102.

road to victory. A contest in which one does not intend to counterattack should not be fought at all. "The final aim of a defensive action can never be an absolute negation," according to Clausewitz. "Even for the weakest there must be something whereby he can become a threat to his adversary, endanger him."[20]

Mao insisted repeatedly that guerrilla operations are incapable of producing a decision. "There can be no doubt," he wrote, "that our regular forces are alone capable of producing the decision," that without regular warfare one "could not defeat the enemy."[21] Mao is right to stress the need for offensive action, but to insist that offensive success can be gained only by regular forces is wrong. Small nations cannot accept his dicta.

Resistance has to divide, distract, confuse the enemy, and deprive his forces of initiative. Advances must encourage its own nation and weaken the morale of enemy leadership, troops, and home population. All these gains go with attack. But there is no need to seek them in regular battles. They can be achieved by political victories; indeed, they are political victories.

Political attack is the best offensive strategy—safer, less costly, more effective. Not only can a well-predisposed nation survive an attack; it can actively damage the enemy. Occupation brings enemy agents into close contact with the defenders. Psychologically and politically it "provides an opportunity of winning the second and maybe decisive battle, if the correct tactics are employed," asserted King-Hall.[22] Resistance must use all means to reverse the balance in favor of the defending nation.

Since all conflicts are interactions of opposing forces, the alien can maintain a one-sided superiority only so long as the resisting nation lets its political frailty go unexploited. He may use the defenders' military inferiority and overrun the country.

---

[20] Carl von Clausewitz, *Vom Kriege* (17th Ed.; Bonn: F. Dümmler's Verlag, 1952), Bk. VIII, Ch. 8.

[21] Mao Tse-tung, *Guerrilla Warfare* (London: Cassell, 1962), pp. 32, 41; *On Protracted War*, p. 110.

[22] Stephen King-Hall, *Power Politics in the Nuclear Age* (London: V. Gollancz, 1962), p. 204.

To equal the score, the defenders must hit his political defects hard. Mayor Ernst Reuther of Berlin explained: "You must make the most of the other side's weakness, for their weakness is an essential element of your own strength."[23]

The strongest have vulnerabilities that can be successfully attacked. A Red Chinese general stressed this, commenting on Vietnam in 1965: "What is there for the United States to brag about when this reputed number-one world power, possessing innumerable nuclear missiles, is being battered out of its senses, is fleeing helter-skelter and cannot even protect its own embassy!"[24] No one is immune against blows that seek out a weakness.

Political attack wrests the initiative from the intruder and neutralizes his military superiority. As a result, the chances of frustrating, even defeating, him increase. Where defenders hit his permanent and exclusive infirmities, they are practically immune from retaliation in kind. A small nation has no suppressed peoples under its rule, no citizens exposed in a hostile foreign country; it is politically less vulnerable. Without a corresponding failing of one's own, the advantages can be pressed aggressively without the danger that they may backfire.

Any steps the invader takes in response to political attacks remain defensive in character. For the resisters, the lesson is clear: if their danger is the same, then to attack is the stronger strategy.

Political attack is the only offensive action favoring a small nation unable to afford military offensive. On the battlefield it can never seriously threaten a stronger aggressor; it cannot even dream of invading his home country. Politically, all this can be done.

Diathetic preparation and defense seek to maintain and raise the nation's own strength; political attack seeks to weaken the power of the enemy. But they overlap with, and affect, each other directly as well as indirectly. Often they are indistinguishable, save for analytical purposes. Political thrusts provide the

---

[23] Quoted in *Reader's Digest*, October, 1958, 36.
[24] *New York Times*, May 11, 1965.

offensive means for a small nation against all kinds of aggression by a great power.

Political attacks offer a wide range of opportunities for aggressive action. They strike at eight kinds of targets in three different arenas. In the first arena, the defending country, the targets are (1) the enemy's political forces, (2) collaborators, (3) opportunists, (4) the enemy's technical (military, economic, etc.) personnel, and (5) his political-control apparatus. In the second, the enemy's own country, the available targets are (6) the subject peoples and (7) disaffected groups. In the third, the international arena, the attack hits (8) the aggressor's prestige and his good will.

1. In the Defending Country

Political attack strikes here at the means and the end of conquest: the occupier's servants and apparatus as well as the control itself. Various techniques—violent, non-violent, mixed—are available. The type of the objective, not the technique used, determines the political nature of operations. Whatever means promise the best results should be used.

Enemy personnel fall into two main categories of experts: violence experts and political experts. From the opposite point of view, the two groups can be seen as lacking expertise: the former non-expert in political matters; the latter in violence. Being inexpert, they are more sensitive against weapons they do not know. The logical principle is to hit the violence experts politically and the political experts with violence. Brains are more vulnerable against physical blows; fists and muscles cannot oppose psychological pressure. The enemy must be hit where he is most sensitive.

(1)The *enemy political forces* are relatively immune against psychological attacks, but sensitive to violence. Being the most dangerous of all occupation personnel, they are to be considered a permissible target at all times and are attacked by every means.

The enemy cannot adequately protect his political agents against attacks because their main value, except for the top policy planners, is the ability to stay close to the local population, to supervise and direct. If danger of elimination forces the enemy to keep them in compounds guarded by troops and police, the contact is interrupted and their effectiveness sharply reduced. Violence against them succeeds if it achieves nothing more than this result.

A good example of political attack comes from Irish resistance. On November 21, 1920, a special squad of I.R.A. commandos killed fourteen British agents. The Secret Service never fully recovered from this numerically insignificant blow. This raid was more than a military attack: "England could replace every soldier she lost," an Irish leader explained. "Without her spies England was helpless. Without their police and their agents, how could they find the men they wanted? How could they carry out that 'removal' of our leaders that they considered essential for their victory?" Spies were not as willing to step forward to replace the departed ones as were soldiers. And they were not as able: they could not recover the old man's knowledge. The Irish strike at individual secret agents shook the morale of the entire service.[25]

Political experts are more important in resistance struggles than key officers are in regular war, since the expertise of the latter is easier duplicated. The liquidation of a dozen key experts or secret agents, or twenty to thirty administrators, can shake enemy control badly.

(2) *Collaborators* perform vital services for the enemy. They can do great harm to the resisting nation, a harm more serious than any caused by foreign agents unable to reach what is accessible to renegades. Dealing with them is a major problem of political attack.

A preventive anti-collaborator policy is one of the outstanding features in George Kennan's recommendation for small-nation defense. His plan is to enable the country to tell the aggressor: "You will have a small profit from [overrunning us]; we are in a position to assure that not a single person likely to perform your

---

[25] Quoted in Sean O'Callahan, *The Easter Lily: The Story of the I.R.A.* (London: Allan Wingate, 1956), pp. 42, 48.

political business will be available to you. . . . You will find here no adequate nucleus for a puppet regime."[26] A defender who can say this holds an impenetrable political position. The unexpected inability of the Russians to find a collaborator to step forward and welcome them was a strengthening factor of Czech resistance in 1968. Other nations have to strengthen themselves by attacking the traitors.

Collaborators have close ties with the community; they attack national solidarity and cohesion when they side with the enemy. But their ties to the nation can be used to exert the opposite pull—to split their own loyalties. Except at the very top, these quislings are vulnerable to dissillusionment, to the pull of nationalism, to public pressures and social boycotts against them and their famiiles, as well as to individual persuasion.

In political combat the desertion of an opponent is a greater success than his death. A citizen turned traitor is a heavier blow to the nation than a citizen killed. And it is a better policy to cause a collaborator's return to the national side than to eliminate him. Force should be used with discretion. The aim of violence should be to create a deterrent moderating apprehension among the renegades, to give the threats credibility, rather than to kill great numbers. "The advance guard must always be hit again! This spreads the realization that those in front places almost invariably get killed, and they refuse to occupy the advance positions," advised Guevara.[27] Only the ruthless and dangerous should be attacked. Others are usually spared. (Local-level collaborators—the most dangerous—are discussed in Chapter IX, B 3, below.)

The goal is a political weakening of the occupation regime, not mass destruction. Violence is not used like a military weapon but like a surgical instrument directed against the sensitive points of enemy control. Political back-stabbing must be an art, even when real daggers are used.

(3) The *opportunists*, both enemy nationals and turncoats,

---

[26] George Kennan, *Russia, the Atom and the West* (New York: Harper, 1958), p. 64.

[27] Ernesto Che Guevara, "La Guerra de Guerrillas," *Modern Guerrilla Warfare*, 353.

can become sufficiently unpleasant to warrant counteraction. Citizens of the defending nation are treated like collaborators— according to their merits. Enemy citizens may follow invasion troops as colonizers or as outright scavengers. The opportunists must be shown that there is no real opportunity, that they risk more than they can loot.

(4) *Enemy technical personnel* include various specialists and their dependents: military units; supervisors of production, communications, transportation, exploitation; and consultants in many fields. They may be poisoned by political attacks, usually the best way of dealing with them. Soldiers and others should be persuaded, confused, and demoralized. Only if the invader is not expected to find adequate replacements are key experts to be eliminated.

Among enemy personnel are some especially vulnerable people—members of undigested minorities or of dissatisfied groups. The more there are, the better the opportunity for resistance to find, befriend, and influence them. A Welsh nationalist, imprisoned for refusing military service in Britain, defined the feeling of such men: "I didn't want to do the imperialists' dirty work and keep down nationalism in other places."[28] Citizens of a less-lenient empire may have elected to serve without open protest, but they remain an unreliable tool in oppressing other nations. Their sentiment must always be cultivated and exploited in political warfare.

Every diathetic technique—news, rumors, ridicule, ideological manipulation—can be used against enemy personnel. The stricter his censorship, the greater the impact of otherwise inaccessible news and information supplied to his men in any form. Goebbels knew that "news policy is a weapon of war." He was incensed to find "defeated and conquered nations create difficulties for us with news."[29] Aggressors peddling ideologies and indoctrinating their own citizens make them vulnerable against criticism of the official dogmas: their weaknesses, their clash with reality,

---

[28] *New York Times,* April 5, 1964.
[29] Louis P. Lochner (ed.), *The Goebbels Diaries, 1942–1943* (New York: Doubleday and Company, Inc., 1948), pp. 39, 210.

or their incompatibility with the oppression of other peoples. Ideological attacks involve no danger whatever to resistance, yet they absorb a lot of the enemy's energies. Adroitly handled, they may have an explosive effect.

Both propaganda and violence have been successful in the past, breaking the effectiveness and morale of enemy personnel. Hitler's administrators in Russia were hit by violence. The cautious Stalin saw how vulnerable his subjects were abroad and sent returned prisoners of war to special camps for extensive ideological quarantine and purification. His foresight was indirectly justified later: Russian troops, stationed for longer periods in Germany and Hungary, had unreliable soldiers when the time came to suppress revolts there. American soldiers had to undergo a political decontamination process on returning from Korean and Chinese captivity.

The demoralization of Russian soldiers through political attacks was one of the outstanding features of the invasion of Czechoslovakia. From the very beginning of the invasion, the soldiers were ordered not to talk with the people; but this rule could not be enforced. They had expected to be received as liberators and found themselves in the role of oppressors. The united resistance and hostility of the whole Czech people came as a shock for many of the young men in uniform. Even the morale of the newly arrived replacements was undermined in a couple of days in Prague.

TASS admitted that the situation for the soldiers was "difficult" due to the "anti-revolutionary" popular influence and the lack of food. The call for increased indoctrination indicated the ideological vulnerability of troops exposed to political attack. Some Soviet officers were awarded the Order of the Red Star and the Order for Battle Merit simply for preventing soldiers from talking with the civilians.[30]

One correspondent described the political attacks as "so perfect that they break down very fast all who are not pure barbarians."[31] And the Russians have quite a few people of this

---

[30] *The New York Times*, Aug. 26, 1968; *Czech Black Book*, pp. 88–90.
[31] *Expressen* (Stockholm), Aug. 26, 1968.

kind. They were helpless against questions (Why did you come? Who called you? Where is the counterrevolution?), against Russian-language broadcasts of the free radio, against hostility, against refusals to provide food and water, against leaflets, against the daily demonstrations that could not be stopped even by firing guns close over the heads of the demonstrators. In a Slovak town a citizen asked a bewildered Russian noncommissioned officer: "What happened? Did your leaders lose their mind?" "Seems so . . ." replied the Russian, shrugging.

Scores of the invader's officers spent whole nights removing the most dangerous posters and slogans; as day came, even more daring ones were back on walls and fences. Their impact on the tired, confused, and badly supplied troops could not help being powerful. Trigger-happy behavior, suicides, and other breakdowns are amply documented.

The fear that the soldiers had in their eyes was a peculiar kind. The fear of a man who is holding a submachine gun in his hand and who is backed by almost a million of his fellow soldiers, tanks, and aircraft, who is a member of the largest force in the world, armed to the teeth—this type of fear is really shattering. These soldiers are actually helpless.[32]

(5) Enemy control can be attacked directly and indirectly. Direct attacks weaken or break it by destroying the *control apparatus and enemy agents*. Indirect attacks increase opposition and ungovernability by lowering the morale of enemy agents and raising the spirit of the defenders, or by cultivating the habit of disobedience. All of the attacks hurt the effectiveness of control. Examples from the past show that most possibilities have gone unexploited. But increased resistance consciousness will let the defenders discover new ways to attack enemy rule.

Liberation of political prisoners, exposure of especially ruthless collaborators, publication of data and names connected with secret supervisory networks—their members and activities—be-

---

[32] Resistance newspaper on Aug. 27, 1968; quoted in *The Czech Black Book*, p. 239.

long to tested means of political attack. The revelations of de-
fected secret police Colonel Swiatlo were a telling blow to the
Stalinists in Poland.[33] Revelations about Stalinist practices in
Czechoslovakia to a considerable extent accelerated the liberalization in 1968. When the public received information about the
arrest campaign, during the invasion, the arrests were already
doomed to fail. News that one of the arrested national leaders
had escaped electrified the country; the message "Cisar is free!"
appeared on the walls as a motto of defiance.

Perhaps the most important of all offensive actions is the
cultivation of disobedience. Related to a defensive ignoring of
the enemy and to rejection of his claims to legitimacy, this
weapon breaks down obedience even where enemy control is
established. It can best be based on cultural or economic opposition.

German regulations of prices and sales in the Russian territories they occupied from 1941 to 1944 were uniformly disregarded by the local people and collapsed miserably. The occupation authorities desperately tried to uphold economic control.
"But it was futile to expect complete compliance," wrote a
scholar explaining their failure. "Fines were levied, but black
market operations and black market prices had to be tolerated."
After a while "Berlin yielded on this issue because the phenomenon could not be remedied."[34] In the end, the Germans saw
the futility of trying to stop economic disobedience. In occupied
Poland, in 1943, a German observer found speculation flourish-
ing—"this seemingly unavoidable phenomenon" having corrupted
also the Nazi Party and the Wehrmacht people stationed there.[35]

The connection between economic and strictly political disobedience is so close and logical that failure to recognize and

---

[33] Flora Lewis, *A Case History of Hope: The Story of Poland's Peaceful Revolutions* (Garden City, N.Y.: Doubleday & Co., 1958), pp. 34–36.
[34] Alexander Dallin, *German Rule in Russia, 1941–1945* (London:
Macmillan and Co., 1957), pp. 395, 404.
[35] Hermann Teske, *Die silbernen Spiegel* (Heidelberg: Vowinckel Verlag, 1952), p. 168.

exploit it comes as a real surprise. Economic deprivations have always been politically dangerous to the invaders, while political dispossession tends to be accepted more or less passively. The German Propaganda Minister feared the political effects of food shortages in the East—shortages of potatoes, tobacco, alcohol, and beauty salons in Germany.[36] It is strange that he did not have to worry about the possible effects of a serious lack of liberty. And while the Russians have suppressed political opposition among their subjects, they have repeatedly failed against economic defiance, despite energetic measures (including the death penalty).

Successful speculation and black-marketeering show that a determined, widespread, non-violent resistance cannot be suppressed, that it can continue under any conditions. Why does political oppression prevail where economic oppression fails? Are the lovers of profit truly that much more clever and courageous than the lovers of freedom?

The answer is that political resistance could be just as successful if it used the same strategy and tactics as the speculators: a widespread, determined, non-violent disobedience. The patriots' mistake was to get themselves massacred in quasi-military fighting. After all, the black-marketeers would never have come out on top if they had openly fought against invasion armies, police forces, and teams of economic supervisors!

The patriots did not understand how economic resistance and political resistance fit into the same pattern—that enemy political control is more difficult to establish and maintain than economic control. Illegal moonshine liquor in people's pockets and suitcases is certainly more easily detected and confiscated than the spirit of freedom in their minds. Political resistance breaks down political control just as economic resistance breaks down economic control; the right kind of disobedience is successful and practically irrepressible, whether the nation is deprived of economic goods or of freedom and liberty.

The triumphs of economic resistance under the strictest invaders, and its indestructibility, teach how, *mutatis mutandis,*

---

[36] *The Goebbels Diaries*, pp. 93, 120.

political disobedience can prevail equally well. Resistance is resistance. The two kinds reinforce each other: they combine to foster a general habit of disobedience, break down enemy control, and create ungovernability. "Transgression," said Aristotle, "creeps in unperceived and in the end ruins the state." Political attacks, correctly used, can make future invasion and suppression of nations as much a political liability as are shortages of ladies' stockings, jazz records, and alcohol.

2. *In the Invading Empire*

Political attack should not be limited to the invaded areas but be carried into the aggressor's own empire. Vulnerable spots in his subject areas and in the Motherland itself can be hit with impact.

(6) *Peoples subjugated by the invader* are a promising target. Diversionary political attacks, launched into areas inhabited by the oppressed peoples, create a serious threat. Such thrusts have a maximal impact where historical, national, or emotional bonds tie the resisting nation to the subdued one. The impact of the Polish events on Hungary in October, 1956, was magnified by the historical affinity between the Poles and the Hungarians. The Romanians are traditional friends of the Yugoslavs; they are striving for independence from Moscow in a similar way. "Your cause is our cause!" is a potent rallying cry is such cases.

Hardly ever is invasion a first offense; it is usually committed by a state belonging to the habitual international criminals. "A state may be unjust and may be unjustly attempting to enslave other states, or may have already enslaved them, and may be holding many of them in subjugation," submitted Socrates long ago. "True," even Thrasymachus agreed, "and I will add that the most perfectly unjust state will be most likely to do so."[37] There are sure to be vulnerable subject areas within the borders of every invader. Political attacks in them can upset his digestion.

Such attacks can include practically everything—even a mere

---

[37] Plato, *Republic,* i. 351.

example that basic changes are possible, that there are alternatives available within the limits of the existing system: "More important than direct borrowing of institutions was the infection of Eastern Europe with the spirit prevailing in Yugoslavia," according to J. C. Campbell, "where the freedom of inquiry and experimentation was greater than in any other country ruled by a Communist regime."[38] The subdued people are usually eager to resist—like the Norwegians in the northern part of the country, during World War II. The great majority of them "would have gladly done it if they had had any weapons and any instructions how to set about it. Once the training was started, it would grow like a snowball."[39]

It is no secret that the Czechoslovak liberation had an impact on other subject areas of the Soviet Empire, and that the potential results of this impact were high on the list of Kremlin fears. Among the Politbureau members pushing most strongly for the invasion of the C.S.S.R. were the rulers of the Ukraine (Shelest) and Latvia (Pelshe). Gomulka and Ulbricht, frightened of an infection with liberal tendencies in their assigned regions, demanded the suppression. At the beginning of 1969, the Russians were still extremely fearful that continued Czech resistance might inspire a liberal revolt in the satellite countries. Yugoslavia and Romania, apprehensive of a possible Russian attack, identified themselves openly with the struggle of the Czechs and the Slovaks for freedom; the Romanian chief of state actually used the expression "Your cause is our cause." It would be a serious mistake for the defender not to use the opportunity to land a counterpunch in such sensitive areas of the aggressor's empire.

(7) *Dissatisfied groups* among the enemy's own people are vulnerable, especially if the attacks aim at the regime in power and not against the nation itself.

With the National Socialists rather safely installed in Ger-

---

[38] J. C. Campbell, *Tito's Separate Road* (New York: Harper & Row, 1967), p. 106.

[39] D. Howarth, *We Die Alone* (New York: Macmillan, 1955), p. 5.

many, it is interesting to learn how sensitive its top expert of public opinion had been to the sporadic and clumsy Allied attempts at assailing Nazi rule: "I sense a certain danger in the tendencies [to split the people from the regime]. The less we talk about them, the less easily will political germs become virulent."[40] The Soviets, equally concerned, are reported to have used up to 2,000 interference transmitters to drown out "hot" news items broadcast by only 52 of the senders of the "Voice of America."[41] Even in countries with free reporting, governments suppress certain unfavorable information. Disclosure of such facts can create doubt, uncertainty, conflicts of conscience, defeatism. One example is how reports about oppressive pacification measures in Indochina and Algeria affected the French. A concerted political attack against American policy in Vietnam is in progress in the United States. It is likely to defeat the American efforts there. Lin Piao said hopefully: "Everything is divisible. And so is this colossus of U.S. imperialism. It can be split up and defeated."[42]

Simultaneously with the Czechoslovak liberalization, strong sentiments for a more humane regime were heard in Russia itself. There were expressions of sympathy for the C.S.S.R. and of protest against the invasion. The series of events related to the Czech opposition may not yet be over in the Soviet sphere of domination.

Political attacks can disturb many a regime. Under certain conditions, sabotage campaigns in the mother country of the empire could score a political success.[43]

3. In the International Arena

(8) World opinion, although a secondary factor, is gaining

---

[40] *The Goebbels Diaries*, p. 227.

[41] King-Hall, *Power Politics*, p. 96.

[42] *Lin Piao, Long Live the Victory of People's War!* (Peking: Foreign Languages Press, 1965), p. 56.

[43] O'Callahan, *op. cit.*, pp. 150–57, reviews the I.R.A. sabotage campaign in England in 1939–40. See also the much more ambitious "S-Plan" *ibid.*, pp. 202 ff.

significance. It has affected the outcome of conflicts before. Whatever strategy a defending nation decides to use, it cannot afford to forego the easy and inexpensive appeals to world opinion. Attacks on the aggressor's *good will and prestige* abroad must be prepared in advance. They become increasingly effective as a small nation continues to defend itself with determination. Nothing succeeds like success. And nothing resists like resistance. Nothing evokes more outside support for the political defense of a small nation than a prolonged resistance itself.

The Czechs launched a massive appeal to world opinion from the first day of the invasion; they had, as a matter of fact, secured for their liberalization much support even before. During the initial period of the resistance the Czechoslovaks appealed to practically every significant component of the publics in the West, the neutral countries, even the Communist states. World response to their appeals was overwhelmingly favorable.

Especially effective can be appeals for support of the publics that the imperialist is eager to impress. At the critical time in the C.S.S.R. they were the neutral Communist countries, the Communist Parties in the West, the non-aligned states, and the new administration in the United States. The extremely sharp condemnation of the aggression by these outsiders was an unpleasant surprise to the Russians. There is reason to assume that the negative reaction of world opinion and of the crucial public was extensively discussed in the Kremlin.[44]

The sympathies of the world, in turn, strengthened the morale of the resistance. The citizens of Prague made a point to stop at the statue of St. Vencelas and read the expressions of support that foreign tourists had left with a few flowers in front of what has become a national shrine. The backing from beyond the borders was a matter of considerable pride. "We have lost five allies," read a notice in Prague, "but the whole world is with us."

The events in the C.S.S.R. have shown that the defending country must keep up a steady flow of information to the outside

---

[44] *Dagens Nyheter*, Sept. 3, 1968.

world in order to mobilize its support. In this respect, the Czechs excelled everything seen before. Every day authentic telex, radio, and television news poured out of the invaded country. Even impressive film reports were made on the spot during the struggle. And the work of foreign correspondents in Czechoslovakia was facilitated in every way by the people. The total impact of this information campaign was impressive. The invader's efforts to disorient the world and to distort the facts failed miserably.

One must agree with King-Hall that "political warfare activities are extremely important, perhaps the most important part of our defense arrangements."[45] A failure to exploit political attacks as a deterrent against enemy aggression and as a weapon to be used against his weaknesses would be inexcusable. Political attacks can be launched with little or no risk against many targets. And the superpowers are by no means immune to thrusts against their political weaknesses. These weaknesses are definitely an essential element of a defending small nation's strength.

------

[45] Stephen King-Hall, *Defence in the Nuclear Age* (London: V. Gollancz, 1958), p. 129.

CHAPTER VIII

Ubiquitous Defense

One of the great contributions of the first phase of Czechoslovak resistance to small-nation defense is to have advanced
strategic thinking beyond the restrictive limits placed on it by
people who see resistance as nothing more than an auxiliary
technique of military struggles. Another is the clear proof that
this kind of political defense can succeed.

National resistance is an extended conflict. It is political, and
like politics, it concerns everything in the life of a modern community. Such a resistance must span *all* political elements and
defend *every* political position.

This strategy of small nations derives strength both from its
defensive nature and from its ubiquity. The complication and
extension of the conflict favor the people opposing an alien
enemy. The invader's power weakens as the resistance multiplies
and finally surpasses his ability to control the country. In the
places, at the times, on the levels of resistance that remain free
of alien influence, resistance rules.

The ideal political defense of small nations in unequal conflicts would be all-inclusive. While the ideal can never be
achieved, patriots can take various strategic and tactical steps
to approach it as closely as possible.

A. THE ADVANTAGES OF STRATEGIC DEFENSE

If we think of defense as it should be, it is one with the best
possible preparation of all means; with a capable army; with a
general who awaits the enemy not in a confused and fearful
uncertainty, but by choice, with calm deliberation; with fortresses
that do not fear a siege; finally with a healthy nation which does
not fear its enemy more than it is feared by him. A defense with

such attributes will surely not play the wretched role against an attack, and the latter will not seem so easy and infallible as in the gloomy imagination of those who equate attack only with courage, strength of will, and activity; defense with impotence and paralysis.[1]

Clausewitz wrote this in the first half of the nineteenth century. If we think of political fortresses, not military, the description fits small-nation defense as it should be in the second half of the twentieth century.

The idea that defense was more difficult, wrote Bülow, was based on wrong strategy. "Defense becomes easy," he insisted, "when the attacker operates beyond his own borders." Clausewitz agreed that a defensive strategy "gives the defender a general superiority," and that it never favors the invader on hostile territory. He clearly distinguished between the offensive and the defensive, stressing that "for defensive wars even the means of small states are infinitely great." The Swede Victor Rydberg perceived the basic difference, referring to Switzerland as a "great power defensively." They based their conclusions primarily on the political advantages of defending their country with the help of the people. Both the Germans and the Allies had great respect for Swiss defense during the Second World War.[2]

In political resistance the advantages of defense are even greater than in warfare. The defenders, supported by the sympathies of the nation, can force the invader to fight for every political position; they can choose to hold what they can hold best. The invader, however, must take and hold all positions: he needs them all as means of enforcing political control. A failure at any point blocks his advance. Even having lost their army, government, administrative machinery, political parties, national and provincial organizations, the defenders are not yet subdued. From local power positions they can still have *de facto* control

---

[1] Carl von Clausewitz, *Vom Kriege* (17th ed.; Bonn: F. Dümmler's Verlag, 1952), Bk. VI, Ch. 5.

[2] Hans Rudolf Kurz, *Die Schweiz in der Planung der kriegführenden Mächte während des zweiten Weltkrieges* (Biel: Schweizerischer Unteroffiziersverband, 1957), describes the respect of the big powers on both sides.

of the country. The invader's failure to take over any one of them frustrates a conquest; all rival political foci can rally and lead opposition.

At the start of a conflict the small nation commands every political strong point in the country. They must be defended: as long as they are defended with ingenuity, the invasion falls short of its aim. Clausewitz reminded his readers that "war is more useful for the defender than for the conqueror. The conqueror is always a lover of peace; he would gladly enter our state quietly; to make this impossible for him we must want war and prepare for war." (*Vom Kriege*, VII, 5). Exactly—the invader's purposes are best served if he is not opposed. A defender's strength, therefore, grows with the extension of resistance.

Political strongholds, however, like natural obstacles or fortifications, are effective only if defended. The more is defended, the stronger is defense. To use all advantages, every position must be defended, on all levels. Nothing defensible must be lost by default.

Hitherto, political positions were conquered not because they were indefensible but because they were undefended. An invader could capture all political strongholds of a country by taking only the weakest, the central government. A single breakthrough would topple the entire defense structure. Most, and often the strongest, defensive positions were simply abandoned because of mistaken strategic thinking.

Now the aggressor must subdue them all, even the least accessible. The defended political positions now resemble a network of independent but mutually supporting strong points, all of which have to be overcome before a conquest is completed. No part is lost without a fight; no fight is lost until all are subdued.

Mere preliminary reverses do not decide anything. Informal groups and resistance positions on local levels are often stronger and can resist much longer than central or governmental organs. It does not matter how many reverses the defenders have suffered, how many leaders have perished: as long as the national will to resist survives nothing is irrevocably lost.

The strategic advantages increase when opposition extends—in time, dimension, and depth—to cover every power position in the community. Each defensive position can (1) stop, (2) divert, or (3) delay enemy efforts. The best ways to extend the status of indecision are (1) to defy the enemy at every point that he would like to take over quietly, (2) to take up alternative political positions—prepared in advance, if possible—when forced to abandon the initial ones, rather than give up resistance, and (3) to hold out, if only by passive defense, until active opposition can rise again.

Once a quick victory eludes the invader, time starts working for the defending nation. So do space and complexity. All of them are guardian saints of defense.

A resistance struggle requires more fighting, albeit political fighting, and perseverance than regular war. Resistance must defend everything and be everywhere. A defense truly national in extent would be invincible.

B. THE STRENGTH OF UBIQUITY

A fable tells how the seemingly impossible can be accomplished with a little strategy: It relates how a hare was defeated in a race with a turtle, who placed his brother at the other end of the line. No matter how fast the hare sprinted from one end to the other, when he arrived exhausted, there was always a turtle on the spot. And when he had to leave and race off, a turtle always remained behind.

The invader in an occupied country, just like the hare in the fable, keeps rushing around to create an appearance of control, while the defending nation is at all times present—everywhere! Correctly exploited, ubiquity of the defenders makes the invader's position untenable in the long run. Wherever his military or political forces arrive, the population is in charge; whenever they withdraw—for short or long, completely or partially—the people take over. The defenders regain control to the extent of enemy withdrawal. The omnipresent opposition, like a compressed spring, is held down only in proportion to enemy pressure; it is always ready to snap back. Where the enemy cannot control everything, sizable areas remain *free*. The spreading opposition can take them over uncontested. The people achieve all this by their mere presence—without fighting.

Clausewitz knew that an armed nation's resistance must be everywhere. Lawrence wrote that "dispersal was strength" for his irregulars: "Our virtue lay in depth, not in face. Consequently we must extend our front to its maximum." Ubiquity was the indispensable virtue of his strategy; his strength was "the widest dissipation of force in time and place." Modern political defense must always strive to be as widely present as possible.

As resistance extends, it reaches a point beyond which the invader loses hold of the situation. Wherever there is defiance, he must have a supervisor to keep control. The ideal defense would be to force him to supervise every Dane, Czech, or Pole —at least every two or three of them. No empire on earth could muster four, ten, or thirty million interpreters and controllers; political domination would have to break down. Admittedly resistance does not reach this extent. But no invader could manage to put up more than a small fraction of the required numbers. His capacity to supervise is quite narrowly circumscribed and not difficult to surpass. (The more than half a million U.S. troops in South Vietnam cannot even hope to supervise every town!) An extending opposition progressively strengthens defense and weakens the alien regime, rapidly approaching the point at which its control collapses altogether.

The defending side's strength is ubiquity: the invader's, his capacity for violence. The correct defensive strategy, therefore, is to make the conflict more extensive and less intensive—to seek the greatest dispersion, extension, and complication. Instead of a few large-scale outbreaks of slaughter, the defending nation must rely on many political operations, independent but concerted. An extensive and complex struggle makes violent clashes, and defeats, less likely. And indecision more permanent.

1. Complicated and Controlled Conflict

Ubiquitous resistance prevents enemy control by complicating the struggle. A complicated struggle offers wide choices of alternative courses of action. A controlled opposition can defy the enemy most effectively.

COMPLICATION.—Deliberate complication helps the opposition, and makes it more difficult for the invader to suppress, even to find, its various elements. Beyond a certain degree of complication, the struggle becomes so confused that defiance can no longer be checked. One of Bülow's basic ideas was the creation of disorder to split, dislocate, distract the attacking forces, to render him unable to cope with the multiplicity of opposition. Diversions and disorder were important strategic devices. And Lawrence said that "the Arabs beat the Turks by their uncertainty."

An invader profits most from simplification and centralization when trying to secure political control. Resistance relies on decentralization and complication of the contest. If the defending people's loyalty and cohesion cannot be split, a scattering of resistance only makes control more difficult. And where physical control fails, loyalty decides.

A loyal nation enhances its own strength when it complicates resistance. This makes the invader's problems practically endless. Opposition can spring from many sources and appear in many forms. A deliberately complicated opposition can become unmanageable and keep the enemy off balance. Where this succeeds, his military superiority is neutralized: the organization of disorder has been achieved.

The invader resembles a juggler who manipulates a certain number of objects. The wider their variety and the more complicated the circumstances, the more difficult it is to control them and the less likely he is to succeed.

CONTROL OF RESISTANCE.—Control and complication strengthen each other; they belong together. Complicated resistance opens new choices and widens the scope of opposition—it adds more strength. Controlled resistance permits the best choice of responses to enemy action. Control transforms raw strength into purposeful power and directs it against the appropriate target. Between the death of every patriot on the barricades or in the trenches and the willing obedience to the invader's orders, the defenders have a wide choice as to the intensity, extent, and manner of defiance. Adequate control and self-control let them exercise their options best.

Resistance itself is an alternative to regular war. It is neither a surrender nor a fight "to the bitter end." For national resistance, planning and doing something else must be an immutable rule: in strategy as well as in tactics, on all levels, in all phases of opposition. Only a flexible defense can neutralize the import of enemy pressure, evade his blows, and preserve the ability to fight on. As soon as the enemy brings unbearable pressure against one point, it must switch to something else. "The further we turn to the West," wrote Miksche, "the more cunning becomes the waging of clandestine war and the less we find force operating in the open."[3]

Ubiquitous resistance is selective, steadily shifting, and flexible. It rejects no alternative *a priori*. But since the invader's personnel are mostly expert in violence and the defenders' in political and technical matters, opposition naturally tends to move from the violent to the mixed and non-violent forms. If the military is seen as the lower level, the technical as the intermediate, and the political as the higher, then it can be said that the higher its level of resistance the more immune the defending nation is against violence, even against supervision. Defiance, therefore, shifts to the political and non-violent means with increasing enemy pressure, filters back to the technical and mixed forms as pressure eases. The struggle can always be shifted to grasp the defending nation's main advantage.

Choice reduces the need for forced or predictable moves that may be dangerous and wasteful if the enemy can plan his responses. Choice lessens reliance on open or violent resistance. Unorthodox, unpredictable defenders using what T. E. Lawrence called "a hodgepodge" of sundry strategic, technical, and tactical moves are apt to outmaneuver regular forces. The Turks in Arabia were not exceptionally stupid, nor were the Japanese in

---

[3] F. O. Miksche, *Secret Forces* (London: Faber and Faber, 1950), p. 86.

China, the Germans in Yugoslavia, the British on Cyprus, the French in Algeria, the Americans in Vietnam, or the Russians in Czechoslovakia. Unfortunately for all of them, their opponents saw the weaknesses of regular forces and picked a strategy against which regulars could not succeed.

Both nuclear power and the tremendous force dormant in a nation are best utilized not in a single burst of violence blowing everything to bits, but in a slow, sustained, controlled reaction. Successful resistance leaders have always preferred ubiquitous opposition, controlled in intensity. Lawrence refused to call a general uprising of the Arabs, despite pressures from many sides; and he was proved right. So was Mao, who advised his Chinese to rely on a protracted war: "Unlike the reckless gamblers, we do not advocate the theory of staking everything on a single throw of dice."[4]

A political struggle is best fought in disciplined silence and invisibly. Ostentation may lead to disaster. In quasi-military action, the best weapons are silent ones. In non-military struggles against a violent enemy, silence and invisibility protect from discovery and destruction, increase the chances of surprise, and multiply the psychological effect on the enemy. His morale is weakened, his countermoves are dislocated most, by unknown danger.

It is just as important to know when and how to fight as it is to know when and how not to fight. Control reduces losses. Defense often has to yield and let the invader through; but it should be ready to rise again and man its positions, as soon as the worst is over. Without control and self-discipline this is impossible.

A resistance controlled in intensity and manner can enjoy many advantages, escape disadvantages, and select optimum conditions for its operations. If a situation favors attack, it can attack; if defense is easier, it can defend. If the situation is bad, the fighters can disperse, to reassert themselves when things improve. Suspended for a day, a week, a year, resistance con-

---

[4] Mao Tse-tung, *On Protracted War* (Peking: Foreign Languages Press, 1954), p. 130.

tinues to hang over the invader like the sword of Damocles. Sufficient control to be able to rise again is the only requirement. Without being able to remain under conspiratory cover in the cities or in the countryside, opposition rarely could survive for long.

Why does a deliberate complication of the struggle confound an alien invader more than the defenders? How can patriots preserve the necessary minimum control of the situation if the alien cannot? The answer is (1) that nationalism provides a stable loyalty and cohesion, a reliable guide for the resisters, (2) that co-ordination among the patriots helps to orient them, and (3) that most opposition takes place on the local level. Local political resistance is autonomous: unlike a military organization, it needs no detailed, central lead. Reasonable self-control and co-ordination will usually do.

Can the needed control and self-control be achieved? The demands on the citizens are, admittedly, very high. A critic strongly doubted the practicability of national resistance because "it requires a higher collective discipline and fortitude than an army has achieved, but requires this to be attained by the nation as a whole."[5] A few years ago the Algerians showed unbelievable self-control during the final Secret Army campaign of terror, aimed especially at provoking uncontrolled retaliation. The provocation failed completely, demonstrating that the opposition could be successfully controlled.

The critic, Liddell Hart conceded that "members of a religious or political movement that is cohesive in spirit" may have the required self-control. I submit that a loyal and united small nation, facing an alien enemy, often resembles such a political organization, and is able to muster all the fortitude needed.

The Czechs and the Slovaks displayed unprecedented self-control. During the critical days of the invasion, even without a leadership, the resisters effectively controlled their opposition. Expectant collaborators were restrained. An informed population could not be inflamed by repeated provocations.

---

[5] B. H. Liddell Hart, *Deterrent or Defence* (London: Stevens and Sons, 1960), p. 221.

After the national leaders had returned from Moscow, Russian tanks and patrols were again moved into the center of Prague in a final attempt to provoke bloody fighting and institute a terror regime—despite everything, the control remained strong. Especially outstanding was the controlled opposition of the adolescents and young people.

The control of resistance was of such high order that practically no clashes took place, while opposition was going on without pause. Suggestions that street signs be changed were carried out within a few hours in most cities of the land. Throngs of determined patriots assembled for demonstrations and dispersed when called to do so by the news media and resistance people: time and again enemy attempts to get the defiance to solidify so that it could be smashed were frustrated by the controlled reactions of the population. And the strength of controlled resistance was excellently expressed in a street poster in Prague: "Composure, unity, and steady nerves are more formidable weapons than the barrels of guns!"

The required discipline and fortitude have been achieved before and can be achieved again. The new emphasis on political action, and the depreciation of military fighting, help make it possible. So do the wider range of available alternatives and the fact that in political defense patriots can resist within the fields they know best, where they see the limits of effectiveness and safety. It has been repeatedly observed how well people in invaded countries adjust to the exact amount of enemy pressure, how ably they control their reactions.

Will a particular defending nation be able to muster the needed fortitude, and control, at a particular time in the future? This cannot be safely predicted in advance. One would have to make at best an educated guess.

Sufficiently controlled resistance can withstand even the most determined adversary. Discipline breeds discipline: the successes of controlled action will inspire a calmer response in later emergencies. It may even enable the patriots to experiment with new resistance techniques.

The Czechs had enough cohesion and self-control to apply

the *relay effect* that increased the strength and endurance of their opposition. The idea in the relay is to pass around resistance tasks, not to give them up. When excessive enemy pressure is directed against one group of patriots, other groups pick up and continue to perform the same function. The relay effect (1) allows important activities to continue practically without interruption (as did the broadcast of the Free Czechoslovak Radio during the invasion), (2) makes it practically impossible for the enemy to know for sure which group is going to take over what function next (the Russians did not know which station would follow on the air), (3) enables the groups previously active to resume the functions at a favorable moment (after an interval the same stations were broadcasting again), and (4) enables them to perform a resistance function when each group is best able to do so (the one suffering least from enemy pressure, etc.). Political defense using the relay effect becomes extremely flexible.

The free radio began broadcasting from the third floor of Radio House in Prague while the invaders had occupied the first two floors. Discovered, they moved to another studio in Karlin. While Karlin was being searched by the Russians, the Czechs were broadcasting from one of their army camps. But soon after the search they returned to Karlin and worked from the studio which—so the Russians had persuaded themselves—had been abandoned.[6] On the third day of the invasion, the free stations started a country-wide relay broadcasting, one station signing off as another came on the air.

Broadcasting was the most apparent but not the only resistance function using the relay effect in the C.S.S.R. Numerous other tasks passed like the baton of a relay race: As top leaders of Parliament, Government, and the Communist Party were arrested, new patriotic leaders stepped forward. As the offices of many Government and Party organizations, youth organizations, or news media were occupied, the same tasks were performed in emergency sites. Often local organs performed the

---

[6] Slava Volny, "The Saga of Czechoslovak Broadcasting," *East Europe*, No. 12 (1968), 10-15, *passim*.

work of central headquarters. During the winter of 1968–69, the baton of political leadership passed from the Government to the Party, from the Party to the President of the State, from the President to the workers' movement, from the workers to youth and student organizations, from the youth groups to Parliament —back and forth in an endlessly complicated relay. The resulting confusion frustrated the invader repeatedly.

The occupier was even more baffled, and resistance more strengthened, as the Czechoslovaks began to use the relay effect to pass the functions of resistance to different levels, groups, and organizations, beginning in September, 1968. When the Russians demanded censorship of the newspapers, newsreels expressed the feelings of defiance; when Moscow accused the newsreels, the theaters and humorous magazines steadily and quite strongly expressed the will to resist. When the threat of censorship became serious, leaflets appeared on the streets and chain letters explained the situation to citizens. Writers called protest strikes; unions informed the public. When the invaders accused right-wing elements of backing the resistance of Czech and Slovak workers, labor unions and Communist youth groups shouldered the main tasks. When the Russians condemned the opposition of Club 231 (former prisoners of Communism), the League of Anti-Fascist Fighters (former prisoners of Nazism) voiced defiance with the same vigor. At one time the multiple Olympic gold-medal winners Zatopek and Caslavska were in the center of attention: at others, the Academy of Sciences, the ice-hockey team, the organization of journalists, or young Jan Palach and others who chose death by fire in protest.

Resistance using the relay effect can avoid being pinned down and destroyed. And it can recoup lost political ground: when one focus of opposition becomes the target of concentrated enemy forces, his hold elsewhere eases; there, others can spring back into action. The Czechs gained considerable flexibility using this tactic between levels of defense, organizations, activities, etc. Other nations can strengthen their own political defense by using the relay: and by inventing new tactical variations.

Complicated resistance opens new choices and widens the

scope of defiance; adequately controlled resistance increases security and efficiency. Both add to the strength of extended opposition.

2. Extended Conflict

Political control is the sum total of a great number of particular controls, a mosaic of control fragments. To succeed, the invader must secure his own control. And he must eliminate national control from the picture to make his conquest safe. He can physically take and hold almost any point in the invaded country; he can also take over by force the top positions of administrative apparatus.

Yet despite his ability to seize practically anything, the aggressor can never take and hold everything. The shrewdest invader, like the most agile juggler, can manage only a limited number of objects. Once this number is exceeded, command over the objects collapses. An alien's capacity for supervision and control has definite limits.

The task of defense strategy is to find the limits and to extend resistance beyond them. If the aggressor can control a number of points or objects, then opposition extended to twice, five, or ten times that number—a task well within the ability of a ubiquitous population—reduces his influence to 50, 20, or 10 per cent of the contested total. A maximal extension would diminish it to a mere fraction of the active resistance fragments, perhaps near the "one thousandth" of Arab territory Lawrence said the Turks were welcome to hold "until Doomsday." As extension progresses, what the invader holds falls well below the minimum required to keep up as much as a semblance of effective rule.

Lawrence called this "the mathematical advantage." While the Arabs were concentrated things went rather badly for them. "Once they began to stretch out, the scales turned the other way," explained Liddell Hart. "And the more they became separated the worse had become their enemy's plight."[7] An

---

[7] B. H. Liddell Hart, *T. E. Lawrence in Arabia and After* (London: Jonathan Cape, 1934), pp. 171–72.

infantryman and a nuclear strategist know the value of dispersal as a defensive means. Extension serves a similar purpose in political struggles.

A defending nation multiplies its strength as it extends its opposition. Widespread opposition denies the aggressor a final victory that averts defeat by one blow, or by a few blows. At most points of a well-extended struggle the invader is absent, and defense, therefore, successful. Where the invader concentrates, he achieves some success. But while concentrated at one point, he is weak at others where opposition can immediately reassert itself. Resistance thus seeks victory through the cumulative effect of its numerous actions. No action is decisive standing alone, but together they can foil the invaders.

MULTIPLICATION.—The simplest method to extend is to increase the number of resistance points, to divide the available forces into more units. Multiplied defiance splits enemy efforts, hampers his supervision and control.

In military defense 150 units of 100 men each are harder to subdue than five units of 3,000 or one unit of 15,000 men. With luck the invader may destroy the large unit in a single action. The small units require at least 150 attacks. Staff work, intelligence, preparation, co-ordination, and the element of chance complicate attempts to eliminate the greater number.

In political opposition, multiplication is even stronger. Resisting composite organizations (labor unions, Boy Scouts, Y.M.C.A.'s) can divide into independent units. They can divide geographically or simply split into smaller teams. When forming new opposition groups, the more the better. The same applies to activities: their number is often more important than the size or strength of any single effort. The Prague radio usually operates in one building; during the invasion it broke into many smaller groups and quickly set up new broadcast centers. The Russians could easily control one transmitter but not the many scattered units. Dividing the defenders increase their own strength, especially if their activities are coordinated.

Multiplication reduces the danger of supervision, infiltration, and destruction of the defense groups. Operating at many points, opposition exceeds the invader's capacity to control. It is a simple technique but a very effective one.

DIVERSIFICATION.—Diversification goes beyond multiplication. It pushes further the practically unlimited possibilities of extension, making opposition truly multifarious. The endless variety of social activities likely to sustain resistance can never be subdued.

Variety, the spice of life, is also the spice of opposition. Diversification can mix enough spice into defiance to upset the most hardened conqueror's digestion. The practical possibilities are unlimited. A national student organization, for example, can divide into local groups of its members inscribed in each institution, each faculty and department, each year of study; from each of the different home provinces; according to their various extracurricular hobbies and interests, etc. Every group can be a separate circle of resistance, acting autonomously. Members of labor unions, to give another instance, can vary their opposition into circles operating in locals, places of work, different jobs, and so forth. Labor and most other similar organizations can form separate groups of senior members, regulars, youth and women's auxiliaries, associated Boy Scout and Girl Scout patrols. Each of the groups can resist in a different way.

Diversification is a true "organization of disorder." It creates a sophisticated political resistance—wider, more secure, and longer-lasting. The resulting diffuse defiance robs the enemy of a solid target. Specialization of functions ensures efficiency and taps the nation's skills best, lets everyone contribute what he knows well and does gladly. All individuals and groups can participate: men and women, children, teen-agers, and the aged. Each fights in his own manner: rallying the people, maintaining discipline; informing the resisting nation and the outside world; misinforming the enemy, ignoring the invaders and refusing to co-operate with or help him in any way; distributing leaflets, painting slogans, carrying messages from one opposition group to another; or talking to enemy soldiers to break down their morale. Political defense is far broader than war; popular participation in it can be all-embracing.

An individual has a wide choice of resistance circles and activities. A member of a national organization may join at its headquarters, in a provincial and town group, or in an affiliated youth team. He may be employed in the administrative machinery of the government (or any other parallel apparatus of control) and be able to counter the invader's designs at his place of work. Or he may join a local commando, a philatelic club, a bowling team, a group of a few anglers, a circle of close relatives. He may not be active in any one of them, or he may be in more than one. Who is going to unravel this maze of possibilities?

Diversification aggravates the enemy's problems of detection, supervision, and elimination. To suppress military resistance the invader needs only military specialists, and he has them in unlimited numbers. Against well-diversified national opposition, he needs a number and variety of experts hardly possible to recruit. But where expert supervisors are not available, control remains ineffective. One example is the use of the national language: every enemy agent must either understand it himself or have it translated. Translation itself is a formidable task if the defenders do not help. But the defenders can diversify the difficulties of the enemy translators by using many dialects (people who know High German cannot understand Swiss German), jargons, and terms of reference known only to certain professions, different generations, to people specialized in national literature, history, mythology, to families or groups of friends, and so on. The possibilities are endless.

Multiplication increases the foci of resistance. Diversification adds new ways of doing things, making defiance diffuse as well as multifarious. Combined, they produce opposition so varied that to control all but a minor part of it is out of the question.

But the patriots should not stop with a defensive extension of resistance. They should push on beyond the limits of enemy supervision to where the recoil sets in. The further they extend defiance beyond the invader's grasp, the more offensive defiance becomes. In the end it may break down enemy influence altogether.

LOCALIZATION.—Localization too can be used both defensively

and offensively. It can (*a*) either keep out enemy influence, or (*b*) revive resistance in some parts of an area generally controlled by the alien invader. Local resistance is strongest—attacking or defending—because it is closest to the people. Compatriots in daily contact are the most cohesive and can maintain the best security. The smaller localities are easier to defend and recapture because the people's strength is tapped directly.

Localization cuts the invader's contacts with a certain place and eliminates his agents there. An invader, like any unpopular ruler, depends on centralized supervision and enforcement to obtain control. But unlike the indigenous despot, he lacks the political specialists to man local machines, to supervise, to direct violence. Like the cyclops Polyphemus, he has only one eye—his collaborators on the spot. Either when his arms of violence cannot reach a locality, or when he is blinded by the loss of his collaborators there, the invader's control fails.

Keeping out his forces or knocking out his agents can be called localization. Without the informers, violence remains aimless and useless. The ability to distinguish targets and to direct violence against them is as essential as the capacity to terrorize. Knocked out through localization, both must be restored—a long and difficult process—before alien control can be effective again.

Localization smashes the Government machinery the invader has built; it cuts his chain of control. It cleans the air of fear and suspicion, restores the patriots' morale and mutual contacts. The people can again freeze out the returning enemy. On retaking a localized place, he has to start from scratch. He has lost his agents and informers, and the records and facilities destroyed by resistance. To infiltrate a second set of agents into a place, where people know or can observe everyone present, is just as hard as before. Where the patriots have learned from previous experience, it is even harder. Agents cannot be kept out physically, but if they are known, their utility is lost. The eye of Polyphemus grows back very slowly, just as slowly do the tentacles of enemy control revive after localization.

Localization does not have to be permanent or even semipermanent. Its tangible and intangible effects are lasting. The national leadership will utilize even short periods of localization when the defenders on the spot have the upper hand. A few days —as little as two days annually—should be enough to recharge opposition and to frustrate enemy domination forever. A mere threat of localization may strain enemy resources and reduce the impact of his regime. Two days annually will indeed suffice in most cases in which the people's will to resist is strong. An alien invader's effort of 180 days can thus be undone in a single day by resistance supported by the nation; in such situations one could safely say that national resistance is, at least statistically, a hundred times stronger than the enemy!

Localization is a far cry from military reconquest and much easier to bring about: (*a*)a co-ordinated coup against the invader's communications may do it; (*b*) political resistance may be so strong in a town or district that the control of the regime lapses; (*c*) enemy forces may be withdrawn, creating *de facto* localization; (*d*) natural phenomena, such as blizzards, floods, fog, heavy rainfall, often sever all communications, practically insulating a place against enemy action and supervision for a time. The Danube floods in June 1965, isolated a town in Slovakia, forcing the inhabitants to seek refuge in Hungary. Elsewhere, Hungarians had to flee to Yugoslavia. In many similar cases, isolation, although less than complete, can be easily completed by selective sabotage. The results are the same.

Effective supervision and control are difficult to achieve, even in one's own country. Western countries do not feel this difficulty because their governments are satisfied with fragmentary supervision. In Russia, at least 2,000,000 supervisors, divided into 350,000 groups and committees, are reported watching bureaucrats, managers, and workers in the administrative and technical fields.[8] Premier Khrushchev was, nevertheless, dissatisfied with the results and in a reform—later rescinded by his successors—assigned to the 10,000,000 members of the Communist Party the task of supervising agricultural and industrial

---

[8] *Dagens Nyheter*, March 25, 1963.

production. In addition, Russia of course has a few hundred thousands of police, secret police, and agents for political supervision. China is reported to have an even more extensive control system in all localities, enterprises, professions, and organizations. In Cuba, ten years after coming to power, the Castro regime has an estimated 2,000,000 Cubans watching the slightly more than 6,000,000 of their neighbors and each other.[9]

Such huge numbers of supervising agents are necessary—and do not succeed completely—within their own countries, governed by established regimes, where problems of supervision are certainly much easier to solve than amid a foreign, hostile nation. Extended resistance can easily spread beyond an invader's capacity to control.

3. A Network of Observers

Ubiquity gives the defending nation a great superiority in the struggle for information and intelligence. Lawrence explained his own near-perfect knowledge as a result of Arab ubiquity and friendship: "The civil population of the enemy area was wholly ours, without pay or persuasion. In consequence our intelligence service was the widest, fullest and most certain imaginable."[10] Danish resistance leader Muus achieved good results dividing the country into six regions with one wireless station each to communicate with London. His countryman, resistance scholar Haestrup, wrote that under German occupation "at least from 1944 hardly a gun could be moved, hardly a platoon change place or a ship leave harbour, without their knowing in London, if necessary by wireless telegraph."[11] The surprisingly good Vietminh intelligence on French and American dispositions and morale in Indochina has been amply docu-

---

[9] *New York Times,* Dec. 14, 1969.

[10] T. E. Lawrence, *Seven Pillars of Wisdom* (New York; Dell Publishing Co., 1962), p. 386.

[11] J. Haestrup, "Exposé" in Henri Michel (ed.), *European Resistance Movements, 1939–1945,* p. 157.

mented. It was more of a surprise to hear that even in the Congo the native tribes and the local administration had more complete information about the movements and activities of the United Nations' forces than their own G-2 branch. "When we did not know where one of our units was, or what it was doing, we would ask the Congolese—and they would tell us," declared Norwegian Colonel Ägge, the former chief of U.N. forces' intelligence in the Congo. "I still do not know how they did it, maybe with drums. . . ."

Any small nation can duplicate such feats on its own territory by establishing an observation net of people trained to watch the enemy, and providing good equipment to transmit the information fast and accurately. The observers should be at selected places, able to reconnoiter in darkness and in all kinds of weather. The network should cover the entire country, leaving the enemy no chance to escape detection.

For resistance, such a network provides *control by observation,* an indispensable condition of success. If the moves of enemy forces can be detected in time and charted, the defenders can deprive them of targets and make the intended blows miss the mark. The Vietcong have, obviously, achieved this hundreds of times! The system can easily be converted from war status to resistance status in an invaded territory. To avoid unnecessary difficulties in the main stage of clandestine resistance, it should be organized secretly and with an eye on resistance needs from the very beginning.

An observation net is easy to build before the conflict, in time of peace, on home territory. An aggressor will transplant the network to his own rear simply by invading the country. As soon as the enemy arrives, a ready-made intelligence organization goes into action. It can provide information both to local resistance and to the central leadership. Information supplied to the Soviet military leadership is said to be the main achievement of Russian partisans. "We have certainly underestimated the partisans' contributions who guided the Red Army to the weakest spots at the German front," analyzed Dixon and Heilbrunn. They estimated that "an occupying army cannot count for one minute on keeping major movements from its opponents" in areas where an observation net operates.[12]

Fighting "in the crowd" and the use of free areas will become more significant in the future. In the political community and in the free elements, the side with better intelligence will be able to beat its opponent. The greatest strength is to be informed; the badly informed are defeated by weaker adversaries. "Once one has an accurate knowledge of the adversary's strength and weakness," wrote Banse, "the victory is really his already, provided he keeps his head and does not flag in the struggle."[13] Many examples confirm the value of local radio-equipped observers, even if they are only partially effective.

The ubiquitous population is an always ready network of observers. Small nations can exploit this great asset simply by providing the people with the necessary communications. No serious technical problems are involved, nor is the cost of equipment excessive. Sweden's Civil Defense Organization has 8,000 transmitters, both stationary and mobile types, the latter broadcasting from vehicles and planes, divided over the entire country. They use 320 channels. The total cost was estimated around ten million dollars, quite a moderate sum.[14] In a conflict the network can serve civil defense, military defense, or political opposition. Only two adjustments are required for resistance purposes: (1) the personnel need special preparation; (2) they have to be able to operate secretly. The changes are not difficult to make. Analyzing Vietnam experiences, the U.S. Army's chief of staff predicted that devices to keep "battlefields or combat areas under 24-hour surveillance" would "revolutionize the battlefield of the future."[15] Any small country can afford to strengthen military and resistance defenses with this type of organization and equipment.

---

[12] C. Aubrey Dixon and Otto Heilbrunn, *Communist Guerilla Warfare* (London: Allen & Unwin, 1954), pp. 188, 93.

[13] Ewald Banse, *Germany Prepares for War* (New York: Harcourt, Brace and Co., 1934), p. 74.

[14] *Dagens Nyheter*, Jan. 31, 1963.

[15] *New York Times*, Oct. 15, 1969.

C. FREE COMPONENTS OF RESISTANCE

Extended resistance prevents the invader from checking every point of opposition. His limited numbers of experts cannot supervise and control the whole territory of the defending state. He will have to decide what he wants to hold firmly, what to check fairly regularly. The rest becomes a virtual no-man's-land in the conflict—the *empty,* or *free, space.*

It has long been known that armed forces cannot hold more than a fraction of a sizable territory. Xenophon proposed to avoid the enemy, not to attack him: "It is much better to try to steal some part of the empty space and get around unseen, if we can, than to attack fortifications and men prepared to fight." The maneuver succeeded. The Greeks marched through the "empty space" to safety, demonstrating that unguarded ground favors the side with more enterprise and imagination. Bülow wrote: "You cannot hurt the enemy more than by going where he is not!" Clausewitz advised the *Landstorm* (a citizen's militia) to use the territory left unoccupied by an advancing enemy; to limit him to narrow strips of land; to contest his control over places "where he has no troops at all or only weak detachments."[16]

T. E. Lawrence built his strategy on the use of empty Arabian desert spaces: "In Arabia range was more than force, space greater than the power of armies." Repeatedly he stressed the significance of territory beyond enemy grasp: "the Arab war was geographical." The Turk was welcome to all his railroads and communication lines, "as long as he gave us the other nine hundred and ninety-nine thousandths of the Arab world. His stupidity would be our ally, for he would like to hold, or think he held, as much of his old provinces as possible. This would keep him in his present absurd position—all flanks

---

[16] Xenophon, *Anabasis* iv; Carl von Clausewitz. "Das Wesentliche in der organisation eines Landsturms und einer Miliz," *Beihefte zum Militair-Wochenblatt pro Januar bis inclusive October 1846* (Berlin), 70.

and no front."[17] Lawrence's aim was to keep the enemy over-stretched, to have as much of inadequately occupied—meaning empty—space as he could.

"It is in the matter of securing the blank spaces on the check-er-board that the strategic role of the guerrilla base areas behind the enemy lines reveals its great significance," taught Mao. During the Sino-Japanese War, he saw that "a great vacuum appeared in enemy occupied areas in North China," available for "a free development of the guerrillas."[18] Vast areas in the Japanese rear remained in the hands of the Red guerrillas throughout the war; Maoist administration was established there on a scale to resemble "a state in miniature."[19]

Empty spaces develop in regular wars. Even the Russians could not hold wide areas during the Winter War against Fin-land. The German war with Russia moved back and forth across the wide plains of Eastern Europe. The *Blitz* thrusts went best advancing through the empty spaces. Frustration resulted when, disregarding Bülow's advice, they ran against fortified points and enemy concentrations. But neither side knew how to use the opportunities waiting in the open spaces, beyond a limited patrol activity. The accepted procedure remained to "grab the bull by the horns," to go where the enemy was—to move against the enemy, not to avoid him.

Irregular warfare provides spectacular examples of the use of empty space. Revolutionary pressure in Ireland forced the English to give up outposts in the countryside and concentrate in well-guarded towns. The Sinn Fein were thus able to gain most of the country—and victory. Russian guerrillas held vast empty areas behind the German front. In some forest and marsh areas behind the Central Front, no German ever set foot during the three years of occupation. The populace lived under a Soviet regime, and delivered food and fodder to the guerrillas. By 1943 and 1944, the partisan-ruled spaces were more ex-tensive than those controlled by the *Wehrmacht*.

---

[17] Lawrence, *Seven Pillars*, p. 199, 228.

[18] Mao Tse-tung, *Strategic Problems in the Anti-Japanese Guerrilla War* (Peking: 1954), p. 45; *On Protracted War*, pp. 64, 113.

[19] Lin Piao, *op. cit.*, pp. 23, 25.

French resistance showed that guerrillas can dominate a perimeter around their mountain redoubt up to a depth of as much as one or two hundred miles.[20] The *redoutes* were no fortifications; they were empty areas in German-occupied France. Yet they were more than mere forts; they were outside the effective reach of the invader. Yugoslavia's partisans operated throughout large areas not penetrated by the Germans and without the backing of an army of their own—a remarkable feat at that time. In small Lithuania, nationalist guerrillas held out for years, after World War II, in wooded areas that the Russian Army could not police.[21] At the peak of the anti-Kurd offensive, 1962, half of the Kurdish provinces were held by the nationalist forces against the Iraqi troops.[22] The Kurdish resistance, as old as written history, is by the way still alive; 1970 may be the year of victory for the Kurds. And in South Vietnam, in 1963, Government troops and American teams, according to a newspaper report, "held cities, large posts and some hamlets. The Viets moved freely everywhere."[23] These examples should suffice.

In modern conflicts military and political pressures for a speedy victory make the invader lunge for the main military and administrative objectives, leaving most of the attacked country uncovered. (Where a possibility of nuclear counter-action dictates a wide dispersion of forces, large spaces remain unoccupied.) British commandos and Rommel's regulars were rather imaginative in the North African campaign, where an empty southern flank permitted daring maneuvers by both sides. Attacks launched through the desert found enemy weak spots always vulnerable. But in North Africa only one flank was exposed. In an invaded country the occupation forces have uncontrolled areas all around them: there they truly are in a position with "all flanks and no front."

---

[20] Miksche, *op. cit.*, p 153.

[21] K. V. Tauras, *Guerrilla Warfare on the Amber Coast* (New York: Voyages Press, 1962), p. 51.

[22] *Dagens Nyheter*, Aug. 16, 1962.

[23] *New York Herald Tribune*, Dec. 9, 1963.

In an invaded country there are extensive unoccupied spaces where neither the enemy army nor the armed units of the defender hold sway. They may well be called *empty* spaces controlled by neither friend nor foe.

To enjoy the advantages of empty spaces the defenders need the sympathies of the local people or an enemy who depends on their coerced obedience. A nation determined to resist, and sufficiently politicized to support the struggle actively, turns the *empty* space into *free* space: i.e., territory controlled by partisans of the defending side. Such a defiant community always dominates a much larger part of the country, by their numbers and presence, than any enemy could: there are 14,000,000 Czechoslovaks in the C.S.S.R.; the Russians cannot assemble in similar numbers there.

Political defense is strong because it enables practically the entire population to participate in a ubiquitous opposition and use the free space. The hold of an invader on newly taken territory is weak. It is easier for the defenders to secure and use free space against him. There is always enough of such space available to resistance.

The resisting nation can dominate most of the country. The greatest part of it will be areas (1) where the invader has never been and is not likely to go, or (2) where his forces may not stay for an appreciable length of time. Such areas belong to the inhabitants. The impact of short enemy "visiting periods" does not establish his physical or political control. In a third type of area, he is not present in sufficient strength to exercise more than minimal, or symbolic, occupation—the illusion but not the substance of domination. A vicious circle of cause and effect begins there, if the resisters are clever: the more expanded the opposition, the thinner the enemy has to spread his forces; the thinner his forces, the easier they are evaded.

Enemy pressure and domination varies not only in space but in time as well. Resistance can take advantage of *free times* as it can of free spaces. Any locality, otherwise adequately held, may be impossible to dominate with the available forces at certain periods. A report from Poland described the typical situation of this kind. In 1946, the Russians were in full possession of certain areas by day; "but we are the masters at night," wrote an officer of the resistance forces. The occupier's difficulty of coping with the empty *spaces* is, thus, compounded by the additional difficulty that his rule is ineffective at certain *times*.

Certain places usually remain beyond an invader's reach— the predominantly mountainous regions in Norway, in the Alps, in the Balkans. Finland and Sweden have large territories; their size makes any but fragmentary occupation impossible. To this element of space we must add free times: they are bound to occur in the northern latitudes of Europe, where winter, in addition to hampering troop mobility, brings long nights, lasting for weeks (even months) in some places. Very little imagination is needed to realize the advantages resistance enjoys in such areas.

The elements of free space and time get less attention than they deserve; extensive free areas are not adequately used. One reason for this is psychological: operations are led by army personnel and land-oriented people. Lawrence wrote that operations in empty spaces "should be like naval war, in mobility, ubiquity, independence of bases and communications, ignoring of ground features, of strategic areas, of fixed directions, of fixed points." Rommel, another great desert captain, had similar thoughts about the parallels with naval war. Just as no navy in the world can dominate the seas to the exclusion of every adversary, no occupation army is able to exclude all resistance. The more landlocked minds among the military still do not grasp the extent to which the command of free areas—just as the command of the sea or of Lawrence's Arabian desert— favors resistance.

The discussion of free space and time merely introduced the most important point of this section: the need to find other *free resistance components*. Many socio-political elements can be brought into play to support national defense and be kept outside enemy reach. In one sense, the whole aim of a national resistance is but to find and use the countless free components of national life. Whatever (1) remains outside, or (2) can be kept outside, or (3) is removed from enemy control strengthens defense.

Many activities are completely, or greatly, free from the invader's domination, even his supervision and interference. And often it is not difficult to discern the limits between enemy supervised and *free fields, matters, levels,* and *functions.* Spiritual resistance for one is entirely beyond enemy reach; this was already pointed out as its great strength. Many other kinds of political resistance remain free. Most activities in technical fields are likely to be beyond the invader's effective influence. (The information media of Czechoslovakia were free in the crucial first phase of occupation: they helped annul the impact of the military invasion.) Most are free on local levels. Although the exact degree of domination or freedom over various political and technical functions cannot be measured in advance, we can safely assume that the intruder, unable to dominate the territory, will not be able to dominate the more complex technical functions in a hostile country.

How effectively a certain matter is within enemy reach may differ considerably throughout a struggle. Many of its aspects may remain free. Often controls conflict. People in invaded countries usually estimate rather accurately what the alien is and is not able to do—in which activities there is a conflict of influences, which are free from enemy interference. In a political national defense the advantages of all *free* resistance components accrue to the side favored by the people.

Ubiquity and flexibility multiply and help exploit the free components of opposition. Searching out the enemy and locking horns with him must give way to defiance as far as possible outside his reach. Opposition extended to more places, times, levels, activities, and organized groups soon reaches a point beyond which the intruder cannot match it, at least not match it adequately. Resistance must go where it is free to act with a greater impact. It must act where the enemy is absent and take what he cannot hold. Resistance cannot hurt the enemy more than by going where he is not, or is not at his strongest.

CHAPTER IX

Specialized Conflict

Since the days when the tribal chief was the final authority in all matters—the symbol of power, the government, the god-priest, the court, the commander of warriors, the owner of everything, the holder of the purse—a long development of civilization has produced a complicated and specialized system in Government and in all other activities of national life. To run the Government, the religious services, the judicial, military, economic, administrative and other highly technical machineries, in modern society requires the combined expertise of countless specialists.

War itself has become more complex. Once a conquest was final when the invader had killed or chased away the chieftain and a few of his aides. Thereafter, everything could be taken easily. Nowadays, the invading and killing are minor parts of a complicated political and technical take-over: too many things have to be secured and converted to different purposes.

Conquest and control are no longer decided by a battle or by a massacre, but by an involved process in which one side causes, or fails to cause, the erosion of the other side's political position. Ultimate victory is a sum total of countless political and technical contests. Resistance can stop an invader at any one of the numerous points where he needs to prevail for final success.

A. TECHNICAL RESISTANCE

A political struggle includes many politically relevant elements. Technical resistance—a part of the over-all political contest—embraces all fields of specialized activities and all individuals able to influence some function of society because of their skill, experience, or training. Military action—a branch of technical defiance—includes irregular warfare.

The wide variety of specialized functions requires an equally wide variety of experts. Non-experts are easily outwitted in their attempts to exercise control. Military experts are never able to master the functions of an entire developed society; the military machine itself needs expert civilian assistance to run smoothly. Governing and looting of occupied countries fails without the help and collaboration of national specialists.

Technical resistance includes all functions that require special skills to perform, or to perform well. In specialized fields resistance enjoys a great advantage over alien personnel. A systematic exploitation of this superiority is an important part of national defense.

To begin with the most important, political conquest calls for special knowledge of the people and the country. Without it, a military success soon turns into a political defeat. Hitler's mistakes in Eastern Europe are a classic example of a gross political clumsiness. The Russians have shown equal mastery in arousing political resentment in Czechoslovakia. Since August, 1968, their initial tragi-comedy of errors and their subsequent difficulties were caused by an inability to understand the peoples they were trying to subdue. Obviously, the defenders' knowledge of their own nation surpasses that of the aliens. The resulting advantages should not remain unexploited.

Most technical activities will be outside an invader's reach. He will not be able to dominate even the fields he considers important, at least not during the first years. The Germans could not supervise Norwegian education; it was a free activity for the duration of their stay. In neighboring Denmark they could neither control the local police and court system nor maintain order themselves.

In one technical field—the military—neither ten, a hundred, nor a thousand soldiers can dominate an invaded country (even without opposition), simply because their number will be too small. In other technical branches the situation is similar.

But there is a decisive difference: the invader can bring in enough soldiers to complete a military take-over; he cannot find the experts to take over hundreds of technical functions. An extended technical resistance creates more problems than a conqueror can solve.

The invader's difficulty is fivefold: he needs experts (1) with a certain degree of competence, (2) familiar with local conditions, (3) in adequate numbers, (4) on all levels, (5) for each speciality. Without them he cannot control the country. This problem is by no means limited to high levels or some selected fields. It embraces every specialized activity—engineers and printers, teachers, linguists, soil analysts, harbor pilots, statisticians, and maintenance men—anything that can be done effectively only by a part of the population.

The need for a large number of experts on the lower levels greatly limits an invader's ability to supervise and control. He may be able to find a few professors to staff a university, but never the thousands of teachers for elementary schools. (See Chapter VII, A2.) Yet it would be much more important to exploit the vast opportunities for indoctrinating the younger children than the graduate students, whose views are already formed. In every other field the situation is similar: the most important struggles take place on the lower levels; the greatest opportunities are there—and the invader is weakest there.

Domestic Soviet experience gives an impressive example: the extraordinary learning necessary to catch up with the American lead in nuclear physics was achieved within a few years; the relatively simple goal of raising Soviet agriculture to American standards will not be achieved in decades to come because it requires tens of thousands of loyal experts. It is clear that passive opposition, or non-co-operation, of the peasants partly accounts for the failure. But both difficulties are interrelated: a less-adequate supervision is easier to evade.

In a hostile country technical opposition is even harder to overcome. The aggressor's inability to supply his own experts, especially on the lower levels, forces him to rely on citizens of the defending nation. But the patriots holding technical positions have an opportunity to exploit the weak spots and extend technical resistance to most activities. Five years after the Bolshevik revolution, Lenin complained that "we lack sufficiently educated forces to exercise real control over the vast army of government employees. Actually, at the top the machine functions somehow; but down below, where the state officials are in control, they often counteract our measures. There are hundreds of thousands of officials who, sometimes unconsciously and sometimes consciously, work against us." He admitted reluctantly that *"nothing could be done"* against that, that *"many years* will be required to improve the machine, to reform it, and to recruit new forces."[1]

Since collaborator specialists are not available in adequate numbers, and reliable incompetents will not do (intelligent resisters can easily fool them), the alien will have to work with national experts for a long time, making political and material concessions to keep their services. He cannot achieve optimum results by violence. Dismissals do not work as a policy since only a limited number of people are capable of operating essential services. The more specialized the activities, the less enforceable they are. The exercise of personal intelligence, inventiveness, or the best performance cannot be enforced.

Alien control of political and technical activities is often quite illusory. Even the fact that machinery of supervision exists does not necessarily mean that it can do the job adequately. The intruder may deceive himself, even others, that he is the master, but he will not prevail against an alert opposition. Analyses of control—political, military, economic, etc.—tend to accept as decisive the mere presence of any formal control apparatus, without finding out whether it is effective and how effective it is. But a formal setup does not rule anything by its mere existence.

In German-occupied Russia and the Ukraine, Soviet administration had collapsed, and the occupiers built a new monopoly

---

[1] Quoted in M. Fainsod, *How Russia Is Ruled* (Cambridge: Harvard University Press, 1957), p. 330 (my emphasis).

organization to collect and distribute products. "They established a network of hundreds of offices supervising close to a million indigenous personnel; at the peak of operations, it managed over 4,000 plants."[2] Of course the network could neither *supervise* nor *manage* this multitude with any degree of efficiency. How exactly could the work of a million local collecting and distributing personnel, in a newly conquered territory, be supervised from a few hundred offices? Merely stating the question shows the impossibility. In practice, they knew little more than the names of the million subordinates. And how could each of the same offices in addition manage dozens of plants?

Did the corps of 14,000 German "specialists" really supervise agricultural production in the Eastern Territories? Not all of this large mass could be competent experts, to begin with. Surely, not many of them could speak Russian, Ukrainian, or other local languages. Few if any were familiar with local conditions. Consequently, as a member of the occupation headquarters put it, "if you reckon the resistance of the peasants, you can place an agricultural supervisor behind every cow, and yet he would be cheated out of cream."[3] And the typical area under every supervisor was far more than a single cow: it was around 80,000 hectares of land and 25,000 people. Even first-rate experts could not cope with a minimum of non-co-operation there; the effectiveness of second-rate supervisors was bound to remain inadequate. What a splendid opportunity for technical counter-action!

Despite ten thousands of imported administrative personnel, the invader could do little without the co-operation of the local people. When the German exploitation failed, Goering questioned a top administrator: "If you get police forces, do you believe you can get more out of the region?" "On the contrary," was the reply, "I believe we will get still less if we use force."[4] Other

---

[2] Alexander Dallin, *German Rule in Russia, 1941–1945.* (London: Macmillan and Co., 1957), p. 339.

[3] Peter Kleist, *Zwischen Hitler und Stalin* (Bonn: Athenaeum Verlag, 1950), p. 158.

[4] Dallin, *op. cit.*, p. 188.

examples show that despite violence and pressures, Russian agricultural exploitation has failed in their own country, as well as in Eastern Europe. The officially admitted disproportion of productivity between collective or state land and the private plots of the peasants is startling.

Political defense headquarters need a technical resistance section, qualified to guide the planning and execution of technical counteraction. Trained specialists should search out ways to oppose an invader in all areas. They should be familiar with various activities and equipment. A few "inefficiency experts" can direct others and cause impressive breakdowns themselves. Technical resistance must not be a mere irritant but one of the main weapons in the struggle. Complicating, endangering, jamming, can foil enemy control, attract public attention, prevent economic exploitation, and weaken the invader's military hold on the country. If sufficiently extended, it can paralyze his rule.

One specialist can stall more than a thousand soldiers can repair. Modern invasion and occupation depend on special facilities, services, and equipment. Complexity increases their vulnerability. Their sensitive points or vital processes—the bottle-necks—can be found and attacked: with slowdowns practiced by the population or precision demolition by teams of technical experts. A widening of technical defiance not only increases chances of success but also decreases enemy ability to repair the resulting damage and to suppress technical opposition.

In the hands of an entire nation, technical resistance can become a popular political campaign conducted on the technical level. Every man and woman can discover the significance of a job, a study, a hobby; its part in related processes; its vulnerabilities. Anyone can add sugar or syrup to gasoline. If aliens do not know the make of a machine, people can cause delays and stoppages by hiding operating instructions or lists of spare parts. Everyone can participate in non-co-operation, slowdowns, and slackness. Some results may be felt immediately; others may merely accelerate or aggravate natural malfunctions. The total effect of the common effort will be considerable.

Every technical function has its critical bottlenecks. Students and technicians will soon discover how a machine, depending on the simultaneous operation of all parts, can be blocked by stalling one of them. Resistance can do this with few men in small actions; hardly ever is violence called for. If it is, special commando teams must complete the demolitions by selective blocking and jamming.

Much of it is, obviously, sabotage. It is called blocking and jamming to emphasize the possibility of succeeding without violence. In resistance struggles, violence is secondary and must be applied with discretion. Sabotage is but a tool, a precision instrument. Selected technical targets are hit with pinpoint accuracy, avoiding unnecessary damage. Miksche wrote that "sabotage is a science. Clever sabotage can inflict serious damage on the enemy by a series of small but well-directed thrusts. A simple short circuit can have more effect than a large explosion."[5] Expertly aimed blows combine a minimum of violence with a maximum of technical impact.

The effects of technical resistance increase when (1) its actions are multiplied and diversified; when (2) more people are participating; when (3) new methods are discovered to clog the machineries of administration, production, collection, transportation, and others; when (4) its measures are co-ordinated; and when (5) it concentrates on steps that have multiple effects and complement each other.

The citizens of Czechoslovakia cleverly frustrated the invaders' attempts to stage a wave of arrests of political and intellectual leaders, thereby to disorganize resistance and create an atmosphere of terror and despair in 1968. The people did not help Russian agents find their way around their cities, did not answer when addressed in Russian. Stores and newsstands did not sell any maps of the cities; people removed street names, house numbers, floor numbers, name plates on apartments. Even street lights were switched off at night to make orientation more difficult. To create utter confusion, wrong names and

[5] F. O. Miksche, *Secret Forces* (London: Faber and Faber, 1950), p. 125.

numbers went up: a suburban street would appear in the center of Prague; the left-side numbers would be on the right side of a street; names like U Thant appeared on doors. Free radio warned people who were threatened by arrests, broadcast the numbers of cars used in arresting people; the cars were then intercepted by Czech police or citizens and the prisoners released. Prison personnel refused to accept prisoners from the Russians. Members of the police released the names of threatened persons, the names of collaborators trying to help the K.G.B. and the description of their vehicles; they even released the captives the Russians brought to their headquarters. Finally the invaders were helpless, and the collaborators began to fear reprisals against their own families. News of attempts to terrorize were broadcast abroad to inform world opinion. Every new move of the enemy was anticipated and parried. When the campaign of arrests failed, the invasion misfired.

Specialized resistance penetrates practically every field and function, including administration, production, communications, and transportation. Its administrative aspect is examined in Section B, following.

The production process can be broken at any of its links. Industrial enterprises can be easily paralyzed, or their productivity reduced, by people familiar with their functions. The director of a French factory producing for the Germany Army stayed on the job to make sure that the work would be done as slowly as possible. His efforts were successful. They remained undiscovered: the Germans never suspected him; the French nearly shot him as a collaborator after the war.[6] In the 1969-1970 non-co-operation campaign, Czech and Slovak workers organized slackness, reducing the output of industrial production considerably. How could supervisors deal with such sabotage? Sending Russian soldiers to the factories did practically nothing to improve the situation.

Communications are vulnerable to technical attacks. Their

---

[6] Stephen King-Hall, *Power Politics in the Nuclear Age* (London: V. Gollancz, 1962), p. 189.

Specialized Conflict 235

breakdowns affect every step of the invader. They can weaken supervision and control, or result in the localization of certain areas. Mere interruptions of communications create an atmosphere of insecurity and psychological stress, especially among enemy agents and collaborators outside the main centers.

Unhindered transportation on land and water depends mainly on facilities operated by citizens of the resisting nation. They can remove and change road signs, refuse directions, block tunnels, tracks, bridges, channels, and locks. They can interfere with road, rail, water, and air traffic, with signal and repair equipment, in many ways.

A German officer described how the fate of an entire front sector in Russia hung on one short, wooden railway bridge.[7] As the only supply route for a tank army, the railroad had to be kept operating. The bridge had to stand, despite intensive Russian bombardment. Similarly critical constructions, and the opportunities for destroying them, are numerous. Any essential construction of a road or railway is, in effect, critical for its operation. And in difficult terrain (the Alps, the Scandinavian and Balkan mountains), it is easier to disrupt and more difficult to repair them than in the level country of central Russia, where the German bridge had to stand.

A Czech railroad worker described how a Russian train with jamming equipment against resistance radio was stopped before it reached Prague: it got entangled in trolley wires thrown across the tracks and broke into three parts. The maintenance man collapsed. A piece of track was dismantled at another point; further along the line a stalled trolley car blocked the tracks; and so on. "Every one of us knows a lot of ways of crippling traffic."[8]

Technical resisters must always look for critical bottlenecks where the invader can be hit best, and for the *free* activities

---

[7] Hermann Teske, *Die silbernen Spiegel* (Heidelberg: Vowinckel Verlag, 1952), p. 209.

[8] R. Littell (ed.), *The Czech Black Book* (New York: Praeger, 1969), pp. 215–16, 116.

they can take over. The inability of the invader to detect or jam free radio and television was exploited with excellent results by the Czechs and the Slovaks. Resistance radio stations broadcast between eighteen and twenty-four hours a day; they even started foreign language programs. Television used five channels, while only two had been used before the invasion. The Russians were unable to operate four strong radio transmitters their armies had secretly installed during the July "maneuvers" in Czechoslovakia simply because the local electricians switched off the current they needed. Czech television also managed to interfere with the invader's TV broadcasts. The Russians could not prevent the printing and distribution of resistance newspapers and leaflets; the patriots used this to gain a decisive advantage in the diathetic struggle. The aliens had no specialists to publish any newspapers, except the East German *Zpravy* written in faulty Czech. Local collaborators could prepare many editions, but printers repeatedly refused to print them.

Technical intelligence will be an important part of the struggle. It will be best if collected on a day-to-day basis to show—like a weather chart—points and areas of high, low, or medium enemy pressure—to make short-term and long-term predictions about the movements of his forces and pressures. Such charts can be prepared for each field and activity. One of the main purposes is to determine what areas will remain *free* from enemy interference: there resistance rules. It was very important to know that telex transmissions from Prague could be continued practically without interruption during the entire critical first week of invasion. Even statisticians found important resistance tasks: they released data concerning the damage caused by the invasion and they helped prepare the extremely important opinion polls, even in 1969.

The importance of the invader's own technical experts for his political and technical control was stressed before. Attacks on them, a part of political attacks, can contribute greatly to technical resistance. Since enemy weakness is the resisting nation's strength, no means should be neglected to break the enemy hold on any political or technical activity.

B. ORGANIZED AND ADMINISTRATIVE RESISTANCE

A nation is, in effect, an organization embracing every citizen and commanding the strongest loyalty—nationalism. The organized nature gives national resistance many advantages: (1) Resistance uses the strength of combined and co-ordinated actions. (2) Organized groups and circles extend and diversify opposition, widen participation, increase cohesion and communication among compatriots, and tap more group loyalties to strengthen the movement. (3) Most defiance takes place within closed circles immune to supervision and infiltration. The number of such *free* groups—those beyond effective enemy interference—varies; but close friends, families, and many other small circles can elude all supervision even under the most severe reign of terror. Where, as in Denmark under the German occupation or in Czechoslovakia under the Russians, the invader's pressure is less effective, even nationwide organizations may be able to participate actively in resistance.

Many fields are always open to organized resistance. They include opposition by informal and formal organizations, administrative counteraction from within the control apparatus, and dealing with local collaborator administrators.

1. Organized Resistance

The sociologist Philip Selznick spoke of "the organizational weapon." He stressed the tremendous power dormant in organized groups, regardless of their original goals:

> Organizations established for limited purposes (trade unions, civic groups, etc.) develop strength that may be diverted to other, more far-reaching aims. This incidental ability may be exploited without regard to the limitations set by the initial charter of the group to include new areas within which power is generated and won. It is in those areas of power not yet fully recognized or not readily controlled, that a struggle may take place.[9]

---

[9] Philip Selznick, *The Organizational Weapon: A Study of Bolshevik Strategy and Tactics* (New York: McGraw-Hill, 1952), pp. 3–4, *passim.*

Cohesive informal circles have, of course, similar strengths and advantages. The fact that areas where organized power is effective may not be easily controlled is a definite plus for resistance.

The conquerors, actual and expectant, know this well. Hitler went so far as to doubt the wisdom of permitting free religious activities in occupied Russia, despite the recommendations of most experts. His main concern, according to one analyst, was "to prevent the emergence of any organizations—social, communal, political, or religious—that might become nuclei for opposition movements."[10] Stalin applied strongest pressure, after World War II, to have patriotic organizations prohibited in Eastern Europe, while at the same time demanding the formation of Russophile organizations—a purposeful policy, indeed.

Just as political parties are schools of resistance struggle, organizations and small circles are training grounds for cooperation and concerted action—its invaluable resistance assets. A nation is only as strong as the people and groups that form it. To preserve and strengthen all groups capable of acting purposefully must be an important task of national defense. A wide use of groups adds the benefits of organized and extended defiance; it also helps increase the *relay effect* of resistance (see Chapter VI, C).

A national defense fought within the political community goes beyond traditional usage in two respects: (1) it extends the concept of organizations to include all informal groups and circles, and (2) it gives organizations a far greater role in the political campaign.

(1) For the purposes of resistance *all* organizations in the *polis* are political. They are all a part of the community, whether or not usually considered political. All units of people able to act in concert can participate; all are potential nuclei of power and pressure; all can become foci of resistance. A group of stamp collectors can be as effective as a secret army—more so at times —because of its innocuous appearance. People can contribute to the common defense as members of churches, schools, unions, hospitals, book and record clubs, veterans' groups, and many

---

[10] Dallin, *op. cit.*, p. 480.

more. Their co-ordinated activities sustain the entire defense effort. Strongest are the organizations linked to the active fighters: youth, workers, political cadres. Safest are the groups further from enemy interference: friendships, families, and other primary groups. Since resistance is a struggle of the people, national strength would be wasted by excluding some of them.

(2) The obsolete notion that war is for soldiers and peace for civilians is long dead; this is only a logical conclusion of its belated demise. Every organization has a positive purpose, expressed or implied, to promote the welfare of the nation or some of its citizens. To oppose an invader is to do just that. In quiet times many resent, as the subjects of totalitarian regimes do, attempts to charge their actions with a militant political content. In the hour of national danger, however, all patriots will seek to join the common struggle. The leadership should not fail to give every group an opportunity to participate. The housewives in Slovakia were among the most apolitical of all groups; they were politicized and contributed significantly to the opposition after the Russian tanks rolled in.

Organizations are political fortresses in an invaded country. Their variety—from geographic subdivisions to circles of friends —is endless. All are potential obstacles to conquest. All may act to multiply the enemy's control problems in an already confusing political conflict.

Geographic subdivisions, from historic provinces and districts to the small localities, are often sufficiently cohesive to act as independent organizations. Local subdivisions are an asset, for instance, in Switzerland's strength. Local loyalties—to canton, half-canton, and commune—are extremely strong, rooted in history. Internally they can be, and often are, a source of division and irritation. But any sufficiently foreign threat rallies the local efforts for a common defense.

Circles of individuals, such as friendships and families, have the closest ties. That is why modern totalitarian regimes do not trust such primary groups: "They do not build upon, but on the contrary, destroy, family and friendship ties."[11] Even two or three

---

[11] Selznick, *op. cit.,* p. 288.

friends can be valuable: they know each other best; they are able to work together efficiently and secretly. Families are basic traditional units bound together by loyalty, safe from infiltration, hardly capable of being paralyzed even by terror, able to resist under any conditions. National and religious ideas are transplanted from one generation to another in the family. The Swiss believe that "defensive strength has its proper place not only in the armories, barracks and training areas, but also in home life."[12]

Small groups—including all kinds of cliques, many with durable loyalties—have similar strengths. They excel in co-operation and security. Especially when prepared in advance, they could be valuable contributors to resistance. If members of the groups are specialists in any important field, they can perform crucial defense functions.

Informal organizations can add much to the national effort. The co-workers in a plant, the members of the Class of 1955, the patients in a hospital, even the readers of a local newspaper or football enthusiasts, can co-operate to oppose the invader. The range of their activities is wide, and it is hardly possible to discover or supervise them.

Formal organizations can prevent an invader's control of the population in many ways, especially during the initial phases of the conflict. Their organized structure, established connections, and extensive membership are obvious assets in a political struggle. To be able to resist over a long period, they must be able to defy infiltration and take-over.

Enemy attempts to split up or outlaw organizations are not the main danger. Even if successful, they do not strengthen the invader's control. Country-wide organizations can carry on as local groups of members or as mere friendships very effectively if they keep up essential contacts and co-operation with other such groups.

Central and local leaders must provide in time for a possible

---

12 *Soldatenbuch: Auf Dich kommt es an!* (Bern: Eidgenössische Drucksachen- und Materialzentrale, 1959), p. 15.

conversion to resistance work, for independent local activities and communications in case of need. A well-prepared national organization can resist on all levels—national, provincial, local. Its smaller units should not scatter to the winds or obey the enemy but continue their work underground. Resisting as a whole, and with its separate parts, an organization can offer multiple opposition sufficiently varied to confound outside control. The formidable Mafia demonstrates—over many centuries, in many countries—how difficult it is to find out and destroy deeply rooted, cohesive, and cleverly managed organizations.

In invaded Czechoslovakia, the Communist Party, the trade unions, academic institutions, and others were uniquely effective, even when the occupiers arrested their main leaders, occupied their central offices, or when their governing bodies had to meet in secret. New leaders stepped forward; local units, presidia, committees, assumed command for a time; or groups of members simply acted on their own. There is no reason why equally good results could not be achieved in other countries.

Governmental organizations—executive, administrative, legislative—bear the brunt in the first stage of the struggle for political control. They are the primary targets of enemy attempts to infiltrate, subvert, take over, and destroy. Their opposition is essential to the whole contest, even if it is but a delaying action to gain a few days or weeks. Resistance of governmental organizations has many important results: (1) The organizations exclude enemy rule from the places they control. (2) They divert the invader's attacks to themselves, being his primary targets, and thus leave other organizations free to rally and act as long as they are not subdued. (3) They reduce alien influence to the extent of their resistance, be it only local or fragmentary. (4) They protect, by holding on to a position anywhere, practically all the lower levels in the hierarchical pyramid. Even where the strength of a contested position is partly reduced, it can still serve as a political fortress covering its subordinate bureaucratic positions. (5) They delay enemy advances and threaten to recover lost political ground until they are finally subdued. (6) They can, as a matter of fact, continue as a threat to dislodge the invader for a long time to come. If the functionaries keep alive the will to resist, they remain a potential rival machinery of control after the enemy has taken over the Government.

Napoleon was convinced to his dying day that Spanish resistance would never have grown enough to stop him if the Bourbons of Spain had fled the country, as had been their original intention. King Leopold of Belgium shocked the world by remaining in his occupied realm in May, 1940; but his act impeded Hitler's wiping out the Belgian governmental organization, establishing full occupation rule, and splitting the state in two. In French North Africa, General Weygand rebuilt units of the French Army, hid considerable quantities of matériel from the Germans, and took up contacts with the Allies, while serving the Vichy Government.[13] And the Pétain Government itself performed a service to France in the territory which it controlled —simply by keeping out German administration.

If the Czechoslovak leadership had either called for armed resistance or escaped to the West, the orthodox Russian leaders would have been quite able to deal with the situation. When the chiefs of Government and Party refused to flee or to fight with military means but chose determined political resistance, the Kremlin was confused: they did not understand the situation. The defenders understood already on the second day that "the military invasion has succeeded, but the political invasion has failed."[14]

One reason why Russian influence was shaky in the C.S.S.R. was the continued existence, and resistance, of the Czechoslovak federal structure. Moscow was attacking almost exclusively the central Government in Prague, applying only fragmentary pressure to the state organs. Provincial, district, local governments were left *free* of any enemy influence for a considerable time. The top Government and Party leaders were holding onto their positions, despite massive Soviet interference, to stop Russian

---

[13] Karl Heinz Hoffman and Otto Mayr-Arnold, *Okänd Armé* (Stockholm: Hörsta Förlag, 1959), p. 168; L. M. Weygand, *Mémoires* (Paris: Flammarion, 1950), pp. 395, 470.

[14] *New York Times*, Aug. 23, 1968.

influence on the top level. Moscow also found it more difficult to dominate because in the C.S.S.R., as in other Communist countries, there were two governmental structures—the Government proper and the Communist Party—both resisting vigorously.

Resistance must not abandon its weapons of organized defiance, just as a soldier must not throw away his arms in combat. Every organization is an additional obstacle on the invader's road to control. He must overcome them, every one of their levels, against opposition, before he can reach his goal. All of them should be defended.

Orthodox strategy draws a distinction between peace, military defense, and resistance. When armed defense is overcome, the military organizations disintegrate. Thereafter, new groups must form from scratch. During the last war, the Communists usually had the best setup simply because they used their established subversive organizations. Other resisters had to lose time and opportunities, as well as to expose themselves to more danger to find people of similar convictions, sound them out, create a pattern of co-operation with them. Many analysts were impressed with the formidable advantages of using such a ready-made organization.

In national resistance, the entire community defies the invader. Resistance is a part of daily life. It relies on existing organizations: whatever their peacetime function, after invasion their task is to resist. With adequate predisposition, planning, and information the change to a defense function in case of need is easily accomplished. Existing organizations are more efficient and secure; they know their members and rely on established loyalties and patterns of co-operation.

The mere presence of national organizations, their resistance potential, is a strategic element of political strength. The Church contributes an organization and spiritual support. The national Army and police forces influence the situation simply by remaining inactive; so do the workers and the news media. The Paris constabulary turned on the Germans days before the arrival of Allied armies. The fear of a similar coup in Denmark led to the dissolution of the Copenhagen police in September, 1944.[15] The Russians disarmed units of Czech police; they failed to get the security (political) police to support them: both remained, on the whole, loyal and a potential threat to the invaders. Army units, even if surrounded and supervised by superior enemy force, retain the capability either to fight or to disperse and take up guerrilla warfare. The invader must repeatedly practice moderation to avoid open clashes. There is evidence that some Czechoslovak Army units, especially in Slovakia, were ready for partisan struggle in case the Soviets failed to release the arrested national leaders at the end of August, 1968. In the C.S.S.R., the workers were as much a strategic threat to the invaders as the armed forces. Organized in active trade unions, they were able to stage slowdowns or strikes at any time. Besides, they controlled the armed People's Militia. The news media had excellent experience in clandestine operations; if the oppression became too strong, they could again go underground. All this tends to restrain the invader.

> Before his arrest and deportation by Russian troops, on August 21, 1968, Dubcek smuggled out a message in which he appealed to Prague citizens, and above all to workers, particularly in large plants, to hold on to their factories and remain there together, for such a concentration of strength would offer the capital city protection and a guarantee. This could be an important and perhaps even decisive force, the message concludes, which in case of need could be put to use.[16]

The small nations would do well to tell the people how narrow are the limits of governmental power. Actually, the Government has *no* power of its own; all of its power is delegated to it by the nation: the more accurately a Government expresses the will of the people, the more power does it hold; the less it follows the people's will, the less is its power. If the nation is united, politically aware, and willing to resist the misuse of Govern-

---

[15] Jørgen Trolle, *Syv Maaneder uden Politi* (København: Nyt Nordisk Førlag, 1945), describes an occupied metropolis without police.

[16] *The Czech Black Book*, pp. 98-99, 177, 191.

ment functions, this is no mere argument of political theory but a quite realistic rule of political practice. An imposed alien regime may come close to having no power at all. Police and Army receive orders from the Government, but they are part of the population and are strongly influenced by popular opinion. In the last analysis, the Government depends on the support of its constituents as any other organization depends on its members. It is but one of the national organizations.

The population should know and understand how important it is (a) to support a popular government and (b) to oppose an imposed alien regime. They should know the ways in which non-governmental organizations and private groups can exercise their political influence. A consciousness of popular strength, and of the strength of popular institutions, coupled with a feeling of shared power and shared responsibility in a political struggle always profits resistance.

The examination of political control showed that the invader must complete four steps to keep power: (1) eliminate national organizations, (2) establish his own, (3) maintain his own, and (4) prevent the re-emergence of new national foci of power. Against organized resistance this is difficult to accomplish.

(1) No invader could hope to eliminate all widely dispersed and varied groups capable of organized defiance. Neither legal nor military power, nor a combination of the two, can effectively overcome it. Loosely organized and scattered organizations are likely to remain in loyal hands for some time, turning into political fortresses. The enemy can issue orders to organizations, imprison or shoot some of their members; but the orders cannot be enforced; persecuting some patriots rouses the defiance of others. Attempts to dissolve or outlaw groups wholesale are nothing but a bluff. Taking over some high positions, or the entire headquarters, of an organization are superficial measures: local units can continue operating, regardless.

The invader, able to attack only some and capture but a few of the organizations operating in the open, will certainly threaten and pressure many of them, hoping to induce gratuitous surrender. But he cannot seize all the groups he attacks.

(2) Even if the invader does seize an organization, he practically never gets as much political power or is able to exert as much leverage as the resisters could from the same positions. (Reasons for this inequality were discussed in Chapter VI, C.)

(3) The invader cannot hold permanently all the organizations he manages to seize at one time or another. Where the defenders see and exploit this inability, his efforts to end resistance and gain final control are the less likely to succeed.

(4) In all phases of the contest patriotic organizations play a *defensive* and an *offensive* role. In the defensive political struggle they are like fortresses resisting after occupation of the country—strong points that repel, delay, divert, confuse, bind enemy forces. Offensively, they are rival apparatus of control—Mao's parallel hierarchies, the backbone of the formidable Vietcong resistance—and foci of defiance gathering opposition and directing it against the enemy. There are always opportunities to attack politically in an organized manner; they must be exploited. Even on the offensive, resistance enjoys advantages: it can attack any one of the weak links of the enemy system or organization. Any organized unit, being a rival power center, can itself resist and it can lead others in offensive counteraction.

Existing organizations are not the only threat to the enemy: old groups can be reactivated, and new ones can be formed. "Shadow organizations" prepared in advance to spring into action at certain times can rally the community. Almost any group will do. A local newspaper may marshal the strength of the people guiding its readers; a church, a hockey club, or a choir may turn into a focus of defiance. The opportunities are there: the resisting nation is always looking for leaders; and anyone able to translate national determination into action can lead.

Enemy take-over should never be treated as a steady and irreversible process. It is more like the tides—advancing and receding. In the organizational field, as in other areas, resistance must use every opportunity to reverse an invader's gains. Even the governmental machinery should not be given up for lost—at least not on the lower levels, where enemy influence naturally remains limited. Retaking local units of the administration, or special agencies, or organizations will often succeed if persistently explored. Local power positions can be used to cushion pressures from the center and to invalidate the aggressor's orders by misinterpretation, misapplication, and other techniques. They have an important place in political resistance.

Nothing, at least no political position, should be considered lost forever. Nothing lasts forever, not even an invader's domination. His generally disliked, hastily built regime is certain to have many weaknesses. Where probes disclose them, the defending nation must retake lost positions. The spring effect of national resistance, its recoil power, must be given full play.

2. *Administrative Resistance*

Administrative resistance enters the picture while an organization or a part of it is under enemy influence: after defensive organizational resistance has been overcome, before they have been recaptured by the patriots. Defiance can continue even in this stage, exploiting the fact that no alien can fill all administrative positions with his own reliable agents. Within governmental and other organizations formally run by the enemy, the defenders can counteract his moves. This form of resistance may be called administrative resistance.

The invader can choose between two tactics: (1) to leave national organizations intact and try to supervise them, or (2) to take them over or replace them with his own. The first alternative lets these organizations function and possibly elude supervision. The second lets patriots infiltrate nominally enemy organizations. Where he uses the first tactics, the enemy faces organized resistance; where he uses the second, administrative resistance erupts.

Organized resistance is open disobedience. Its administrative counterpart is an apparent consent while actually counteracting the enemy. The border guard, for instance, can openly oppose orders to shoot refugees fleeing the country. Once the invader dominates the organization and commands the men to kill without warning, guards and patrols can still overlook the escapees or miss them intentionally. (East German guards have done this often.)

Administrative defiance is secure and flexible. It is not easy to detect. A typical case is that of the French factory director who actually frustrated German plans for years while pretending to collaborate with them. In administrative matters the borderline between intentional manipulation and mistakes or natural breakdowns can seldom be determined. Everyone knows how difficult it is to eliminate crimes and corruption among holders of administrative positions (thence their desirability for patronage) in normal times. When political warfare rages, administrative manipulation has far greater leeway and can remain undetected.

"From the standpoint of power struggle," wrote Selznick, "the official position functions as a weapon."[17] In a resistance campaign this weapon can be used against the alien. And practically every position (each of the million local employees of the German collection and distribution system in the occupied Soviet territories during the war!) can be useful. Czar Nicolas I bluntly admitted: "Russia is not ruled by me, but by my forty thousand clerks!" Lenin, another Russian ruler, described how the irreplaceable administrative experts in effect determined the policies of institutions under formal Communist control: "To tell the truth, the Communists are not doing the directing, they are being directed."[18]

During the Second World War, Danish police and court officers practiced organized and administrative resistance extensively. At first the Germans left the Danish police intact; it soon established "not only intimate, but also especially extensive contacts" with, and "rendered valuable services to, the underground."[19] Dissatisfied with the performance and loyalty of Danish police organizations, the Germans dissolved it, sup-

---

17 Selznick, *op. cit.*, p. 3.

18 Quoted in Fainsod's *How Russia Is Ruled*, p. 92.

19 Jørgen Haestrup, *Kontakt med England* (København: Thaning & Appels, 1954), pp. 229, 232.

pressed its administrative apparatus, and arrested some of its members. The criminal police were put "under house arrest" in Copenhagen but refused to co-operate. The invaders could find no replacements. The capital city, with close to one million people, was without police for seven months. When the occupiers authorized an unarmed Guard Force to maintain a semblance of order, the Danes turned the force into a national organization, recruiting two hundred active resistance men (one-third of the total) but not a single informer. A German order to deliver all captured weapons to the invasion forces was resisted: a common effort of the Guard Force and the Public Prosecutor's Office kept all weapons in Danish hands. The same two organizations succesfully conspired not to investigate or prosecute crimes suspected of being political. Judicial officers accepted only Danish proof: when the evidence originated from German sources, the suspects were automatically acquitted.[20]

Administrative resistance prevailed because a lack of experts rendered the invader practically helpless. Germany could not muster the specialists in Danish law to dispense with national judges and court clerks in occupied Denmark. What the Danes accomplished can be duplicated by people in administrative positions elsewhere.

"A modern society such as exists in Britain cannot possibly be operated by a horde of non-English-speaking foreigners," as King-Hall pointed out.[21] Had the Germans been able to invade Britain, they would certainly have failed to control it. A German administrative expert explained the conquerors' predicament in the 2,000,000 square kilometers (750,000 square miles) of the Occupied Eastern Territories: "If one put there a huge administrative apparatus of 20,000 people—and I do not know where you would get a mere fraction of the interpreters and specialists—you would have on each hundred square kilometers [forty square miles] one man and one secretary." Even the small Baltic states could not be ruled with a German administration: "It was im-

---

20 Trolle, *op. cit.*, pp. 13, 15, 19, 36, 177.
21 King-Hall, *Power Politics*, p. 198.

possible to muster 30,000 and more administrative officials and
gendarmes for each of these small states in the middle of the
war." National administrations had to be respected there, since
"without them one would have been helpless from the very first
day."[22]

In some respects small nations are better off: experts of their
language, customs, culture, and society are scarce. And 30,000
supervisors would not suffice to control effectively even the
smaller states.

The defiant patriots must keep or obtain positions from
which they can counteract the alien without openly challenging
his rule. They must distort, misinterpret, contradict his orders;
delay them, omit essential steps, fail to carry them out in
proper sequence; neutralize their effect by premature disclosure;
and so on. They can exploit inconsistencies and contradictions
in enemy administration and orders and rivalries among enemy
agents.

Patriots do not necessarily have to hold the higher positions
in enemy-directed organizations; any clerk and bureaucrat can
do his share to pervert organizational aims and activities. Enemy
directors cannot check internal defiance. In an organization it
means less who issues the orders than who are its personnel and
how they perform. The analogy with technical machinery, where
the operator sits at the controls and runs the whole system, is
misleading. Instead of mechanical control levers and the operating parts in an engine, the control links in resistance-infiltrated
organizations are human beings—unfriendly and un-co-operative
—whose psychology the aliens hardly understand. In every
section of the mechanism, down to the last human operating
part, the political influence of these people becomes decisive.
Who sits in the driver's seat, or in the director's office, is of
secondary import when the machinery does not obey.

Even some administrative positions that give only formal
powers can be worth holding: their value for resistance may
extend beyond these powers. Rather insignificant in the hands

---

22 Kleist, *op. cit., pp.* 154, 158, 160.

of the enemy, they may be much stronger as a resistance position. The reasons for this have been explained elsewhere in this treatise: the superior effectiveness of resistance and of certain positions in the hands of resistance (Chapter VI, C), the ability of positions higher in the bureaucratic hierarchy to protect activities below that level (touched upon in the immediately preceding subsection on organized resistance).

Throughout the administrative pyramid the opportunities are legion and can be exploited with impunity. As orders are conveyed down the chain of control, they can be frustrated at every link. "Certain types of sabotage, especially those committed within administrative organizations, very often remain undiscovered and only make their effects felt after a long time. The authors are often never brought to book."[23] The longer the invader fails to identify the resisters, the longer lasts the instability of his regime. Should he dismiss some employees and hire others, he still could not be sure that the new ones will be more reliable.

The impact of administrative resistance multiplies when it is concerted—by a number of friends who function as a team, co-ordinating information and actions toward the same target. Such circles or cliques use organizational and administrative advantages. Their combined organized-administrative resistance can be sufficiently strong for defensive as well as offensive action —taking over or subverting whole branches of enemy organizations such as local Party or Government bureaus, exploitation offices, subversion centers, or police departments.

The invader's domination is limited in time, in place, and in extent. When, where, and to what extent he applies direct pressure, orders will be obeyed, or at least not openly ignored. But such coercion is less general than people tend to assume. The rest are *free* times, areas, and levels where *de facto* disobedience can change the picture. Ingenious national leaders and an unbroken spirit help the resisting nation exploit lapses in enemy pressure.

---

[23] Miksche, *op. cit.*, p. 125.

Organizations under the formal control of the invader can effectively resist him in a hostile country. Like all internal opposition, administrative resistance often hits the enemy hard. Local people working for the invader's railroad system caused the main damage to German transportation facilities in Belgium and in Russia.[24] In Lithuania, after 1945, nationalist guerrillas received badly needed information and help from patriots working in the Russian administration at a time when that apparatus was their deadliest enemy.[25] In Czechoslovakia, most organizations remained in the hands of patriots after the invasion; organized rather than administrative resistance was the main form there. Within the Czech Secret Police units taken over by collaborators, patriotic agents managed to frustrate the arrest campaign. As the pressure of collaborators and occupants hardened, the opposition gradually retreated to administrative defiance and to local levels.

3. Local Administrators

The ultimate contest is fought locally, where the defending nation is strongest and the invader weakest. Local administrators in the control machinery—be they loyal national officials or enemy collaborators—deserve special attention because they are closest to, and in direct contact with, the mainstay of national defiance—the mass of the resisters.

A central Government rules directly little more than the national and provincial capitals. Provinces, districts, towns, and villages are supervised and administered by local officials. No matter how modest their positions, they may be the most important part of a political machinery: they are the links of the regime's chain of power. Only a mistaken overvaluation of government power has led people to depreciate the role of local functionaries.

In resistance struggles the importance of the local agents is

---

[24] Teske, *op. cit.*, p. 206.

[25] K. V. Tauras, *Guerrilla Warfare on the Amber Coast* (New York: Voyages Press, 1962), p. 97.

much greater than under a legitimate national Government. Lacking legitimacy, loyalty, and an established administrative machinery of his own, an invader would be helpless against a hostile nation, were it not for the collaboration of the officials below. In the closely controlled world of a concentration camp, according to the Soviet alumnus Solzhenitsyn, "your gang boss is everything; even an assistant gang boss is a big shot of sorts, and more depends on him than on the Commandant."[26] Without the help of similar aides, an occupation, like a concentration camp, remains a failure. In no case can unpopular rule be secured if the lower administrators do not co-operate. Without them the chain of power breaks before it reaches the people; contact with the localities is lost; control remains ineffective, exploitation impossible. (In Denmark under the Nazis, and in Czechoslovakia during the first year under Russian invasion, enemy pressure could not reach the local levels; in both cases alien control outside the capital was almost non-existent.)

Sed quis custodiet ipsos custodes? The problem of guarding the guardians was touched upon in Chapter VII, B. Most of what was said there applies here also: placed between the invader and the resisters, they experience conflicts of interest and loyalty, as well as social pressures; the invader cannot protect them in case of danger; they are in a precarious position as long as the contest is not decided; it is better to reform them than to liquidate them—better to split their loyalties than their skulls. They may eventually succumb to the pull of nationalism and help in the national struggle.

Local collaborators deserve far more attention in resistance theory and practice than they have received—certainly more than the few pages here. Their role should be kept in mind while examining all other threads of the web of resistance; their influence extends throughout. Here again we may learn from the Mafia gangsters the importance of using and neutralizing local administrators.

---

[26] Alexander Solzhenitsyn, *One Day in the Life of Ivan Denisovich* (New York: Bantam-Praeger, 1963), pp. 50, 26.

Merely writing them off as traitors and quislings will not do. A more flexible approach is needed. To state it candidly: (*a*) Traitors must strive to preserve their nation (at least partially), since without it they would have nothing to betray and would be out of a job. (*b*) Collaborator administrators depend on some co-operation of the people and, failing that, risk to lose their positions—and more. But to obtain co-operation, they must make concessions. (*c*) Once the nation starts reprisals against the collaborators, they may be safer siding with the people. Resistance successes diminish their sense of being on the safe winning side in the struggle. Many factors combine to create a psychological *squeeze*—coercion and temptations from above, counterpressures from below—forcing the local administration to seek a way out of the predicament.

A correct policy is to aggravate the split of their loyalties, to edge them closer to the people—to encourage their "neutrality" in the conflict, their bare formal service to the invader, or their outright return to the national side. To turn collaborators into resistance helpers is a worthy undertaking: their services and advice, open or clandestine, can be very valuable.

Every collaborator genuinely desiring to rejoin his own nation in its struggle for survival should have an opportunity to correct his errors. This choice prevents forced alienation from the collaborators' compatriots. It weakens the invader's hold over them. An open way back for its members is the most corrosive antidote against the control machinery of the enemy.

Nothing resists like resistance. A strong opposition is the best wedge to drive between the alien regime and its collaborators. A possible need to change sides in order to survive exerts a restraining pressure on the renegades. Realization of how dependent the turncoats are on the people's co-operation strengthens the position of the patriots, the sensitivity of traitors to public opinion. The unexpected upsurge of resistance, in 1968, seems to have been the reason for the unexpected timidity of Czechoslovak collaborators. As soon as it became evident that the outcome of the political struggle was in doubt, and the resisters assured them publicly, "We will not forget anything!"

the number of active traitors dwindled to a mere few dozen Czechs and Slovaks. Boycott, social ostracism, and counterpressures are other persuasive weapons in the political armory of the defending nation.

On the local level the strength of resistance confronts the weakness of the invader. There the collaborators are most vulnerable. And the defenders have the best chances of gaining political victory there. Even partial success has a beneficial effect. Opportunistic hesitation or neutrality of the administrators weakens the invader's control and encourages resistance. The vital role of local administrators, and the need to give them a way out, deserve serious attention.

Specialized resistance—technical, organized, or administrative—is part of the decisive political struggle. Even a great power able to overrun a small country militarily may well be defeated by intelligent national opposition.

C. MILITARY RESISTANCE

Small-nation strategy tries to reduce the significance of enemy military force. The passive measures of the defenders aim to deprive the invader's army of targets; the active measures aim to reduce its combat effectiveness. Either can the defenders order their forces not to resist or they can keep under arms only a smaller force of highly trained professional soldiers, thus leaving the enemy with fewer targets to attack. And they can assign civilian experts to disrupt essential functions of the invading army by technical means.

In unequal conflicts between a big-power aggressor and a defending small nation, military fighting is best studied as a branch of specialized resistance, one of many techniques of the political struggle. Depending on the circumstances, the national leadership may not use armed forces at all, or keep them in reserve as a strategic factor. When quasi-military and military action is indicated, the task is left to well-trained troops rather than to recruits. If fighting is to be done, let experts do it.

By the same token, many technical tasks previously assigned

to uniformed semi-experts should be given to civilian specialists. Civilians can take better care of communications, reconnaissance and intelligence, supply, even of demolitions and sabotage and the like. If need be, they can have commando protection. This diminishes the need for large uniformed forces vulnerable to enemy attacks. And it lets the soldiers become really effective military specialists, able to achieve better results with smaller losses.

It is important to note that most of the soldiers are assigned to non-combattant tasks in modern armies. Armies depend on these technical services and cannot function effectively without them. That is the reason why civilian specialists can paralyze military units when they interrupt the technical services. Army draftees often lack the motivation and the professionals lack the expertise: civilians outperform them in many fields.

The Swiss have a new approach to achieve military results without using regular soldiers. The Constitution of Switzerland permits neither the Federation nor the cantons to have any standing troops. There is a total of only five hundred professional soldiers in the entire country.[27] Surprisingly, even the acquisition of modern equipment in large quantities has not caused an increase in the number of professional soldiers. The practical Helvetians assign as pilots, telegraphers, and other technical experts men with similar civilian occupations. They hire specialists to maintain and service the equipment; having no military duties, the men devote their full attention to technical tasks. In case of foreign invasion they would be able to operate the equipment in anger.

Soldiers are assigned the technical tasks not because of their greater expertise but because of their availability. When a big-power army is operating abroad, it has no choice but to depend on the uniformed semi-specialists for the essential technical services. A defending small nation is fighting at home in its own country, where the best experts are available; their participation ensures top efficiency of resistance.

---

[27] Karl Brunner, "The Fundamental Ideas Behind Swiss National Defense" (mimeographed, 1959), p. 4.

Victory on the battlefield may or may not be gained without fighting; all other military objectives can be reached peacefully. Militarily inferior small nations have a wide variety of expedients when forced to rely on technical methods in the military field. Lawrence had the correct strategy for Arabs in such a position: "to find a weak link in the Turkish military system and bear on that till time made the mass of it fall." After World War II Colonel Miksche recognized a significant trend: "The more armies depend on economic and industrial production, the more vulnerable they are to blows directed against the hinterland that supports them; and this consists not only of the mother country but also of the occupied territory."[28]

The resisting small nation, and the militarily inferior side, should exploit the bottlenecks and blind spots in the military system of the enemy. A tank division on the battle line is in military combat. But the production of tanks and supporting equipment; the training, feeding, clothing of its men; maintenance, overhaul, repairs, fueling—all are peaceful technical activities. Their failure can defeat the division as completely as a month-long battle. If it depends on a supply bottleneck formed by a wooden bridge (as did an entire Panzer army in Russia), a civilian can saw through the wooden supports and thus cut off the supplies. The division is forced to retreat quite peacefully and just as effectively as by a massive offensive! Sugar in the fuel halts a military vehicle as effectively as a mine; sand in the lubricant stops a vessel as surely as a torpedo. To achieve this requires only technical know-how.

The guarding of prisoners of war, to name a "purely military" activity, is not immune to non-violent interference. A British commando leader in North Africa saw the technical impossibility of fully guarding and controlling P.O.W.'s in transit camps, and organized numerous escapes.[29] After the collapse of Germany, the Allies could not supervise the prisoners they had taken. Uncounted thousands slipped out of captivity, became civilians, and could not be recaptured, despite a general atmos-

---

[28] Miksche, *op. cit.*, p. 39.
[29] Vladimir Peniakoff, *Popskis Privatarmé* (Stockholm, 1951), p. 151.

phere of resignation and the docility of the Germans. A spiritually undefeated nation can organize escapes and reintegration, and have a large part of its captured soldiers free in a few weeks, without firing a single shot.

National resistance may well suceed without military fighting. But it is good to have elite formations available in case of need. Besides being a strategic factor, they can counteract the worst enemy abuses of violence. They provide the necessary counterviolence for some types of political attack, for the temporary localization of certain places, for patrolling; and they diversify resistance in other ways. In addition, the knowledge that the invading army is not completely unopposed, that there are "real soldiers" opposing it—even if only on a small scale—is sure to raise the resisters' morale. This diathetic effect alone more than justifies the use of some armed forces.

Small fighting teams can be tactically effective. In China, according to Lin Piao, a popular method of fighting behind Japanese lines was the so-called sparrow warfare: "It was used diffusely, like the flight of sparrows; and it was used flexibly by guerrillas and militiamen, operating in threes and fives, appearing and disappearing unexpectedly and wounding, killing, depleting and wearing down the enemy forces."[30] The local people themselves can organize such small teams to protect their interests without waiting for outside help from the commandos. It gives the patriots more strength and self-confidence. In some localities the small units of the people may practically exclude the alien. An eyewitness of the fighting between Russians and Georgians in Georgia, in 1956, was talking about "inhabitants of the mountain regions" and about "the guerrillas." Both terms turned out to mean the same people: the grievance had produced the fighters.

One of the strategic advantages of national resistance is the wide choice of means available to a multiform struggle. It is basically political. But it should not reject any form of defense, including military defense, *a priori*. Since military defense re-

---

[30] Lin Piao, *Long Live the Victory of People's War!* (Peking: Foreign Languages Press, 1965), p. 33.

quires a long preparation to be successful, it would be poor strategy to abandon this weapon before the specific conditions of the struggle are known.

Many small nations owe their survival to military strength and knowledge. As long as they can maintain this happy position, they are fortunate indeed. But they should not consider themselves helpless if, for one reason or another, their military defenses fail.

My aim here is not to give military resistance all the attention it deserves. Qualified military experts have written exensively on this subject; their works provide the needed guidance. I intended merely to point out some of the vital *technical* aspects of military defense and the technical possibilities of political resistance in unequal conflicts.

Military fighting should be only a minor part of a resistance struggle. Liddell Hart observed that even in regular war some of the most successful campaigns are losing their exclusively military character. In the Battle of France, "the effect of cutting the opposing armies' communications, and dislocating their control system in the deeply penetrating drive is hard to distinguish from its accompanying effect of shaking the people's morale and disrupting civic organization."[31] If the disrupting effects can be achieved by technical and political means, the military fighting may become irrelevant and superfluous.

Military power can influence the outcome of a resistance struggle, but the crucial role belongs always to its political elements.

To survive in today's world, small states need all the strength they can muster: non-military as well as military. They must, in addition, use the strength to their best advantage if they want to succeed. But increased fighting does not necessarily increase—in unequal conflicts it often fatally reduces—the efficiency of their defense. Increased politicizing always strengthens small-nation defense in militarily unequal conflicts.

In any case, a purely military defense makes little sense. Small-nation resistance must be primarily political.

---

[31] B. H. Liddell Hart, *Strategy* (New York: Praeger, 1954), p. 360.

Conclusion

After the partition of Poland an interesting ritual was observed at formal receptions in Constantinople. The official charged with introducing foreign diplomats at the Sultan's Court always announced, "His Excellency, the Ambassador of Poland!" Invariably another functionary was assigned to answer, "The diplomat, momentarily unable to attend, asked to be excused for not being present."[1]

For more than a century this seemed a futile gesture. When the Polish state re-emerged during World War I, the Turkish ritual proved to have reflected the actual facts far better than "more realistic" assumptions that Poland had ceased to exist in 1795. The Kurds have been incorporated into foreign empires and states since time immemorial, but it would be risky to claim that they are not a nation or that they have no future as a nation. In the Polish as well as in the Kurdish case the crucial factors were political—a surviving national spirit and a strong will to resist alien domination.

The political elements of small nation defense had become decisive by the time of the Great Revolutions; since then the importance of military force has receded even more. Nowadays a politically strong small nation, fighting for freedom on its own soil and among its own citizens, can succeed even if it cannot win the preliminary military jousting. The seeming weakness of small nations stems mainly from a failure to appreciate their political strength.

The basic condition for small nation survival is a new strategy, one designed to stress the political nature of unequal con-

---

[1] Weygand. *Mémoires*, p. 79.

flicts. This strategy must aim to neutralize the aggressor's military predominance as it exploits the political superiority of the defending nation. The conflict remains unequal, but the inequality is no longer one-sided. Since political elements are the primary ones in modern conflicts, the political inferiority of an alien power can, when correctly exploited, lead to the ultimate victory of the defenders.

The main strategic task is to mobilize the nation's sociopolitical strength. Most of the preparations can be made openly; their deterrent effect is a fringe benefit not to be underestimated.

As the actual conflict begins, national strength is rallied and directed against the aggressor. If the members of the defending nation are determined to defend their freedom and independence, if they recognize defense as a common cause, if their national loyalty and cohesion are strong enough to sustain an extended struggle, the foundations for successful resistance are laid.

Once the flame of resistance is lit and the people have withstood the initial shocks of enemy pressure or invasion, a first success is achieved. If the defenders use their political and spiritual strength, if they communicate among themselves and have a resolute leadership which is aware of the nature of the struggle and the opportunities that present themselves, the auguries for ultimate victory are favorable. The struggle is far less violent but also far more extensive than regular or guerrilla war; often it turns into a protracted conflict.

With sufficient time to extend and diversify the struggle, the cumulative effect of a national resistance will begin to tell. A multiform organized and specialized opposition will spread, even throughout a country occupied by alien forces or ruled by their agents, and finally escape enemy interference and paralyze enemy rule. A ubiquitous and extended resistance on the political level is more than a match for any control apparatus that an imposed regime can muster.

The rest is operational strategy and tactics, the determined and flexible use of various resistance techniques. No rigid scheme can be applied, since no two cases will ever be alike; war is antinomian, as T.E. Lawrence explained. The very nature of the political conflict causes wide differences in actual situations, psycho-political factors varying more than military ones. And complication is one of the strategic assets of the defenders.

National resistance fuses politics and rebellion; as a struggle within the defending political community, it has a revolutionary character. Its base—the entire nation—is much wider than that of military force; its sword-points—the specialists counteracting the aggressor in their respective fields—are more precise and ultimately more effective than sledgehammer blows of regular military units.

Small nations may have to mobilize their political strength in various emergencies: against political pressure from abroad, against subversive acts, against a regime imposed by an alien power, or against military invasion. The strategy and tactics suggested in this book will, as a rule, apply to all of them: in all of them the crucial elements are political. The political community—the *polis*—and its enduring resistance will decide whether the conflict is fought with soldiers, sticks and stones, or subversion. "War can be hot, tepid or cold; military, political, psychological or economic," remarked King-Hall, "but it is always in its essentials a conflict of ideas; a clash of policies; a contest of wills."[2]

I do not consider military power unimportant. It has often decided the outcome of struggles between large and small states. But there are, especially in recent history, many examples showing its reduced impact. I reviewed some of the latter instances and searched for common patterns in cases where militarily inferior small nations did survive. I found that armed force, if correctly opposed, does not gain political control, but rather can be prevented from achieving ultimate victory.

I conclude that (1) the basic objective of small nation defense is political; (2) political means lead directly, and most effectively, to that objective; (3) even the use of military violence

---

[2] Stephen King-Hall, *Common Sense in Defence* (London: K-H Services Ltd., 1960), p. 29.

should serve exclusively political purposes; and (4) in certain situations a small nation can achieve victory by political means against a military preponderant invader. And I consider a purely political victory not only a logical but a *quite practical* possibility. (The political victory of the Czechs and Slovaks in 1968 supports my point.)

Some small nations, like Switzerland and Sweden, rely on military defense. But even they can greatly improve their chances of survival by exploiting their socio-political strengths. Political elements enhance the over-all defense strength during the pre-military deterrence stage, at the time of military operations, and in the post-military contest. In the first stage political strength is at least as important as military preparedness; in the last stage it is decisive.

Enemy occupation may be unavoidable where the aggressor credibly threatens nuclear destruction as the only alternative to military surrender; in such a case the small nation is left with political resistance as its only defense. This applies wherever the whole or part of a country is occupied by an invader, either temporarily or permanently.

The mixed military-political nature of conflict is obvious in the case of Finland. Even after the successful conclusion of their military defense in 1944, the Finns could maintain their independence against vicious outside pressure only due to a unique political fortitude in 1948. It is clear that no small nation can afford to neglect the political elements of its strength.

Sometimes a small nation's territory is absorbed by an empire, and often its state completely disappears from the map. In such cases, too, spiritual and political strength can still preserve the nation. If such a nation resists, it can expect that changed power relationships in the area will provide it with an opportunity to reassert its independence after decades (Yugoslavia and Romania emerging from their subjugation at the end of World War II), even centuries (Poland emerging after its partition in 1795). The Kurds in Iraq are asserting their independence after thousands of years under alien rule!

Small nations can use political resistance whenever a great

power, or any state disproportionately superior in military force, acts to deprive them, in whole or in part, of their physical existence, national identity or independence. This is the safest and, in most cases, the most effective opposition to outright absorption into an empire, colonization, satellitization, active or passive imposition of an alien regime, or an undue influence over a small nation's external or internal policy. Another great advantage is that this resistance can be used not only defensively, but also in an offensive campaign to regain any of the lost components of national independence.

The political strength of a nation, like the nation itself, grows in the course of history; it can hardly be destroyed by the ephemeral impact of military defeats. This deep foundation is the reason for the surprising power of nationalism in political struggles. T. E. Lawrence devised a winning strategy based on Arab nationalism, a force so strong that "the presence or absence of the enemy became a secondary matter."[3] Clausewitz was impressed by the resistance of Spanish nationalism:

> Where the nation itself joins the struggle, where it does the main part of fighting in a national war, one will understand that this is no mere increase of popular assistance, but that a truly new force comes into being.[4]

Modern resistance expert Miksche described the political "people's war" as an extremely powerful weapon, comparing it to the atomic bomb.[5]

The united strength of an entire nation is indeed a tremendous force. This force can be mobilized and directed against an alien aggressor. A correct strategy for small nations is to apply their national strength in a political struggle, where most advantages favor the defending community. Correctly utilized, it may insure national survival.

---

[3] *Seven Pillars* . . . , p. 200.
[4] *Vom Kriege*, Book V, ch. 1.
[5] *Secret Forces*, p. 17.

Bibliography

BOOKS CITED

Aristotle. *Politics*. Jowett translation. (Modern Library.) New York: Random House, 1943.

Aubry, Octave. *Napoléon*. Paris: Flammarion, 1936.

_____. *Les pages immortelles de Napoléon*. Paris: Corrèa, 1941.

Banse, Ewald. *Germany Prepares for War*. New York: Harcourt, Brace and Company, 1934.

Bülow, A.H.D. von. *Geist des Neuern Kriegssystems*. Hamburg: Benjamin Gottlieb Hoffman, 1799.

_____. *Der Feldzug von 1800 militärisch-politisch betrachtet*. Berlin: Heinrich Frölich, 1801.

_____. *Lehrsatze des neuern Krieges*. Berlin: Heinrich Frölich, 1805.

_____. *Neue Taktik der Neuern wie sie seyn sollte*. Leipzig: Johann Ambrosius Barth, 1805.

_____. *Der Feldzug von 1805 militärisch-politisch betrachtet*. Berlin, 1806.

Campbell, John C. *Tito's Separate Road; America and Yugoslavia in World Politics*. New York: Harper & Row, 1967.

Cases, Compte de las. *Le Mémorial de Sainte-Hélène*. Paris: Garnier Frères, 1895.

Clausewitz, Carl von. *Vom Kriege*. 17th ed. Bonn: Fred Dümmler's Verlag, 1952.

Cole, G. D. H. *Europe, Russia and the Future*. London: Macmillan, 1941.

Dallin, Alexander. *German Rule in Russia 1941-1945; A Study of Occupation Policies*. London: Macmillan and Co., 1957.

Dixon, C. Aubrey and Otto Heilbrunn. *Communist Guerrilla Warfare*. London: Allen and Unwin, 1954.

Emerson, Rupert. *From Empire to Nation*. Cambridge: Harvard University Press, 1960.

Fainsod, Merle. *How Russia Is Ruled*. Cambridge: Harvard University Press, 1957.

268 _Small Nation Survival_

Falls, Cyril. *The Art of War.* New York: Oxford University Press, 1961.
Fuller, J. F. C. *Armament and History.* London: C. Scribner's Sons, 1945.
Gandhi, M. K. *Non-Violent Resistance: Satyagraha.* New York: Schocken, 1961.
Garnett, David (ed.). *The Essential T. E. Lawrence.* London: Jonathan Cape, 1951.
Garthoff, Raymond L. *Soviet Strategy in the Nuclear Age.* New York: Frederick A. Praeger, 1958.
Goebbels, Joseph. *The Goebbels Diaries 1942-1943.* Edited by Louis P. Lochner. New York: Doubleday and Company, Inc., 1948.
Goodrich, Austin. *Study in Sisu: Finland's Fight for Independence.* New York: Ballantine Books, 1960.
Grafström, Anders. *The Swedish Army.* Stockholm: Hörsta Förlag, 1954.
Haestrup, Jørgen. *Kontakt med England.* København: Thaning & Appels, 1954.
Hoffmann, Karl Heinz, and Otto Mayr-Arnold. *Okänd Armé.* Stockholm: Hörsta Förlag, 1959.
Höhn, Reinhard. *Revolution-Heer-Kriegsbild.* Darmstadt: Wittich Verlag, 1944.
Howarth, D. *We Die Alone.* New York: The Macmillan Company, 1955.
Hubatsch, Walther. *Weserübung.* 2nd. ed. Göttingen: Musterschmidt Verlag, 1960.
Kennan, George. *Russia, the Atom and the West.* New York: Harper, 1958.
Khrushchev, Nikita S. *The Anatomy of Terror; Revelations about Stalin's Regime.* Washington, D.C. Public Affairs Press, 1956.
King-Hall, Stephen. *Defence in the Nuclear Age.* London: Victor Gollancz Ltd., 1958.
————. *Common Sense in Defence.* London: K-H Services Ltd., 1960.
————. *Power Politics in the Nuclear Age.* London: Victor Gollancz Ltd., 1962.
Kleist, Peter. *Zwischen Hitler und Stalin 1939-1945.* Bonn: Athenaeum, 1950.
Kurz, H. R. *Die Schweiz in der Planung der kriegführenden Mächte während des Zweiten Weltkrieges.* Biel: Schweizerischer Unteroffizierverband, 1957.
————. *Die Schweizer Armee Heute.* Thun: Verlags-Aktiengesellschaft, 1964.
Lawrence, T. E. *Seven Pillars of Wisdom.* New York: Dell Publishing Co., 1962.

Lewis, Flora. *A Case History of Hope: The Story of Poland's Peaceful Revolutions.* Garden City, N.Y.: Doubleday and Company, Inc., 1958.

Liddell Hart, B. H. *Great Captains Unveiled.* Boston: Little, Brown and Co., 1928.

————. *T. E. Lawrence in Arabia and After.* London: Jonathan Cape, 1934.

————. (ed.). *T. E. Lawrence to His Biographer Liddell Hart.* New York: Doubleday, Doran and Co., 1938.

————. *The Revolution in Warfare.* New Haven: Yale University Press, 1947.

————. *Defence of the West.* London: Cassell, 1950.

————. *Strategy.* New York: Frederick A. Praeger, 1954.

————. *The German Generals Talk.* New York: Berkley Publishing Corp., 1958.

————. *Deterrent or Defence.* London: Stevens and Sons, 1960.

Lin Piao. *Long Live the Victory of People's War!* Peking: Foreign Languages Press, 1965.

Littell, Robert (ed.). *The Czech Black Book.* New York: Frederick A. Praeger, 1969.

Luther, Hans. *Der französische Widerstand gegen die deutsche Besatzungsmacht und seine Bekämpfung.* Tübingen: Institut für Besatzungsfragen, 1957.

Madelin, Louis. *L'Affaire d'Espagne 1807-1809.* Paris: Hachette, 1943.

Mao Tse-tung. *Strategic Problems in the Anti-Japanese Guerrilla War.* Peking: Foreign Languages Press, 1954.

————. *On Protracted War.* Peking: Foreign Languages Press, 1954.

Mao Tse-tung and Che Guevara. *Guerrilla Warfare.* London: Cassell, 1962.

Marbot, Baron de. *Mémoires du Général Baron de Marbot.* Paris: E. Plon, Nourrit et Cie., 1891.

Michel, Henri (ed.). *European Resistance Movements 1939-1945.* London, 1960.

Mikes, George. *The Hungarian Revolution.* London: André Deutsch, 1957.

Miksche, F. O. *Secret Forces.* London: Faber and Faber, 1950.

Mill, John Stuart. *Considerations on Representative Government.* New York: Harper and Brothers, Publishers, 1867.

Muus, Fleming B. *The Spark and the Flame.* London: Museum Press Ltd., 1956.

Nutting, Anthony. *Lawrence of Arabia: the Man and the Motive.* New York: Signet Books, 1962.

O'Callahan, Sean. *The Easter Lily: The Story of the I.R.A.* London: Allan Wingate, 1956.

Om kriget kommer. Stockholm: Kungl inrikesdepartementet, 1952.

Osanka, Franklin Mark (ed.). *Modern Guerrilla Warfare.* New York: Free Press of Glencoe, 1962.

Peniakoff, Vladimir. *Popskis Privatarmé.* Stockholm: Natur och Kultur, 1951.

Plato. *The Republic.* Jowett translation. (Vintage Books.) New York: Random House, n.d.

Prawdin, Michael. *Tschingis-Chan und sein Erbe.* Stuttgart: Deutsche Verlags-Anstalt, 1938.

Rauschning, Herman. *The Voice of Destruction.* New York: G. P. Putnam's Sons, 1940.

Redelis, Valdis. *Partisanenkrieg.* (Wehrmacht im Kampf, No. 17.) Heidelberg: Vowinckel Verlag, 1958.

Rydberg, Viktor. *Huru kan Sverige bevara sin sjelfständighet?* Göteborg, 1859.

Selznick, Philip. *The Organizational Weapon: A Study of Bolshevik Strategy and Tactics.* New York: McGraw-Hill, 1952.

Soldatenbuch: Auf Dich kommt es an! Bern: Eidgenössische Drucksachen- und Materialzentrale, 1959.

Solzhenitsyn, Alexander. *One Day in the Life of Ivan Denisovich.* New York: Bantam-Praeger, 1963.

Tauras, K. V. *Guerrilla Warfare on the Amber Coast.* New York: Voyages Press, 1962.

Teske, Hermann. *Die silbernen Spiegel.* Heidelberg: Vowinckel Verlag, 1952.

Trolle, Jørgen. *Syv Maaneder uden Politi.* København: Nyt Nordisk Førlag, 1945.

Vztah Čechů a Slováků k Dějinám 1918-1968 Praha: Ústav Pro Výzkum Veřejného Mině ni ČSAV, 1968.

Weygand, L. M. *Mémoires: Mirages et Réalité.* Paris: Flammarion, 1957.

Xenophon. *Anabasis.* W. H. D. Rouse translation. New York: Mentor Books, 1959.

ARTICLES CITED

Brunner, Karl. "The Fundamental Ideas Behind Swiss National Defense," distributed by the Consulate General of Switzerland in New York City, 1959.

Burnham, James. "Sticks, Stones, and Atoms," *Modern Guerrilla Warfare,* ed., Franklin Mark Osanka (New York: Free Press of Glencoe, 1962), 417-24.

Clausewitz, Carl von. "Das Wesentliche in der Organisation eines Landsturms und einer Miliz," *Beihefte zum Militair-Wochenblatt pro Januar bis inclusive October 1846* (Berlin), 70-71.

Dürenmatt, Peter. "Wehrpolitik in der Demokratie," in *Die Schweizer Armee Heute*, ed. H. R. Kurz (Thun: Verlags-Aktiengesellschaft, 1964), 204-10

Geneste, Marc E. "Guerrilla Warfare," in *Modern Guerrilla Warfare* (New York: Free Press of Glencoe, 1962), 264-67.

Guevara, Ernesto "Che." "La Guerra de Guerrillas," in *Modern Guerrilla Warfare* (New York: Free Press of Glencoe, 1962), 336-75.

Haestrup, J. "Exposé," in *European Resistance Movements 1939-1945*, ed., Henri Michel (London, 1960), 150-62.

Hitler, Adolf. "Auszug aus der Ansprache des Führers and die Heeresgruppenführer am 1.7.43 abends," *Vierteljahrshefte für Zeitgeschichte* (Stuttgart) 3, (1954), 309-12.

Jungstedt, Ernst. "Polarräven, en tysk anfallsplan mot Sverige under andra Världskriget," *Krigshistoriska Studier* (Stockholm, 1950), 100-114.

Lawrence, T. E. "The Evolution of a Revolt," *The Army Quarterly* (London), No. 1 (1920), 55-69.

————. "Guerrilla Warfare, World War I," Encyclopaedia Britannica, Vol. X (1960), 950-950D.

Meerheimb, F. von. "Behrenhorst und Bülow," *Historische Zeitschrift* (München-Berlin), VI (1861), 46-74.

Monfort, H. R. "Force et Faiblesse des Armées de Milice," *Révue Militaire Générale*, (1959), 465-75.

Nemo (pseud.). "La Guerre dans le milieu social," *Révue de Défense Nationale*, (1956), 605-23.

————. "La Guerre dans la foulle," *Révue de Défense Nationale*, (1956), 721-39.

Rupp, Torsten. "Ur OB-svaret 62," *Tidskrift för värnpliktiga Officerare* (Stockholm), No. 5 (1962), 7-15.

Sanakoyev, Sh. "Internationalism and Socialist Patriotism," *International Affairs* (Moscow), No. 12 (1961), 8-13.

Ugeux, W. "Quelques Considérations Techniques et Morales sur l'Expérience de Guerre Psychologique Menée en Belgique Occupée Entre 1940 et 1945," in *European Resistance Movements 1939-1945* (London, 1960), 170-81.

Velde, R. W. van de. "The Neglected Deterrent," *Military Review* (Fort Leavenworth, Kansas), XXXVIII (August, 1958), 3-10.

Villa-Real, Louis A. "Huk Hunting," *The Army Combat Forces Journal* (Washington, D.C.), 5 (1954), 32-36.

Volny, Slava (pseud.). "The Saga of Czechoslovak Broadcasting," *East Europe* (New York), No. 12 (1968), 10-15.

355.0218
Sv968

115 905